12/2?

RAPID
PSYCHOLOGICAL
ASSESSMENT

RAPID
PSYCHOLOGICAL
ASSESSMENT

JASON T. OLIN
CAROLYN KEATINGE

JOHN WILEY & SONS, INC.

New York • Chichester • Weinheim • Brisbane • Singapore • Toronto

This book is printed on acid-free paper. ⊚

Copyright © 1998 by John Wiley & Sons. All rights reserved.

Published simultaneously in Canada.

This publication is designed to provide accurate and authoritative information in regard to the subject matter covered. It is sold with the understanding that the publisher is not engaged in rendering professional services. If professional advice or other expert assistance is required, the services of a competent professional person should be sought.

Library of Congress Cataloging-in-Publication Data:

Olin, Jason T., 1964–
      Rapid psychological assessment / Jason T. Olin, Carolyn Keatinge.
          p.   cm.
      Includes bibliographical references and index.
      ISBN 0-471-18181-1 (hardcover : alk. paper)
      1. Psychodiagnostics—Handbooks, manuals, etc.   I. Keatinge,
Carolyn.   II. Title.
RC469.038   1998
616.89′075—dc21   97-45506

Printed in the United States of America.

10 9 8 7 6 5 4 3 2 1

To Serene, for your love and inspiration.

J. O.

To A. J. B., love, thoughts, and thanks, as always.

C. K.

Preface

THERE ARE many excellent published assessment texts, but few are geared toward everyday clinical use. Our experience, as licensed psychologists, has been to rely on pertinent portions of certain texts, ignoring much of what was written. In addition, it is time consuming to comb through different texts and articles, identifying the information needed to do effective assessments. Nor can we take our reference libraries with us when we go see a client. We needed a practical and concise assessment book that contains essential information for clinical assessment of clients of all ages.

Most books labeled as assessment handbooks serve little purpose out in the field. They tend to be bulky and are primarily designed as textbooks for graduate students. Many of the smaller handbooks tend to be written like test catalogs, which is useful when trying to identify what tests to administer, but provide little help when making interpretations. Our book offers clear descriptions of the most commonly used tests and most frequently seen disorders. We provide methods for integrating the explanation into a concise report and include numerous practical tips for specific populations.

Assessment texts, like most psychology texts, do not consider the real-world constraints that affect our work. Clinicians no longer have the luxury of seeing clients for numerous visits with the assurance of being paid. Seldom is it possible to give lengthy test batteries with the hope of later identifying data to support our diagnostic impressions. Thus, it is crucial to know in advance which tests are the most effective and efficient, given the referral question. It is also important to know the key diagnostic signs that differentiate between competing diagnoses. It was our intention to create a handy text that contains the most practical assessment information, enabling clinicians to work rapidly and effectively.

Rapid Psychological Assessment was developed for novice and advanced clinicians involved in assessment, including clinical, counseling, and school psychologists, graduate students, academics who teach assessment courses, and other professionals who have been trained to administer psychological tests (e.g., social workers, marriage and family counselors). Clinicians who work with managed care companies may find this book useful because it provides quick and sensible methods to interpret and report psychological tests.

JASON T. OLIN
CAROLYN KEATINGE

March 1998

Acknowledgments

THIS BOOK WAS INSPIRED by a workshop we presented in 1995, titled "Speedy Psychological Assessments," at the Annual Meeting of the Los Angeles County Psychological Association (LACPA). Thus, we first want to thank Patricia Fricker, M.A., the Executive Administrator of LACPA, who brought our workshop to John Wiley & Sons' attention, leading to the creation of this book. Second, we wish to thank Kelly A. Franklin, our editor at Wiley, for her expert guidance and creativity.

Many people contributed to the creation of this text. Adam Bezark helped us to persevere and edit. Karen Berg, Ph.D., Joyce Crowfoot, Ph.D., and Mary Large, Ph.D., edited early drafts providing excellent feedback. Patricia Villaseñor helped track down references. Lauren Fox, M.A. had the daunting task of creating many of the appendixes in this book, and she helped to fashion a seamless fit between our two writing styles.

Special thanks is due to Serene Olin, Ph.D., who was instrumental in providing current information on psychological and neuropsychological assessment of children and adolescents. She reviewed all of the content of this text pertaining to children, and her numerous suggestions on assessment, diagnosis, interpretation, and treatment were vital.

Both authors would like to thank the numerous mentors who have helped serve as an inspiration for their love of psychological assessment: Jerry Borofsky, Ph.D., James Choca, Ph.D., Elaine Eaton, Ph.D., James Kelly, Ph.D., Michael Ward, Ph.D., and Charles Peterson, Ph.D.

Jason Olin was supported by a grant from the National Institute of Health (MH01368) during the preparation of this book.

J. T. O.
C. K.

Contents

SECTION III

Testing Tips

SECTION I

ASSESSMENT OVERVIEW

CHAPTER 1

An Introduction to the Role of Assessment and the DSM-IV

Reasons for Psychological Assessment

PSYCHOLOGICAL ASSESSMENT plays a central role in diagnosis and treatment and there are several primary reasons for conducting an evaluation. In every case, your role is to be a consultant who can help answer specific questions and aid in making relevant decisions (Groth-Marnat, 1997). The five most common reasons for assessment are now described.

DIAGNOSIS

Referring clinicians want to know the diagnosis of a client, and sometimes they're unsure. This most commonly occurs when the client presents with symptoms shared by multiple diagnoses or when there is a possibility that one disorder is being masked by the symptoms of another.

TREATMENT PLANNING

While referring clinicians often are familiar with a client's diagnosis, they may not be sure what types of treatment are appropriate. Because assessment typically considers critical issues such as a client's impulse control, crisis issues, and available emotional and cognitive resources, it is possible for you to make thoughtful decisions about treatment. For example, you may be able to help decide whether a client can participate in psychotherapy, be maintained in a day treatment program, or live alone.

IDENTIFYING FUNCTIONAL STATUS

Functional status is an assessment of a client's cognitive and emotional abilities and skills. This information can be used to assist in treatment planning or to make decisions about the client's living arrangements or employment. Thus, psychological assessment can easily identify a client's abilities and then make specific recommendations based on those findings.

SELF-CONTROL

Psychological assessment is often used to identify the factors impinging on a client's level of self-control, particularly when there are concerns of suicidality, dangerousness, or substance abuse.

HISTORY

A history is gathered by most clinicians who have any contact with a client, but it is rare to find a history as detailed as that found in a psychological assessment.

Diagnosis is often a component of an assessment, even though it may not be part of the referring question. In the following section, we review the diagnostic nomenclature currently used.

Differential Diagnosis: *DSM-IV* Primer

Psychiatric diagnoses are made based on the nomenclature developed by the American Psychiatric Association and used in the *Diagnostic and Statistical Manual of Mental Disorders* (*DSM-IV*; American Psychiatric Association, 1994). We recommend that you purchase the *Quick Reference to the Diagnostic Criteria from DSM-IV* because it includes the key information in a very compact book.

DSM-IV has shortcomings. The criteria that form each disorder do not adequately fit with the heterogeneous population seen by clinicians. In addition, *DSM-IV* diagnoses have greater reliability at the expense of their validity. At its worst, *DSM-IV* is merely one method of categorizing and labeling individuals who suffer from clinical and psychiatric symptoms.

DSM-IV clusters disorders into 17 major categories:

1. Disorders usually first diagnosed in infancy, childhood, or adolescence.
2. Delirium, dementia, and amnestic and other cognitive disorders.
3. Mental disorders due to a general medical condition not elsewhere classified.

   4. Substance-related disorders.
   5. Schizophrenia and other psychotic disorders.
   6. Mood disorders.
   7. Anxiety disorders.
   8. Somatoform disorders.
   9. Factitious disorders.
   10. Dissociative disorders.
   11. Sexual and gender identity disorders.
   12. Eating disorders.
   13. Sleep disorders.
   14. Impulse control disorders.
   15. Adjustment disorders.
   16. Personality disorders.
   17. Other conditions that may be a focus of clinical attention.

MAKING A DIAGNOSIS

Once you arrive at a diagnosis (or diagnoses), you need to record them in a specific way. *DSM-IV* assigns diagnoses to a set of five axes.

Axis I   Used for all disorders except Mental Retardation and the Personality Disorders.

Axis II   Personality Disorders or Mental Retardation.

Axis III   General Medical Conditions potentially relevant to the disorder.

Axis IV   Psychosocial and Environmental Problems. These problems are grouped into nine categories:

Problems with primary support group.

Problems related to the social environment.

Educational problems.

Occupational problems.

Housing problems.

Economic problems.

Problems with access to health care services.

Problems related to interaction with the legal system/crime.

Other psychosocial and environmental problems.

Axis V   Global Assessment of Functioning (GAF). The GAF is a 100-point scale, with 100 being the highest level. GAF is usually rated at the time of diagnosis, but it can also be rated in terms of the highest level during the past year, or at the previous evaluation.

In a perfect world, clients would neatly fit into the *DSM-IV* diagnostic categories. However, it is common to find clients with complex symptomatology that cannot be easily pigeonholed into a diagnosis. A psychological assessment usually provides critical data that can help create a more understandable diagnosis.

A Model for the Assessment Process

To perform rapid assessments, it is necessary to have a working model of the assessment process in hand to assist you. Our model is adapted loosely from Cushman and Scherer (1995) and includes the following steps:

1. Determine the information you need to answer the referral question(s) (e.g., knowing whether the client's hallucinations are due to psychosis, mania, or substance abuse).
2. Identify who is to be involved.
3. Obtain informed consent and releases.
4. Collect and examine medical records.
5. Identify what is to be measured (e.g., cognitive function, mood, personality, etc.).
6. Identify and select your measures (Chapters 4 and 5 describe the most popular ones).
7. Administer your assessment. Modify as needed.
8. Score measures; analyze and interpret results.
9. Seek consultation if you are unable to make sense of the results.
10. Write report (Chapter 12 provides sample report formats).
11. Provide feedback to client and other appropriate parties.

Format and Organization of This Text

This text is divided into three sections. Although the book may be read in sequence, experienced clinicians may find the text most useful by relying on the Testing Tips located in shaded boxes throughout each chapter.

ASSESSMENT OVERVIEW

The first section documents critical information needed to perform effective and rapid psychological assessments. These chapters provide both a crash course in assessment and pointers from the pros. Chapter 2 offers methods and strategies for performing effective interviews and mental status examinations. Chapter 3 summarizes methods for choosing various tests, using both traditional (e.g., validity) and practical methods. Chapters 4 and 5 focus on assessment methods for adults and children respectively. We describe the most current versions of tests available today because of their better standardization.

DIFFERENTIAL DIAGNOSIS

Most referrals focus on diagnostic issues, but few texts consider differential diagnosis when performing assessments. The chapters in Section II consider common dimensions in differential diagnosis: Mood (Chapter 6), Behavior (Chapter 7), Reality Testing (Chapter 8), Self-Control (Chapter 9), Personality (Chapter 10), and Cognitive Function (Chapter 11). They are organized similarly. We first describe the key criteria in each diagnostic category. Each chapter includes summary tables that list symptoms and test results by diagnosis. Variations that occur with children, adolescents, and older adults are also described. Finally, we provide guidelines for frequent diagnostic differentials.

INTERPRETATION AND REPORT WRITING

Section III includes a chapter to help you organize, interpret, and write your assessment.

Rapid Assessment

Our goal throughout this book is to provide standard assessment methods and enable readers to use them as relevantly and rapidly as possible. Pay close attention to our Testing Tips: They will give you the key points to make your assessments rapid and more effective.

CHAPTER 2

Setting the Stage: Clinical Interviews and Mental Status Exams

---

Practical Issues in Rapid Assessment

Like Finn and Tonsager (1995), we consider assessment to work best when it is a collaborative process between you and the client. If possible, the assessment should begin with you and the client working to identify questions that could be addressed by the evaluation. Although this cannot occur with every client, for example, in clients who lack insight into their psychopathology, allowing the client to participate in the assessment makes it easier for you to provide needed feedback after the testing is complete.

CONSENT AND RELEASES

Prior to performing an assessment, you need to obtain the client's consent. Some states require the client to sign a consent form, and minimally, you should document in your notes and your report that consent was given. The consent form should simply describe what an assessment is, note the risks (e.g., fatigue), state the costs involved, and clarify the limits of confidentiality. A signed consent form is practically meaningless unless you discuss its details with the client. If necessary, get a copy from a colleague.

You will usually need to have the client sign release forms, too, so you can discuss your findings with other third parties, procure medical records, or allow others to speak with you. A release should specify what information you are allowed to release and discuss, who will be contacted, and for how long the release will be valid.

Testing Tip
Factors to Discuss with the Referring Source Prior to Evaluation

---

These issues can often help you clarify the referral question and help focus the evaluation:

- *Timing.* Why are you being asked to test the client now?
- *Diagnosis.* Are there previous diagnoses?
- *Previous treatment.* Does the previous treatment provide clues?
- *Medications.* Are there medications that might affect testing?
- *Time constraints.* When does the testing need to be completed? When must a report be completed?
- *Breadth of testing.* Does the referring source solely want the referral question answered or a deeper picture of the client?
- *Client factors.* Are there client factors that affect test selection (e.g., disabilities, ethnicity, age, language)?
- *Prior testing.* Is the client familiar with psychological testing? Does the client dislike testing? Are there prior test results?
- *Use of results.* Who will obtain feedback and test results?

CLARIFYING ASSESSMENTS

Many referrals for an assessment are vague, possibly because most referring clinicians do not know exactly what can be gained from your work. A referral may be as short as, "Please evaluate a 45-year-old depressed male for level of cognitive function." Although it is clear that testing is needed, you know little about how the assessment will help your referral source. We recommend that prior to evaluating the client, you *negotiate* a referral question. Discuss with your referring source what information is being sought through testing. Not only will this help save time in your approach to the assessment, but you will be more certain to answer the referral questions.

APPRECIATING THE CLIENT'S NEEDS

Most clients have some anxiety about being assessed because they are asked to reveal sensitive and private information to an unknown clinician. In fact, you should note when clients appear too comfortable because this may signal additional psychopathology. Rapport is the key to a rapid and effective assessment.

There are many ways to establish rapport with a client, so we cannot give you a script. However, you can monitor the comfort level of the client (as well as of yourself) to provide an indication of rapport. If you find it difficult to establish rapport with the client, consider mentioning that you feel he or she is not "with you" in the process. Bringing this dilemma into the open makes it easier for you to address the client's concerns. In addition, by working collaboratively from the onset, you will have a more positive relationship.

PREPARE MATERIALS IN ADVANCE

Prepare a folder containing an intake form, consent form, releases, a history form, and the tests you know you will need. Fill in as much as possible. If you have time, send the forms (not the tests) to your client with instructions to complete them prior to the visit.

USE CURRENT TESTS

Outdated test materials are unethical to use because they can be misinterpreted and the standardization sample may be out of date. In addition, older tests don't integrate current concepts, which can be a problem especially with children and adolescents because diagnostic conceptualizations change more dramatically. Of course, this doesn't mean that you must buy the latest edition of a test the moment it is published, or worse, buy a new test that has insufficient validity. However, you should consider "upgrading" in a timely manner.

PROTECT YOUR MATERIALS

Do not permit outpatients to take the test materials out of the office; the potential threats to test security make such actions unethical. Also, clients may later take the test, and then refuse to return it. In addition, when clients take forms home, you cannot be certain who completed them. Many clinicians find it tempting to allow tests to leave the office: resist this temptation!

OBTAIN PREVIOUS RECORDS OR TALK TO THE OTHER CLINICIAN(S)

Old reports and records are vital in allowing you to rapidly decide what tests you might plan to administer. At the very least, they allow you to gather history and save you the trouble of having to ask this information yourself. At the onset, obtain a release of information to procure the old records.

TESTING AND RETESTING

When a client is referred for a reassessment, establish that there is a valid reason for the evaluation, especially if little time has elapsed since the last one. Be careful about practice and memory effects from readministering tests too soon. Some valid reasons for reassessment are:

- Client has developed new symptoms.
- Client's performance has significantly decreased in school, or in occupational or social functioning.
- Client has been hospitalized.
- Client has made a suicide attempt.
- Client has experienced a significant negative life event.
- Client has made marked gains in school, or in occupational or social functioning.

DEALING WITH A LACK OF COMPREHENSION

If you suspect the client does not understand the test questions, check your suspicions by randomly selecting several test items, and ask the client to read the items and then explain their meaning to you. Do not administer tests that are beyond the client's ability to complete.

WHEN CLIENTS CANNOT COMPLETE A SELF-REPORT
QUESTIONNAIRE DUE TO READING DIFFICULTIES

Occasionally, a client will not be able to read a test form. When this occurs on a multiple-choice test, the items can be read to the client, and the client can enter responses on the answer sheet. To reduce bias, it is important that the reader be unable to see the client's responses, and that the client knows that the reader is unable to see the responses. Make sure to mention these deviations from standard administration in your report. If the client cannot read either the form or the answer sheet, consider giving an alternative test.

MALINGERING AND FUNCTIONAL COMPLAINTS

For varied reasons, individuals may be invested in presenting themselves in an overly positive or negative light. *DSM-IV* defines malingering as the voluntary presentation of false, or grossly exaggerated, physical or psychological symptoms. According to *DSM-IV*, you should be alerted to malingering if any of the following are present:

- Medical/legal context to the referral.
- Discrepancy between objective findings and reported symptoms.
- Compliance problems.
- Antisocial Personality Disorder.

You may also want to consider malingering if any of the following occur:

- High number of obvious, improbable symptoms.
- Symptoms of the disorder that have an unlikely course and severity.
- Sudden onset and vague, inconsistent symptoms.
- Highly inconsistent test results.
- Inexplicable decrease from premorbid functioning.
- Test performance inconsistent with ability.
- Significant monetary or secondary gains in being impaired.

Malingering occurs more frequently in males, in early or middle adulthood. It can be preceded by an actual injury. If you suspect malingering, do not confront the client until testing is complete. Otherwise, the client may alter the response pattern based on your suspicions, making it harder for you to dispute later. In addition, select tests (e.g., MMPI-2) with built-in validity scales. Avoid forensic assessments if you lack sufficient training.

Malingering Tests

One method of assessing for malingering is to use the Structured Interview of Reported Symptoms (Rodgers, Bagby, & Dickens, 1992), a structured interview for adults, 18 years or older. It can identify functional complaints in clients, provided they aren't grossly psychotic or attempting to feign neuropsychological dysfunction. It takes 30 to 45 minutes to administer, and has 12 scales that assess such factors as the client's tendency to report rare symptoms, or improbable symptom combinations. The test has not been validated, however, in clients with cognitive complaints.

One test validated for such clients is the Test of Memory Malingering (Tombaugh, 1995). This test is specifically designed to distinguish between true and malingered memory problems. Clients are shown 50 figures over two trials, and then are given a 2-item forced recognition test. The test provides cutoffs for malingering and for those with genuine cognitive impairment. An advantage to this test is that it does not obviously appear to be a test of malingering.

Practical Issues in Working with Children and Adolescents

RAPPORT AND TRUST

Rapport and a trusting relationship are crucial to child and adolescent assessment, especially when the child's presenting problems include misbehavior. Many children are guarded, suspicious, and disinterested in the assessment because they are typically brought in by others, because testing is an unfamiliar process, and because of their misimpressions of the assessment process. You can counteract this in several ways. First, adopt an accepting, understanding attitude that respects the child. Second, you can explain that the purpose of testing is to identify strengths and weaknesses and to help with certain problems (many children think you are going to fail them). Third, make the assessment a fun process.

For some children, testing needs to be structured in a behavioral manner that engenders rapport. Reinforcers such as toys, stickers, crayons and paper, and sometimes candy may be needed to help a child persist through the evaluation. Identifying what types of rewards are salient to the child should be done prior to the start of testing. Some children will also need limits set when inappropriate behavior occurs. Consequences can include, for example, reducing play time or the number of rewards that have been earned.

Adolescents

When evaluating adolescents, appreciate their need to fit in and their desire to be treated as adults. Acknowledge their resistance while discussing the procedures, and normalize the testing. Respect their need for privacy and trust, and ideally enlist them as collaborators in the process. Always set clear limits.

Parents/Caregivers

Rapport is also needed with the parents or primary caregivers (e.g., foster parents) because they ensure the child's attendance and are often involved later when interventions are introduced. At the onset, explain the nature of the assessment process, obtain informed consent, and encourage the parents to express their concerns. Many parents feel threatened that an assessment will identify problems with parenting; address this concern at the onset to minimize guilt and enhance rapport. You may find that some parents need to be given reassurance more frequently.

ROLE OF THE FAMILY AND PARENTS

To distinguish the contribution of the family and the environment on the child's behavior, an accurate symptom history is essential. You will also want to gather a developmental history, and assess parenting skills. Common questions to ask include having the parents describe how their parenting styles differ, how much time each spends with the child, and what they find both successful and unsuccessful about parenting. Keep in mind the risk factors for child abuse discussed in Chapter 9. For rapid assessment, you may want the parents to complete a developmental questionnaire and intake form prior to the intake, provided that you have already established sufficient rapport and have a clear referral question.

Unrealistic Parental Expectations

Occasionally, the assessment you are doing is one of many assessments that the parents have ordered because of dissatisfaction with earlier report findings. Alternatively, parents may be expecting that the outcome of the assessment will lead to unrealistic change. In either case, process with the parents their expectations so as to maximize the gains of your efforts.

CONFIDENTIALITY, CUSTODY, AND CONSENT

In most child cases, the parents (e.g., biological, foster, etc.), and not the child, authorize treatment and the release of information. Ideally, you would obtain informed consent from both parents before commencing the assessment. In certain states, when the child is the victim of abuse, and sharing the information with the parents would create further harm, the clinician or child client may hold the privilege of confidentiality.

Do not assume that the parent who brought the child for an assessment is the custodial parent. If there has been divorce or separation proceedings, you may need to request a copy of the custody arrangements to identify who can give consent.

Some states permit adolescent minors to consent to treatment if they use drugs or alcohol, or are pregnant. Emancipated minors, too, can consent to treatment on their own. Nevertheless, in most cases, clinicians find that the parents provide needed information and become an integral part of the assessment. If you do not obtain informed consent from both parents, clearly document the reasons why this did not occur and the procedures you followed. Parents may not be financially liable for an evaluation that was conducted without their consent.

Many clinicians use a "no secrets" policy to facilitate open communication within the family. When working with child clients who are concerned about trust (e.g., adolescents), you may need to help the parents respect the child's privacy while you work.

THIRD PARTIES AND RATING SCALES

Child clients can have problems at home, school, and day care centers, involving baby sitters, pediatricians, and others. In addition, you usually need to contact multiple parties to assess for variability in the child's behavior between settings, obtain records, and assist with treatment. In all of these cases, you are required to use a release of information.

One method of gathering data we strongly recommend is to provide rating scales to parents, teachers, and others. For many parents, you will have a greater completion rate if the scales are completed in your office. This can frequently be achieved while the child is being assessed. These forms are discussed in Chapter 5.

Parent reports are less reliable than teacher reports, and it is common for them to have a low correlation with each other. Teacher ratings tend to be more sensitive to hyperactive behavior than parents, who tend to tolerate more and do not have access to normative comparisons. An inaccurate report may be due to the parents' level of education, their limited experience completing forms, and a misappreciation of the data's importance. Teachers, on the other hand, may be reluctant to provide information that suggests failure in managing or helping the client.

DEVELOPMENTAL ISSUES

The child's emotional and behavioral functioning should be placed in a developmental context. Consider whether the child's behavior is consistent and developmentally appropriate or is an exaggeration of a developmentally normal behavior. This may warrant using measures more sensitive to social skills and social behavior as children mature.

ADVOCATING FOR CHANGES IN SCHOOL

Schools and municipalities typically have their own policies and standards for interpreting psychological assessments. When there is a possibility that the test findings will suggest significant changes at school, it is important to know in advance the current state and local policies, in order to assist parents in obtaining additional resources within the school. In some cases, expert consultation or acquiring the services of a school advocate may be warranted.

Practical Issues in the Assessment of Older Adults

Physiological aging as well as cohort differences affect the approach to assessment in the elderly. Here are some critical issues to consider:

- *Choose a location of testing that is free of distractions.* Older adults' cognitive resources are not as resilient as young adults.' Do your testing in a quiet room. If you are testing in a hospital or nursing home, ask the nursing staff to avoid interruptions. Work in a well-lit environment. If these variables cannot be controlled, clarify this in your report, and consider if these distractors account for test findings.
- *Health and medications can confound test results.* Pain and fatigue affect test performance. Age-related deficits in visual and auditory acuity affect test performance. Consider whether loss of appetite and lack of sleep are due to depression or due to physical problems. Identify if the client is taking a neuroleptic (e.g., Haldol [haloperidol], Clozaril [clozapine], Zyprexa [olanzapine], or other medication) that might affect cognitive test performance or behavior. Most older adults have less energy to endure a long test battery. Plan to take more frequent breaks, and give the most demanding tests when the client is most alert.
- *Variability in performance.* Elderly clients will show greater variability over testing occasions than young adults.
- *Response bias.* Older adults are more prone to containing their anxiety rather than acknowledging it. Thus, try to be more perceptive to anxiety-provoking situations. They are also more cautious in their responses, so work to encourage openness.
- *Cohort effects and the age of the tester.* Older adults aged 65 or older were born in the 1930s. Their generation did not grow up with psychotherapists or psychologists. They may approach testing more defensively than someone born in 1960. Of equal importance, they may feel odd about being tested by someone younger. As with children, you may need to explain the testing process in an empathic manner, and attempt to make it enjoyable and interesting.

Clinical Interviews

A clinical interview is the most valuable opportunity to collect the data necessary for making a diagnosis. In most cases, a diagnosis can be made solely with a clinical interview. Thus, if you are able to work efficiently, you can make a diagnosis without having to do any psychological testing.

Unfortunately, a clinical interview can move very slowly. As with other assessment texts, we list content areas for you to consider. Yet, interviewing style varies among clinicians. Just because we list many content areas doesn't mean that it makes sense for you to cover all of them with each patient.

GUIDELINES

Use the Interview to Obtain Data to Assist with Diagnosis and Treatment

Although this may seem obvious, many clinicians gather unnecessary history or ask questions that are already answered in the medical record. Your goal is to gather data that help to identify or answer the referral question, whether that means making a diagnosis, or assessing current functioning.

Types of Questions/Interview Style

Most clients respond better to open-ended questions first, followed by more focused ones later. However, the overarching goal is to maintain rapport. With this in mind, you should choose whatever questions you wish, provided they don't diminish rapport. Sometimes explaining in advance that you are going to start asking more sensitive questions helps the client feel more at ease and feel more understood. In addition, always ask if anything was omitted during the interview.

Create Your Own Standardized Interview Form

This can be initially time consuming, but in the end it will save you a lot of time. Many history forms are already available to mental health professionals. Our experience has been that they are either too lengthy or too sparse. Take an evening and write out the domains that you typically assess in an interview. Feel free to use checklists, but make sure you have room to record unexpected data.

Consider Self-Report Forms When Your Time Is Limited

Some medical history forms are designed to be completed by the client. This can be useful when your time is limited. We recommend that you do this only when you have enough evidence that the client will answer the form in a straightforward manner. The referral source may provide you with this information.

INTERVIEWING CHILDREN AND ADOLESCENTS

Infants and Preschool Children

Because this is a specialized area of assessment, we will describe basics concepts for assessing this age group. First, you will spend much of your time with the parents, identifying their parenting style and family dynamics. Second, you will observe or play with the infant client. Children who are 18 months or older will play more easily. Third, for children who are unable to tell time, you may need to concretely show the client on a clock when you will be stopping. Fourth, you will need to adjust your language to fit the child's developmental level.

School-Age Children

With these clients, you will need toys and playthings to help build rapport (e.g., dolls, stickers, paper). Confidentiality must be discussed, although not all child clients will understand you. We recommend that you tell these clients that anything you will share with the parents or others you will discuss with them first.

Adolescents

Adolescents may appear like adults in many respects, yet must be treated differently. Rapport is established more slowly than with adults. Adolescents are more prone to test your boundaries and patience than adults. As with all clients, the more genuine you can be, the better.

Preparing Children and Adolescents for Psychological Assessment

We recommend that prior to the assessment, you have the parents inform the client about the assessment. Parents should be told to emphasize the following factors:

- The assessment is not being done to punish the child. It is to identify strengths and weaknesses.
- The procedures are not painful. Some clinicians use the term "talking doctor."
- The clinician will explain everything to the child in advance so that there are no surprises, and will provide additional help when needed.

When meeting child and adolescent clients for the first time, it is helpful to reemphasize these points as a way of introduction.

INTERVIEW CONTENT

Table 2.1 summarizes the content areas you may want to discuss during a clinical interview.

Chief Complaint

This is often the first item asked about during an interview, but it is not always necessary to do so. For example, rapport will be diminished if the client is embarrassed about the presenting symptoms, or is having difficulty explaining what is "wrong." When asking about the client's symptoms, it's a good idea to write down symptoms in the client's own words. Once rapport is sufficient, you can start to introduce the opinions of others (e.g., family, staff) to see how that information affects the client's own description.

TABLE 2.1
Outline of Interview Content

Chief Complaint

History Relevant to the Complaint
    Length of the problem
    Precipitants/effects
    Severity
    Pattern of recurrence
    Past treatment for problem

Developmental and Family History
    Parents' occupations
    Birth order and siblings
    Siblings' background
    Relationships
    Cultural considerations
    Developmental history
        Walking, talking, toilet-training

Academic History
    Best and worst classes
    Skipped/held back grades
    GPA/SAT/GRE
    School behavior, extracurricular activities
    Attendance/disciplinary actions

Social and Family History
    Dating/marriage
    Current family
    Friendships
    Occupation(s)
    Hobbies/gang affiliations/social activities

Medical History
    Head trauma
        Loss of consciousness, memory, location of injury, treatment
    Past surgeries
    Chronic illness

Psychiatric History
    Inpatient treatment
        Time and duration of previous hospitalizations
        Reason for past hospitalizations
    Outpatient treatment
        Time and duration of previous treatments
        Reason for treatments
        Name of current therapist
        Medications
            Psychotropic
            Other

History Relevant to the Chief Complaint

You want to have a picture of the client's immediate problem(s), including its duration, precipitating events, severity, whether it is a recurrence, and past treatment. Also assess for a family history of the disorder and the role of the family system. If the chief complaint is psychiatric, you will want to get details on past treatment, and its degree of success. Make sure to obtain the client's perspective on managing with a long-term problem to help identify coping skills.

Developmental and Family History

Knowing whether the client experienced any developmental problems can be illuminating. This information usually includes whether the client's mother had a normal pregnancy, had any birth complications, and whether the client learned to walk and talk at expected ages. Knowledge of whether the client's mother smoked, or used alcohol or drugs during pregnancy can also be relevant. Developmental history also includes birth order, and the client's relationships with family members and significant others. Information about the client's siblings (e.g., career, academic accomplishments, marital history) may also help you to better understand the client.

Academic History

When doing cognitive testing, you need to develop a clear impression of the client's intellectual accomplishments. Information that will help you determine this includes knowing high school and college grade point averages, SAT scores, whether the client skipped or was held back a grade, took advanced or remedial classes, and has been given any developmental diagnoses (e.g., dyslexia). Also identify the client's level of motivation and attendance throughout school.

Social and Family History

Social history includes many facets. You may want to learn how the client spends time when away from school or work. The client's employment or military history is also potentially useful. Marital status and relationship history are a part of this section, too. Finally, inquire about substance and alcohol use and abuse.

Medical History

This usually encompasses identifying relevant past surgeries, medical diagnoses (chronic and current), past physical traumas (e.g., head injury), and medications.

Psychiatric History

This information includes whether the client has had prior treatments, at what time, and for what purpose. Make sure to ask if the client saw counselors in school for any reason. You may need to check the client's report with the medical record, particularly when you get vague answers. This is most likely to occur when the client has sought treatment on numerous occasions. Where there is a known organic component (e.g., stroke, Parkinson's disease), it should be mentioned here.

GUIDELINES FOR PSYCHOLOGICAL TESTING

Rapport is a critical concept in testing as it is with interviews. Clients have to endure a process that is challenging and involves minimal feedback. Here are some specific guidelines to maintain your working relationship.

Give Positive Feedback for Effort

Basically, it doesn't matter how well clients do on tests; it only matters that they try. If you can convey this to the client, then you will maintain better rapport. Most clinicians use statements like, "That's fine; you're doing just fine" instead of "That's correct."

Some Clients Need to Know That Their Level of Performance Is Good

Some anxious clients fear that they are failing on a test, even when they are doing well. If you feel that the level of anxiety is affecting performance, you can give the client minimal positive feedback. This can often occur on the WAIS-III, after the client makes a series of consecutive failures. Remind the client that the test is designed so that most people cannot answer all of the items correctly. If the client remains anxious, consider stating, "You're doing fine on this part, though I can see you don't think so." Make sure to note the client's behavior in your report.

When Clients Refuse to Continue

Clients may refuse to continue for several reasons:

- *Fatigue.* Have you done too much for one day or without a break?
- *Failure.* Has the client done poorly and is now feeling badly?
- *Fear.* Is the client scared to continue because the test taps a known problem area?
- *Function.* Is the client malingering?
- *Frustration.* Does the client feel pushed, misunderstood, and aggravated?

Mental Status Examinations

Mental status exams originated from medical interviews, and are now commonly found in psychological assessments. Essentially, the exam is a summary of the client's cognitive and emotional state and is primarily based on clinical observation.

MENTAL STATUS EXAMINATIONS GIVE A COMPOSITE OF WHO THE CLIENT IS

A mental status examination is a vital component of a psychological assessment. It is the only place in the report that describes how the client appears at that moment in time. If an evaluation takes place over a series of days, make sure to comment on any changes. Here is a sample mental status exam:

> Ms. Jones was assessed in my office. She was well groomed, dressed cleanly and casually, looking younger than her stated age. She is right-handed. Her mood was euthymic, as was her affect, which was appropriate. She denied depressive or anxiety symptoms. Although she was cooperative during the testing, she mentioned that she disliked being tested. No abnormal motor movements were observed. Ms. Jones reported that she has trouble falling asleep, but can sleep through the night. She reported that her appetite is within normal limits, though she has recently gained five pounds. Ms. Jones's speech was at a normal rate and tone. Tangential thinking was not observed. She showed grossly average intellectual function. Her memory was grossly intact, and will be discussed in detail below. She was fully oriented. In contrast to the information provided by her therapist, Ms. Jones denied the presence of hallucinations and delusions. She also denied the presence of both suicidal and homicidal ideation. Impulse control was good; judgment was fair; insight was fair.

KEY SECTIONS IN AN ADULT MENTAL STATUS EXAMINATION

- *Appearance.* Note anything unusual or strange. Comment on grooming, gait, the client's apparent age, limitations in vision or hearing, and if the client is ambulatory. Is there bruising that would indicate abuse?
- *Handedness.* Comment on whether the client is left- or right-handed. Inquire whether the client switched handedness earlier.
- *Mood.* This is the dominant emotion of the client, and is usually described as euthymic (neutral), dysthymic, manic, etc.
- *Affect.* This is the range of emotion observed. Usually the report comments on the affect's content, whether the affect was consistent with mood, and its variability.
- *Behavior.* Comment on the presence of unusual behaviors (tics, etc.) or hyperactivity.
- *Intellectual function.* When testing is done, a gross estimate is recorded here.

- *Language.* Comment on the presence of expressive or receptive aphasia, or concrete use of language. The rate and tone of speech is also described. Mention the presence of an accent, if relevant.
- *Orientation.* Assess orientation to time, place, and person. When correct, it is usually noted as "orientation × 3."
- *Memory.* A gross estimate is recorded here. When testing isn't required, the ability for the client to recall three words is often used.
- *Attention.* Is the client easily distracted? Under what circumstances?
- *Thought process.* Comment on whether the client has hallucinations, delusions, or a thought disorder. Does the client show tangential thinking, circumstantiality, or concrete thinking?
- *Dangerousness.* Is the client dangerous to others or self? Is there ideation, a plan, a past history of dangerousness, poor coping skills, new stressors, or support?
- *Insight.* Comment on the client's awareness of current and past problems.
- *Judgment.* This is based on the client's interview behavior and responses to real life problems that were discussed during the interview.

KEY SECTIONS IN A MENTAL STATUS EXAMINATION OF CHILDREN

Lewis (1996) specifies special areas that are worth including in a child's mental status exam, in addition to those previously mentioned:

- *Physical appearance.* Does the child appear smaller or taller than average?
- *Separation.* Does the child separate from the parents with age-appropriate caution?
- *Manner of relating.* Some initial caution by the child is expected. Gross withdrawal or openness should be a clue for deeper exploration.

Summary

The clinical interview is the opportunity for you to get to know the client, to see whether the client's presentation is consistent with the impression of others, and to gather information that can help answer your referral question. Interviewing is a skill. With these guidelines, and sufficient practice, you will be able to perform rapid and effective clinical interviews.

CHAPTER 3

Criteria for Test Selection

Identifying which test(s) to use in conducting an efficient and effective evaluation involves several clinical, ethical, and practical concerns. This chapter reviews the factors to be considered in the selection of appropriate psychological assessment measures. The basic questions to ask before using a test are:

- Is the test accessible?
- Is the test psychometrically acceptable?
- Is the test clinically useful?
- Is the test appropriate for the client?

These issues will be addressed in more detail throughout this chapter.

Assessment Primer

Before you can do testing, you need to be able to compute and interpret standardized test scores. Moreover, you need to know what it means when we use specific terms such as "impaired" or "average."

STANDARD SCORES AND PERCENTILES

Standardized tests create a score by comparing the client's raw score with that of a comparison group. A standardized score describes how the client performed compared with the normative group. Norms are usually assumed to fall into a classical bell curve. There are several types of standardized scores, which are discussed in this chapter. A conversion table showing specific comparisons is included in Appendix C.

- *Z-scores.* A Z-score describes the client's raw score in terms of its closeness to the normative group's mean score. The mean Z-score is 0, and the standard deviation is 1. A client who scores 1 standard deviation (*SD*) above the normative group's mean would receive a Z-score of +1.00.
- *Standard scores.* The distribution of standard scores has a mean of 10 and a standard deviation of 3. A client who scores 1 standard deviation above the mean would have a standard score of 13. Standard scores are used, for example, on Wechsler subtest scales.
- *T-scores.* The distribution of T-scores has a mean of 50 and a standard deviation of 10. A client who scores 1 standard deviation above the mean would have a T-score of 60. T-scores are used on the MMPI-A and MMPI-2.
- *Percentiles.* A percentile can best be thought of as "How much better am I compared to everyone else?" A client who scores 1 standard deviation above the mean would score at the 84th percentile, meaning that the client scored better than 84% of others who took the test.
- *Descriptive labels.* Reports often describe the performance on standardized tests using words like "superior" or "impaired." These terms, taken from the Wechsler Intelligence Scales, have specific meanings, based on standardized test scores.

Testing Tip
Comparison of Standardized Scores

Standard Deviations	Percentiles	Standard Score	Descriptor
> 2 below the mean	< 2nd percentile	> 4	Impaired
2 below the mean	2nd percentile	4	Borderline
1 below the mean	16th percentile	7	Low average
Mean	50th percentile	10	Average
1 above the mean	84th percentile	13	High average
2 above the mean	98th percentile	16	Very superior

COMPUTING Z-SCORES FROM THE MEAN

If the information in the test manual or research report is limited, you may want to convert a raw score to a Z-score, using the following steps:

1. Obtain the mean and standard deviation of the test.
2. Subtract the client's raw score from the mean.
3. Divide that result by the standard deviation from the test.
4. Use Appendix C to identify the percentile.

STANDARD ERROR AFFECTS TEST INTERPRETATION

Every measure is imperfect to some degree; even a ruler cannot measure inches with 100% accuracy. The extent to which a specific test score reflects the true ability is denoted by a test's standard error. For example, when an IQ test is given to a client, we can assume there is a real score that reflects the client's true ability. This is referred to as the *true test score*. Yet, due to many factors, the score the client receives will not necessarily be the *true test score*. The standard error of the test score is the range in which the true test score is presumed to lie, based on the actual score the client receives. If a test has a standard error of 5, and the client scored 20, we can assume that the client's *true test score* could be anywhere between 15 and 25.

Standard error affects interpretations in several ways. First, when you give a test to a client repeatedly, you may see change that is within the test's standard error, and thus not a reflection of true change. Second, when determining the range of function (e.g., average, high average), you may find that the standard error of the test is wide enough to place the client into two descriptors. For example, the range of the client's score, based on the standard error, may be in both the impaired and borderline ranges.

DEFINING IMPAIRMENT

Many clinicians are surprised that impairment is defined so severely, such that a client performing better than only 16% of the population is considered merely *low average*. The reason for such strict definitions is that low scores can be due to many factors other than the primary one being assessed by the test. For example, depressed adults often score at the 16th percentile on certain memory tests. Moreover, different ethnic or cultural groups can appear to have lower scores if they are underrepresented in the normative sample.

LOSS OF FUNCTION

Testing is also useful because it identifies the client's relative strengths and weaknesses, as well as potential losses in function. For example, a corporate attorney with depression showed low average performance solely on tests of attention and calculation. Although this is not defined as impairment, it is unlikely that he had such weak performance prior to being depressed. These losses can also be identified by comparing the client's occupational history with expected test performance.

Finding Potential Tests

The typical tests used in clinical practice and discussed in this book are well researched measures and are easily obtainable. Most may be ordered from major psychological assessment companies (Appendix A) and are reviewed in many textbooks (e.g., R. Cohen, 1992; Maxmen & Ward, 1995; Newmark, 1996). To become familiar with a particular test that is not listed in this book: (a) Talk to colleagues who use the test, (b) Order the test manual, or (c) Receive free technical documents from the test's publisher (or through the Internet). Alternatively, you may want to consider a test reference source.

REFERENCE TEXTBOOKS

These references are often available in college libraries or can be purchased from test publishers (Appendix A). Three major source books are:

- *The Thirteenth Mental Measurements Yearbook (13th ed.)* (Impara & Plake, 1998). A collection of critical reviews and research for each test, updated approximately every three years.
- *Tests in Print IV* (Murphy, Conoley, & Impara, 1994). Lists basic information on each test, including psychometric properties, population, administration issues, the manual, author, and publisher.
- *A Comprehensive Reference for Assessment in Psychology, Education and Business (4th ed.)* (Maddox, 1997). Reviews over 3,500 tests currently used in psychology, education, and business.

COMPUTER DATABASES AND ON-LINE INFORMATION

There has been a proliferation of on-line information and computerized assessments available for purchase. Most test publishers have a Web site, and search engines help to identify more obscure data (Appendix A).

Selecting Tests

A fundamental decision, when embarking on a psychological evaluation, is the selection of test(s). Thinking through these issues now will make your work more efficient. We consider four major components in selecting tests:

1. Psychometric properties of the test.
2. Clinical utility of the test.
3. Client factors that can affect the test.
4. Clinician variables that can impact the test.

PSYCHOMETRIC PROPERTIES

Most clinicians use tests that they were trained with during graduate school, had exposure to during clinical training, or were introduced to by colleagues in clinical practice. Even if a test comes highly recommended from one of these reputable sources, it needs to meet certain standards and should conform to guidelines published by the American Psychological Association. These standards can be conceptualized in terms of three fundamental psychometric properties: validity, reliability, and standardization.

Validity

Does the test measure what it says it measures? A test does not need to be valid in every way to be useful for your purposes. Most indices of validity are expressed as correlations between the test and a criterion. Correlations above .75 are fairly solid. There are five facets of validity to keep in mind:

1. *Face validity.* Does the test look like it measures what it says? This is the weakest form of validity (e.g., a depression test having questions about sadness).
2. *Content validity.* Do the test items appear to have material relevant to the area being assessed? This is measured by experts identifying that the content in the test is representative of the intended domain. Because content does not always correlate with performance, this measure of validity is relatively weak.
3. *Concurrent/divergent validity.* Does the test correlate with other tests that measure the same domain and not with tests that measure a different domain? If not, then you can draw few conclusions from your client's test score.
4. *Predictive validity.* Does a score on the test predict future performance on another measure (e.g., IQ scores predicting scholastic achievement)?

If not, then you cannot use the test to draw conclusions about the client's future.

5. *Construct validity.* Does the test measure a specific trait or theoretical construct? Construct validity is often assessed with a factor analysis that identifies the underlying factors in a test.

There are also threats to validity to consider when choosing a test:

- *Lack of comprehension.* If the client doesn't understand the test, their responses will not reflect what the test measures.
- *Response set or bias.* A client's response may be influenced by factors such as social desirability, acquiescence, or nay-saying. When doing an assessment, it's important to choose a test that can identify the presence of these biases.
- *Unreliability.* Instability in test scores reduces validity. This is discussed below.

Reliability

In a perfect world, a client receiving an IQ score of 100 would get the same score every time the testing was done. However, there is natural variation in an individual's performance, resulting in a certain amount of variability that will affect reliability. Most indices of reliability are expressed as correlations between the test and itself. Correlations of .70 or better suggest acceptable reliability. Four primary forms of reliability are relevant to psychological assessment:

1. *Test-retest reliability.* Does a client's score remain the same over time? This is usually established by testing a client twice over a brief interval. Test-retest reliability can be affected by practice effects, the time interval between assessments, life events of the client, and variations in the clinician's administration of the test.
2. *Interrater or interscorer reliability.* Can the test be administered or scored consistently by different raters? Standardized administration and scoring contribute to higher interrater and interscorer reliability.
3. *Alternate forms reliability.* When a test has multiple forms, do they lead to similar scores? Even in well-designed tests, there is usually some variation.
4. *Split-half reliability.* Is the test consistent within itself? This is the measure of the test's internal consistency (e.g., the first 10 items in an anxiety test should correlate with the second 10 items).

Standardization and Norms

Most tests are standardized, meaning that a client's score is compared with a group of others who have taken the same test. The group is called the *normative group* or *norm*. The distribution of scores usually forms a bell curve, with the mean falling in the middle of the bell. Although it is frequently not mentioned in an assessment report, most tests are standardized based on age, and some norms also consider gender or education. Standardization is critical because a test's score is meaningless if the norms don't represent the comparison group adequately. In addition, some tests have norms based on specific comparison groups, such as clients with depression or head trauma.

A test may not meet all these criteria, but at the very least, it should be reasonably reliable, and show evidence for concurrent validity.

CLINICAL UTILITY

You should choose tests that will help answer the referral questions. For assistance in clarifying the referral question, see Chapter 2.

Use of Short Forms and Modified Tests

Clinicians sometimes address time constraints by giving shorter version of tests, usually for the MMPI-2, WISC-III, or WAIS-III. However, short forms can reduce the validity and reliability of the results. For the MMPI-2, there is little justification for their use (Graham, 1993). For the Wechsler scales of intelligence, several strategies have been widely researched; Chapter 4 discusses these. Only choose shortened forms that have been researched clinically.

Computerized Testing and Interpretation

There has been exponential growth in the development of computerized assessment measures and software interpretive programs. While these methods save time and increase both test-retest and interrater reliability, many are still considered experimental. Relying solely on computerized cognitive assessments is a disadvantage because it cannot be ruled out that performance was impacted by the skills needed to work well with computer-administered assessments.

Computerized scoring and interpretation of raw test data is more common, with most popular assessment measures having several interpretative programs available (Appendix A). An advantage to interpretive reports is that they document the universe of clinical interpretive data that exists based on a set of scores. Most scoring programs recognize scoring errors, or report indices that are cumbersome to calculate. Scoring the Rorschach Inkblot Test is so cumbersome that it becomes inefficient to hand-score it. However, narrative reports based on personality questionnaires vary dramatically in quality and validity. Such reports may include "Barnum" statements, statements that are so broad they have little specificity. If you use computerized interpretive programs for personality tests, do not overrely on the findings.

CLIENT FACTORS

Diversity

Ethnic and cultural diversity needs to be considered prior to the evaluation. Although the most recent versions of tests have used more representative standardization samples or have developed specific subgroup norms, cultural and ethnic background continue to impact test data (e.g., Bond, 1996; Geisinger, 1992; Uba, 1994). You will find that many of the commonly used tests described in Chapters 4 and 5 continue to use small samples of subjects from ethnic and cultural minorities (which is somewhat justified by using the proportions found in current U.S. census data). Nevertheless, there is increased recognition of substantial variability within cultural groups, suggesting that the client's scores should not be explained away as merely being due to culture or ethnicity.

If your client is from an ethnic minority group, it is important to consider the following factors prior to your evaluation:

- Language, education, and familiarity with American education.
- Level of acculturation.
- Tests with appropriate norms and relevant research.
- Culture-specific findings.
- Need for consultation and special services (e.g., translator).

Age

The age of the client affects which tests to administer, and the length and format of the testing session. As discussed earlier, both older adults and children often require shorter testing periods. Young children may need their parents to be present initially. Older adults may have trouble accepting younger clinicians or admitting to psychological problems.

Level of Education and Reading Level

Most of the major tests have reading-level requirements. Administer tests appropriate to the client's educational level because the client's comprehension of test items is crucial for an accurate assessment.

Physical and Emotional Limitations

If the client has physical limitations, some of the major tests will be inappropriate to administer or will need to be modified. Although there are measures of cognitive functioning specifically designed for clients who are visually-impaired or hearing-impaired, the norms are often limited in scope. Most clinicians give adapted versions of the cognitive tests discussed in Chapters 4 and 5, with the expectation that standardized scores will underestimate cognitive function.

Clients with severe psychopathology often strain the expertise of the clinician performing the assessment. Tests should be chosen that do not compromise rapport, or if necessary, the client should be given adequate emotional preparation. Keep in mind that not every client will be testable. These factors should always be discussed in the test report (see Chapter 12).

Motivation and Test Length

If motivation is an issue, try at the onset to establish strong rapport, or consider modifying the testing sessions, often starting with briefer measures. Test length becomes a significant issue when administering a battery of tests, or when working with clients for whom motivation is the clinical issue (e.g., Oppositional Defiant Disorder).

When There Is a Prior Assessment

If the client has been assessed previously, there are several issues to consider:

- Identify a valid reason for reassessment (see page 11).
- Obtain the earlier assessment, which may be useful as a baseline.
- Decide which tests to readminister, and which new tests to give.
- Obtain raw test data so that results can be compared if the client has moved into a different age group (see Chapter 4).
- Consider whether the client has preconceived notions created from an earlier evaluation that may affect your current assessment.

Financial and Time Constraints

The client's financial and time availability need to be considered when determining the appropriate measures to select.

CLINICIAN VARIABLES

Training and Experience

Ethically, you are obliged to be aware of your limitations and to not practice beyond the scope of your training. Legal difficulties with assessment have often been attributed to inappropriate use and interpretation of tests by inexperienced examiners. Thus, using tests that are easy to administer is not acceptable if you cannot make a skillful interpretation. At the onset, it is important to clarify the training requirements.

Before administering a new test, you should have knowledge of:

- Reliability and validity.
- Legal and ethical issues related to test use.

- Situation(s) that requires the use of the test.
- Conditions that can affect a client's performance.
- Strengths and limitations of the test.
- Impact of diversity on the test.

If you lack experience, obtain consultation and supervision from a colleague. In addition, numerous assessment classes are advertised by local and national psychological publications (e.g., *APA Monitor*), and training also occurs at local and national psychological conventions. Our experience, however, is that these programs, by themselves, do not offer sufficient training to replace a formal assessment curriculum.

Negative Responses to Clients

Monitor your personal feelings for the client. If your feelings impede an objective assessment, seek consultation and consider referring the case to a colleague, while being sensitive not to abandon the client.

When Not to Test

We recommend you consider not testing the client when any of the following indicators are present:

- Numerous recent psychological evaluations.
- Unrealistic expectations of the evaluation.
- Significant negative reactions by you toward the client.
- The presence of a multiple relationship (e.g., testing your psychotherapy client).
- Intoxication in the client during the evaluation.
- Inability to establish rapport.

Test Batteries

DETERMINING THE NUMBER OF TESTS TO GIVE

To prevent your assessment from becoming too cumbersome or too narrow requires having a clear referral question and an awareness of the problem or disorder being assessed. For each referral question, tests should be selected that assess for the presence of the primary disorder or problem, as well as other disorders that share its essential features or typically co-occur (e.g., an assessment for a somatoform disorder should also involve an evaluation of depression). In addition, you must be sensitive to test findings as they occur during the evaluation. Being mindful of test results, as they occur, helps you to select additional tests. This will save you time, particularly when a discrepant finding occurs that can only be resolved through further testing.

TIME AND MONEY

In addition to clinical concerns, consider test length, administration time, format of the test, the type of administration settings, and the ease of administration. Computer scoring is fast, but it can be expensive. In addition, you need to identify how much of your time the client can afford, or how much the insurance company will reimburse.

TEST BATTERIES

Test selection is affected by the other tests you plan to give. Assessments often consider many factors, including diagnosis, strengths and deficits, areas of concern (e.g., suicide, dangerousness, abuse, impulsivity), and treatment. Sometimes these questions can only be answered by administering a series of tests.

Advantages
- Allows for cross-validation of findings.
- Provides more comprehensive evaluation.
- Assesses client's responses to different situations.
- May identify previously unrecognized deficits.

Disadvantages
- More time-consuming.
- Greater expense.
- Completion issues.

We recommend that test batteries be brief, rather than broad. When additional testing is performed, it should be in response to findings made from the earlier tests. In Section II, we provide guidelines for selecting a series of tests, based on specific referral issues.

Testing Tip
Checklist for Test Selection

Questions to answer before selecting a test:

1. Is the test(s) valid and appropriate?
2. Are the measures reliable?
3. Are the norms appropriate or is the client represented in the normative sample?
4. Will it answer the referral question?
5. Are there any diversity or client considerations?
6. Do I have the necessary training?
7. Do I need a single test or a battery of tests?
8. Will additional tests provide new information?
9. Is the administration, scoring, and interpretation standardized?
10. Is the interpretation computerized?

CHAPTER 4

Adult and Older Adult Assessment

T HE FOCUS OF THIS CHAPTER is on adult assessment. We describe the most commonly used assessment measurements of cognitive and emotional functions currently available, and provide methods for quickly understanding and interpreting their use. Readers unfamiliar with standardized tests may wish to read the section titled Assessment Primer in Chapter 3.

Overview of Common Assessment Instruments

While this section includes some of the most current tests available, exclusion of a test does not mean that it is bad. The tests described here are the ones most commonly used, are most likely to answer a broad range of referral questions, and meet the criteria outlined in Chapter 2. Table 4.1 compares basic information for frequently used tests described in the next two chapters.

The following sections provide for each test: (a) descriptive information, (b) key scoring and interpretive information, and (c) integration of the test into a rapid assessment battery.

Wechsler Adult Intelligence Scale-III (WAIS-III)

DESCRIPTION

The publication of the new WAIS-III (Psychological Corporation, 1997; Wechsler, 1997b) positions Wechsler's work into the 21st century as one of the primary measures of intelligence. It can be given to clients between the ages of 16 and 89 years. This latest version comprises 14 subtests, though not all are required. In principle, each subtest is a measure of what the client has learned,

TABLE 4.1
Practical and Clinical Utility of Common Assessment Measures

Test	Wechsler Scales	Minnesota Multiphasic Personality Inventory	Millon	Rorschach	Apperception Tests
Type	Intelligence and cognitive function	Objective test of emotional/ personality function	Objective test of emotional/ personality function with *DSM-IV* diagnoses	Projective test of personality	Projective test of interpersonal conflicts/ issues
Format	WAIS-III: 7 verbal and 7 nonverbal subtests WISC-III: 6 verbal and 7 nonverbal subtests WPPSI-R: 6 verbal and 6 nonverbal subtests	MMPI-2: 567 true-false items MMPI-A: 478 true-false items	MCMI-III: 175 true-false items MACI: 160 true-false items	10 cards are shown, responses are written verbatim; inquiry regarding responses is made	Cards, pictures, or drawings are used to tell a story
Population	WAIS-III: 16–89 yrs WISC-III: 6–17 yrs WPPSI-R: 3–7 yrs	MMPI-2: >18 yrs, 8th grade reading level MMPI-A: 14–18 yrs, 6th grade reading level	MCMI-III: >18 yrs, 8th grade reading level MACI: 13–19 yrs, 6th grade reading	> 4 yrs of age	TAT: >10 yrs RATC: 6–15 yrs CAT: 3–10 yrs SAT: >64 yrs
Testing Situation	1 to 1 administration	Self-report, individual, group, computerized	Self-report, individual, group, computerized	1 to 1 administration	1 to 1 administration
Scoring Options	1. By hand with manual 2. By hand with PC assist	1. By hand with manual (lengthy) 2. PC scoring (fee)	1. By hand with manual (lengthy) 2. PC scoring (fee)	1. By hand with manual (very lengthy) 2. By hand with PC assist	By hand with manual
Format of Results	Total score, scale scores, subtest scores, index scores	Validity scales, clinical scales, supplemental scales	Validity scales, personality disorders, clinical syndromes	Numerous summary scores and indices	Themes, summary scores

as measured under specific experimental circumstances (Kaufman, 1994). Seven of the subtests are considered to be verbal measures and seven are performance measures. Raw scores on the subtests are converted to standard scores. A Verbal IQ Score (VIQ), Performance IQ Score (PIQ), and Full Scale IQ Score (FIQ) are computed based on tallying the standard scores for each age group. These scores have a mean of 100 and a standard deviation of 15.

Testing Tip
WAIS-III

When to Use It
- Identification of client's intellectual function.
- Determination of client's cognitive strengths and weaknesses.
- Determining impact of emotional or psychiatric issues on cognitive function.

Advantages
- Provides comprehensive picture of cognitive abilities and related clinical factors.
- Can give abbreviated versions, depending on referral source.
- Well understood by most referring sources.
- Less likely to show floor or ceiling effects compared with earlier version.
- Standardized with the same subjects as the WMS-III.

Disadvantages
- Full testing can be time-consuming.
- Materials are bulky.

Eleven subtests are used to compute Verbal, Performance, and Full Scale IQ Scores, though a prorated IQ can be derived by using nine subtests. Subtests have a mean of 10 and a standard deviation of 3.

Eleven subtests can be combined to form the following four index scores:
1. Verbal Comprehension (VCI)
    Subtests: Vocabulary, Similarities, Information.
    Reflects verbal reasoning, learning, and academic performance.
2. Perceptual Organization (POI)
    Subtests: Picture Completion, Block Design, Matrix Reasoning.
    Reflects nonverbal reasoning and visually dependent abilities.
3. Working Memory (WMI)
    Subtests: Arithmetic, Digit Span, Letter-Number Sequencing.
    Reflects the attentional components needed to input, process, and respond. Susceptible to anxiety, depression, and distractibility.
4. Processing Speed (PSI)
    Subtests: Digit Symbol-Coding, Symbol Search.
    Reflects the ability to rapidly process visual data. Lower scores may be due to anxiety, depression, or neuropsychological impairment.

Thirteen subtests are required to compute both IQ scores and the index scores.

Wechsler intended his intelligence test to provide both clinical and intellectual data, though this iteration focuses more on intellectual abilities.

Subtest Organization

Each subtest's items are arranged in order of difficulty. Most subtests are set up so that a client is given items until a sequence of consecutive failures occurs (between 2 and 5 items). The assumption is that clients will plateau at their highest ability level. Some items are timed, so that a client has a fixed amount of time to complete the item. For other items, bonus points are awarded for more rapid performance. Speed plays a smaller role in performance for older clients.

The Concept of Intelligence

There are numerous models of describing intellectual function (e.g., global, fluid vs. crystallized; see Kaufman, 1994, for an excellent review). For the purposes of most rapid assessments, intelligence can be considered both globally as well as a reflection of individual abilities. Thus, overall FIQ, PIQ, and VIQ scores give you a general picture of the client, whereas examination of index scores, subtest scales, and qualitative data help provide a more specific picture of the client's intellectual abilities and problem-solving skills. Further discussion of methods of cognitive test interpretation can be found in Chapters 11 and 12.

SCORING AND INTERPRETATION

The Big Picture

In this section, we provide several models for interpreting cognitive test scores. There is no absolute singular method for interpreting test scores. Using a flexible approach allows you to consider as many variables as necessary.

One key to interpreting IQ scores, index scores, and subtest scale scores is to examine the scatter between subtests. In principle, summary scores like IQ and index scores are meaningful because it is presumed the subtests that make them up are reasonably homogeneous. For example, if a client received a VIQ of 100, we would expect that most of the subtests fell within the range of 9–11. When significant scatter does occur, you should use summary scores with greater caution.

How to Identify Significant Scatter

Scatter can be defined in several ways, and the critical values for defining it are located in a series of tables at the back of the WAIS-III manual.

First, identify if there was significant scatter for VIQ by subtracting the highest subtest score from the lowest subtest score. Then, use Table B.5 in the WAIS-III manual and choose the appropriate column based on the number of subtests given. If the scatter occurred with a cumulative frequency of 5% or less, then it is best not to rely on VIQ, and instead plan to use index scores. Repeat these steps for PIQ.

Second, if either VIQ or PIQ showed too much scatter, calculate, if possible, the index scores. Use Table B.4 in the WAIS-III manual to identify if there were statistically significant differences between the subtests that make up each index score. If so, then rely on separate interpretations of each subtest rather than using index scores. In the end, you may find that you are relying on a combination of IQ scores, index scores, and subtest scale scores.

Interpreting WAIS-III Scatter

- *Vocabulary versus Information versus Similarities.* When both Vocabulary and Information are low, relative to Similarities, you may consider whether this was due to poor academic performance. If the opposite occurs, the client may be showing more concrete thinking (which would also be seen on Matrix Reasoning). Higher Information may be due to an interest in trivia.
- *Picture Completion versus Block Design versus Matrix Reasoning.* Always determine if time played a factor in performance, since only Matrix Reasoning is untimed (slowness may be due to depression, anxiety, obsessiveness). Scatter may be due to lack of motivation, which occurs on only one of the subtests. Younger subjects tend to like Picture Completion, which can lead to higher scores.
- *Arithmetic versus Digit Span versus Letter-Number Sequencing.* Check to see if fatigue led to lower scores on the latter tests, due to order effects. Lower Arithmetic might be due to lack of computational skill or problems with executive function (also seen on Block Design and Matrix Reasoning). Lower Letter-Number Sequencing may be due to its being a more demanding active memory task, relative to Digit Span. Higher Arithmetic may be seen in clients who need to use everyday math skills (e.g., accountants).
- *Digit-Symbol Coding versus Symbol Search.* Higher scores on Digit Symbol may be due to the greater role of memory, such that clients learn the items and work faster, and faster motor speed, since the task involves writing. Lower scores on Symbol Search may be due to poor visual scanning or distractibility. Symbol Search also may be lower due to fatigue, as it comes later in the test.

Classical Interpretation of the WAIS-III

First, examine the IQ scores (VIQ, PIQ, and FIQ). Note if scores are consistent with the client's premorbid function, level of education, and career. Use

Table B.1 in the WAIS-III manual to identify if there is a statistically significant difference between VIQ and PIQ scores (around 9 points at the $p < .05$ level). If it is significant, then use Table B.2 to identify how common the difference occurred in the standardization sample. A statistically significant difference is much more meaningful if it occurs with little frequency in the standardization sample. Record these values on the Discrepancy Analysis page of the WAIS-III booklet.

If enough subtests were given, calculate the four index scores. Similarly to the IQ scores, identify using Tables B.1 and B.2 in the WAIS-III manual if there were significant differences between the index scores. These values, too, are recorded on the Discrepancy Analysis page.

To determine individual strengths and weaknesses, separately calculate the mean score for the VIQ and PIQ subtests. Otherwise, you can calculate a mean based on all of the subtests, if they were homogeneous. Use Table B.3 in the WAIS-III manual to identify the mean differences required for statistical significance, and to identify the frequency of the difference in the standardization sample. These values are recorded on the Score Conversion page of the WAIS-III manual.

Table 4.2 lists the variables tapped by the 14 WAIS-III subtests, and this can help you to interpret patterns, strengths, and weaknesses. Finally, look at qualitative differences picked up by the subtests (e.g., anxiety). These, too, are mentioned in Table 4.2.

Remember, IQ and index scores may be suspect if the subtest scores on which they are based are not reasonably homogeneous. Thus, it would make little sense to compare VIQ with PIQ if there were 10 points scatter between the subtests that comprise VIQ. Always identify if there was too much subtest scatter to make interpretation of the summary scores suspect. Comment on this in your report.

Common Interpretations of VIQ-PIQ Differences

Because a first step in interpreting IQ scores is to look at the difference between VIQ and PIQ, it is useful to explicitly state possible explanations for VIQ-PIQ differences.

VIQ > PIQ
- Psychomotor retardation.
- Reduced effort and motivation on timed tasks.
- Reduced visuomotor coordination and processing.
- Stress or anxiety due to time pressure.
- Organic impairment.
- Visual-perceptual-organizational deficits (nonverbal concepts).
- Impulsivity and acting out.

TABLE 4.2

Wechsler Adult Intelligence Scale-III (WAIS-III) Subtest Summary

Subtest and Task Description	WAIS-III Statistical Information		Interpretation and Clinical Consideration*

VERBAL SUBTESTS

Vocabulary 33 items measure knowledge of vocabulary	Split-half reliability Most related to: Information Similarities Least related to: Object assembly Digit span	.93 .77 .76 .44 .45	Standard interpretation [word knowledge & language development]: fund of verbal knowledge, best correlate of VIQ, verbal comprehension, and expression • Administration is slow. • Content is sensitive to aphasia. • Content is less sensitive to organic effects. • Obsessiveness can lead to higher scores. • Sensitive to thought disorder and characterological responses. • Look for content that may reflect clinical issues. • Look for abstract thinking in responses vs. bookish rote answers.
Similarities 19 items measure ability of client to describe how different objects are, in fact, similar	Split-half reliability Most related to: Vocabulary Information Comprehension Least related to: Digit span Coding	.86 .76 .70 .70 .40 .40	Standard interpretation [abstract thinking ability]: verbal concept formation, reasoning • Administration is quick. • Content is sensitive to concrete thinking and psychosis. • Consider degree of abstractness in answers (abstract, concrete, functional). • Obsessiveness can lead to higher scores. • Consider if total score is due to many 1-point or few 2-point responses. • Performance depends little on school-based learning. • Marked concreteness or perseveration can suggest organicity.
Arithmetic 20 items measure ability to perform oral arithmetic problems within a specific time period	Split-half reliability Most related to: Information Vocabulary Least related to: Object assembly Picture comp.	.88 .63 .60 .39 .40	Standard interpretation [computational skill]: sequential processing, facility with numbers, short-term memory, numerical reasoning, speed of processing • Consider whether errors were due to computation, reasoning, lack of attention, or comprehension. • To test limits: Repeat questions, allow pencil/ paper. • Arithmetic is not a measure of academic math achievement. • Depressed clients answer slowly/give up easily. • Look for math phobia as a factor in performance. • Performance is susceptible to anxiety.
Digit Span 30 items measure ability of client to repeat a string of digits forward and backward; strings increase in length	Split-half reliability Most related to: Letter-no. seq Arithmetic Least related to: Object assembly Picture comp.	.90 .57 .52 .26 .30	Standard interpretation [attention]: attention span, sequential processing • Digits backward is more demanding, requiring working memory, spatial visualization, and number manipulation. • Identify whether errors are due to: (a) problems in sequencing, (b) rote memory (e.g., omitting an item), (c) inattention, (d) anxiety. • Better digits backward than forward may suggest variation in effort. • Be wary of conditions that reduce performance (noise, hearing problems). • Performance is susceptible to anxiety. • Norms are now provided to identify significant differences between digits forward and digits backward.

TABLE 4.2 (Continued)

Subtest and Task Description	WAIS-III Statistical Information		Interpretation and Clinical Consideration*
Information 28 items measure common knowledge (holidays, famous figures, science, geography)	Split-half reliability Most related to: Vocabulary Similarities Comprehension Least related to: Digit symbol Digit span Object assembly	.91 .77 .70 .70 .38 .40 .40	Standard interpretation [range of general knowledge]: retention of school-based learning, long-term memory • Subtest is quick to administer and nonthreatening to give (to subjects with average VIQ). • Content elicits rationalizations and excuses. • Failure only on early items may be due to retrieval problems, anxiety, motivation. • Long answers suggest obsessiveness. • Content is sensitive to thought disorder and characterological responses. • Content is sensitive to aphasia and articulation problems. • Failures may be due to cultural and educational background.
Comprehension 18 items measure knowledge of social situations and proverbs	Split-half reliability Most related to: Vocabulary Similarities Information Least related to: Digit symbol Digit span	.84 .75 .70 .70 .37 .39	Standard interpretation [demonstration of practical information, knowledge of conventional standards of behavior]: assesses social knowledge, common sense, reasoning • Administration is fast; scoring is slow. • Culture can impact this test. • Emotional maladjustment lowers scores. • Look for content that may reflect clinical issues. • Content is sensitive to thought disorder and characterological responses. • Do not predict social adjustment with this subtest alone. • Look for abstract thinking in responses vs. bookish rote answers. • Performance correlates with education. • Subtest is less sensitive to organic effects, but may demonstrate aphasia.
Letter-Number Sequencing 21 items measure ability of client to reorder a string of letters and numbers that are presented orally	Split-half reliability Most related to: Digit span Arithmetic Least related to: Object assembly Picture arrang.	.82 .57 .55 .29 .39	Standard interpretation [working memory]: processing demands, sequencing • Items are very demanding. • Performance depends little on school-based learning. • Identify if errors are due to: (a) problems in sequencing, (b) rote memory (e.g., omitting an item), (c) inattention, (d) anxiety. • Be wary of conditions that reduce performance (noise, hearing problems).

PERFORMANCE SUBTESTS

Picture Completion 25 items measure ability, within a fixed time period, to identify missing elements from pictures	Split-half reliability Most related to: Block design Object assembly Least related to: Digit span Arithmetic	.83 .52 .52 .30 .40	Standard interpretation [visual recognition and identification]: attention to detail, familiarity with everyday objects, visual organization, gestalt processing, ability to discriminate essential from nonessential • Most clients like doing this test. • Administration is quick. • Quick responses suggest impulsivity. • Word retrieval problems may suggest aphasia. • Overinclusion errors suggest paranoia or psychosis.

(Continued)

TABLE 4.2 (Continued)

Subtest and Task Description	WAIS-III Statistical Information		Interpretation and Clinical Consideration*
Digit Symbol-Coding Measures ability of client to perform a symbol-replacement task as rapidly as possible	Split-half reliability Most related to: Symbol search Least related to: Object assembly Digit span	.84 .65 .33 .36	Standard interpretation [psychomotor speed]: motor skill, memory, hand-eye coordination, extended concentration • Rule out visual impairment when low scores occur. • Let perfectionistic clients know to perform the test merely legibly. • Examine pacing over 30-sec periods to identify learning curve. • Performance is susceptible to anxiety. • Incidental learning and copy options allow examiner to identify role of memory and orthographic skill on digit symbol-coding.
Block Design 14 items measure ability to rapidly reproduce designs using a set of red and white colored blocks	Split-half reliability Most related to: Object assembly Matrix reasoning Least related to: Digit span Digit symbol	.86 .61 60 .36 .41	Standard interpretation [analysis of whole into component parts, nonverbal concept formation]: visual perception, trial-and-error learning, spatial information processing, speed of processing, synthesis, spatial visualization, flexibility in thinking • Note whether lower scores are due to slowness or lack of ability. • Obsessiveness can lower scores due to slowness. • Subtest is a good marker of right hemisphere damage. • How blocks are used demonstrates problem-solving style. • Test limits: After subtest, do incorrect items with no time limit.
Matrix Reasoning 26 items; an untimed task; an incomplete gridded array is shown, and the subject chooses the missing item from a set	Split-half reliability Most related to: Block design Arithmetic Least related to: Digit symbol Digit span	.90 .60 .58 .40 .42	Standard interpretation [visual processing, visual reasoning, pattern recognition]: executive functioning, whole-part relationships, concept formation • Subtest items purport to measure pattern completion, classification, analogy reasoning, and serial reasoning. • Computation skill is required to solve some items. • Items assess nonverbal reasoning without associated time pressures.
Picture Arrangement 11 items measure ability to rearrange, in a fixed time period, a set of cartoon pictures into their correct order	Split-half reliability Most related to: Information Vocabulary Least related to: Digit span Digit symbol	.74 .54 .53 .33 .37	Standard interpretation [temporal sequencing, anticipation of consequences]: applied social knowledge, visual sequencing, visual perception, common sense, distinguishing essential details, social judgment • Subtest evaluates clients' ability to "get the story." • Almost every story is humorous; clients who are more concrete or depressed will often miss humor as a unifying theme. • Do not predict social adjustment with this subtest alone. • Impulsive clients may work rapidly, but incorrectly. • Test limits: After completing subtest, ask client to tell the stories to incorrect items. • Performance is susceptible to cultural influence. • Thought disorder can lead to illogical stories. • Determine if older adults can perform items correctly with additional time.

TABLE 4.2 (Continued)

Subtest and Task Description	WAIS-III Statistical Information		Interpretation and Clinical Consideration*

Symbol Search
  Measures ability to find, as rapidly as possible, specific symbols that are mixed up within a row of other symbols
	Split-half reliability
	Most related to:
	  Digit symbol
	  Block design
	Least related to:
	  Digit span
	  Comprehension
		.77
		
		.65
		.53
		
		.41
		.44
			Standard interpretation [speed of visual search]: speed of processing, learning ability, visuomotor coordination
			 • Rule out visual impairments before interpreting a low score.
			 • Look to see whether performance is due to obsessiveness, coordination, impulsivity, motivation, visual-perception, anxiety.

Object Assembly
  5 items measure ability to arrange, as rapidly as possible, a set of puzzle pieces together to make a picture of a common object
	Split-half reliability
	Most related to:
	  Block design
	  Picture comp.
	Least related to:
	  Digit span
	  Letter-no. seq.
		.70
		
		.61
		.52
		
		.26
		.29
			Standard interpretation [relationship among parts, ability to benefit from sensory-motor feedback]: flexibility in thinking, holistic processing, reasoning, speed of processing, trial-and-error learning
			 • Administration is slow and cumbersome.
			 • Obsessiveness can lower scores due to slowness.
			 • How pieces are used demonstrates problem-solving style.
			 • Inability to figure out objects may indicate visual-perceptive problems.
			 • Clients who peek behind the screen may be insecure or impulsive.
			 • *This subtest is only required if one of the other performance subtests was spoiled.*

*Specific ability measured solely by each subtest is placed in brackets.
Adapted in part from Kaufman, A. S. (1994). *Intelligent Testing with the WISC-III.* (New York: John Wiley & Sons). Also adapted from Wechsler (1997b).

Testing Tip
WAIS-III Rapid Interpretation

- Describe overall IQ score (e.g., high average, average) and identify whether it is consistent with premorbid level or at an expected level given the client's education and career.
- Identify statistically significant and infrequent differences in VIQ and PIQ (as long as subtests are homogeneous):

    VIQ > PIQ possibly suggests depression, anxiety, organicity, motor slowing, better verbal intellectual abilities.

    PIQ > VIQ possibly suggests lower education, cultural differences, impulsivity, better nonverbal intellectual abilities.

- Identify statistically significant and infrequent differences between index scores (as long as subtests are homogeneous).
- Identify strengths and weaknesses by comparing individual subtest scores to the mean, and identifying significant discrepancies.
- Examine performance on individual subtests and look for reasons to account for scatter.
- Examine qualitative differences and test-taking approach, and look for noncognitive explanations to account for deficits.

PIQ > VIQ
- Lack of formal education or cultural factors.
- Reduced attention span.
- Problems with verbal reasoning.
- Problems with hearing or speech.

Considering IQ Scores Using an Information Processing Model

Like others (e.g., Kaufman, 1994), we think it is useful to consider intelligence with an information processing model. In this model, an intellectual activity might occur in this order:

1. Information passes through sensory modalities to be input.
2. It is stored in memory.
3. It is processed, as necessary.
4. The output is released.

Thus, performance can be traced back to these areas to identify where problems occur.

1. Problems with *input* of information may be seen as PIQ > VIQ or POI > VCI:
   Hearing impairment can underestimate VIQ.
   Cultural differences affect language.
   Slight differences may be due to severe language disability affecting VIQ a lot and PIQ some; they may also reflect global neurological dysfunction.
   VIQ > PIQ or VCI > POI may also suggests visual-perceptual problems.
2. Problems with *storage* may appear as a lower WMI score:
   This index score reflects greater memory demands than other subtests.
3. Problems with *processing* of information may appear as VIQ > PIQ or a lower POI score:
   Such problems reflect the greater processing demands required in performance subtests.
4. Problems with *output* of information may be seen as lower PIQ and PSI:
   Coordination problems can lower PIQ.
   Speed of performance may lower scores although answers are correct.
   Behavioral factors lower speed (e.g., anxiety, immaturity, obsessiveness).

Testing Tip
Rapid Alternatives to Identify IQ Scores

Sometimes, you need an estimate of intellectual function, but are unable to give a sufficient number of WAIS-III subtests. Here are some alternatives, although all are gross estimates of IQ scores and should be interpreted with caution.

National Adult Reading Test (NART)
It can be given to adults ages 18–70. The ability to pronounce a list of words correlates with IQ score. The NART consists of 50 words that can only be pronounced correctly by recognition. It is quick to administer and score, but IQ estimates are based on the earlier WAIS-R, and it is not able to estimate IQ in very bright subjects. In addition, the standardization sample is from England. Overall, it is good as a quick and dirty estimate of intellectual function.

Barona Index
(Barona, Reynolds, & Chastain, 1984; Helmes, 1996). The Barona index is a formula that uses age, gender, and other demographic characteristics to estimate IQ. Consequently, it is a gross measure, and has a wide standard error of measurement (12.1 points). Use the following formula based on the listed codes to calculate a score:

Estimated IQ = 54.96 + .47 (age) + 1.76 (sex) + 4.71 (race)
      + 5.02 (education) + 1.89 (occupation) + .59 (region)

Codes for each variable are:

Age:		Sex:		Education:		
16–17	1	male	2	0–7 years		1
18–19	2	female	1	8		2
20–24	3			9–11		3
25–34	4	Race: black	1	12		4
35–44	5	other	2	13–15		5
45–54	6	white	3	16+		6
55–64	7					
65–69	8	Region (U.S.):	South	1		
70–74	9		North Central	2		
75–79	10		West	3		
80–84	11		Northeast	4		
85–89	12	Region (Canada):	Rural (<2500)	1		
90–94	13		Urban (>2500)	2		
95–99	14					
>100	15					

Occupation:	farm foremen, laborers (unskilled workers)	1
	operatives, service workers, farmers, farm managers	2
	not in the labor force	3
	craftspersons and foremen (skilled workers)	4
	managers, officials, proprietors, clerical and sales workers	5
	professional and technical	6

Noncognitive Factors That Can Affect Test Performance

Performance on Wechsler scales can be due to numerous secondary factors. By examining clinical observations, incorrect responses, and other tests, you may identify the role these factors play on test performance. Whenever a weakness or strength is identified, it is important to identify whether the variation occurred due to a secondary factor. The most common ones include:

- Mood: anxiety, depression, negativism, hostility (decreases scores).
- Immaturity (decreases scores).
- Impulsiveness (decreases scores).
- Obsessiveness to detail, perfectionism (can increase scores, but can also slow client down).
- Motivation/persistence.
- Overlearned "bookishness" (can increase scores, but superficially).
- Lack of socialization (tends to decrease scores).
- Culture/ethnicity/language/education (tends to decrease scores).
- Time pressure.
- Flexibility in thinking (increases scores).

DON'T ALWAYS ADMINISTER THE WHOLE TEST

We do not recommend giving the entire WAIS-III to every client requiring a cognitive assessment because you can usually answer the referral question without it. In particular, Vocabulary is a slow subtest to administer and score. When time is of the essence, we suggest not using it, unless you need the most accurate FIQ and VIQ possible, or are concerned about educational accomplishments.

The FIQ, PIQ, and VIQ scores can be computed based on a prorated version of the test by giving five Verbal subtests and four Performance Subtests (if index scores are subsequently needed, you would still need to give three additional subtests). Also use prorated scores if one of the subtests has been spoiled.

CLIENT FACTORS

Ethnic and Cultural Diversity

The WAIS-III includes a broader sampling of clients than most earlier tests, and items have been designed to reduce ethnic and cultural biases. The standardization sample ($N = 2450$) was collected to match 1995 U.S. Census data, which contains a very small proportion of Asians and Native Americans. Ethnic and cultural groups were oversampled so that statistical comparison and item bias analyses between cultural groups could be made. Nevertheless, this does not mean that the test is free from all cultural and ethnic biases, so always consider their influence in the client's response. For example, clients with lower comprehension and fluency in English are more likely to have lower scores.

The WAIS-III in the Elderly

The WAIS-III has been designed for use in older adults, and is standardized for adults up to age 89, which extends its use by seven years over the previous revision. Unlike its predecessor, the WAIS-III materials are larger and easier for older adults to see. (See the Testing Tips on pages 45 and 47.)

The Minnesota Multiphasic Personality Inventory-II (MMPI-2)

DESCRIPTION

The MMPI-2 (Butcher, Dahlstrom, Graham, Tellegen, & Kaemmer, 1989) is one of the most popular assessments of personality and emotional functioning. It is a 567-item true-false questionnaire that has been extensively validated. It can be given to adults who are 18 years or older who read at an eighth-grade level. The items are summed into 7 validity and 10 clinical scales. The MMPI-2 is easy to administer and score (though you must pay a fee to score it). It takes about 90 minutes to complete. Interpretation can be rapid if a computerized scoring system is used. Although there is a short form of the MMPI-2, we do not recommend using it because of its questionable validity. (See Testing Tip on page 50.)

Scale Scores > 64 Are Considered Clinically Significant

Responses on the individual scales are summed into corrected raw scores, and then converted into T-scores. T-scores have a mean of 50 and a standard deviation of 10. Clinically significant scores are those with a T-score > 64, which is in the 93rd percentile.

SCORING AND INTERPRETATION OF THE VALIDITY SCALES

The first step in scoring is to evaluate the quality of the individual's responses and the validity of the profile.

Time to Completion May Indicate Validity

Clients who finish the MMPI-2 in less than an hour may have an invalid profile. Clients who take 2 hours or more, on the other hand, may have (a) significant psychopathology, (b) below-average IQ or poor reading ability, or (c) cognitive impairment.

Testing Tip
MMPI-2

When to Use It
- To assess emotional functioning.
- To clarify coexisting diagnoses.
- To validate your clinical impression of the client.
- To obtain information about the client's level of psychopathology.

Advantages
- Provides rapid information about emotional and personality function.
- Shows good reliability and validity.
- Familiar to most clinicians.
- Provides scales that assess the test's validity.

Disadvantages
- Few studies of its use in clients with disabilities or in rehabilitation.
- Lengthy for older adults to complete.
- Requires significant motivation.
- Scoring service charges a fee for each testing.

---

*Inspect the Answer Sheet to See That the Client Did Not Select
All True or False Items*

Most assessment texts display the profile of an all-true or all-false respondent. It's easier to examine the answer sheet first.

When More Than Ten Items Are Unanswered, the Profile May Be Invalid

The Cannot Say (?) scale is the sum of unanswered items. Make sure that as many items are completed as possible. There is not a consensus as to the minimum number of items that may be left unanswered on the MMPI-2 for it to remain valid. Answer sheets with 30 or more items missing, however, should not be scored.

The Validity Scales Measure Test-Taking Attitude

These seven scales moderate the interpretation of the clinical scales. They are summarized in Table 4.3.

Profiles Can Be Interpreted Even When Validity Scales Are Significantly Elevated

Clinical judgment should be used in interpreting the clinical scales when the validity scales are elevated. For example, a client showing an inverted V configuration

TABLE 4.3
Minnesota Multiphasic Personality Inventory-II (MMPI-2) Scales and Descriptions

Scale	Description
	VALIDITY SCALES
? (Cannot Say)	This refers to the number of items that aren't completed. More than 10 items should alert you that the client's profile may be invalid. May be due to low education, confusion, obsessiveness, defensiveness.
L Lie	Items are simple frailties that most people admit. Measures tendency for the client to want to appear favorably. High scores (T > 55) suggest dishonesty, unwillingness to admit problems, lack of insight, denial.
F Infrequency	Few people endorse these items. Infrequency is considered a gross indication of psychopathology. Very high scores (T > 100) suggest acute pathology, malingering, plea for help. Typically, when the F scale is highly elevated, clinical scales are elevated, too.
K Correctness	Items are those that were endorsed by known pathological clients who nevertheless had normal clinical profiles. Thought to measure subtle defensiveness, but is correlated with socioeconomic status. High scores may reflect both. Scores > 65 may suggest subtle attempt to fake "good" or deliberately responding false to most items.
Fb Back Page Infrequency	Assesses whether client tends to answer latter items on the test in an uncommon manner, as with the F scale. Elevated scores suggest invalidity, particularly of content and supplemental scales. High scores suggest fatigue, frustration with the test's length, invalidity.
VRIN Variable Response Inconsistency	Assesses whether client tends to answer pairs of similar items in the opposite direction. T-scores > 80 suggest profile invalidity, confusion, random responding.
TRIN True Response Inconsistency	Assesses whether client tends to answer pairs of opposite items in the same direction. T-scores > 80 suggest profile invalidity, response set bias.
	CLINICAL SCALES
1 Hs Hypochondriasis	Elevated scores suggest somatic complaints and somatic disorders, a lack of insight, feelings of misery and hopelessness, hostility, narcissism, and a critical demanding style.
2 D Depression	Elevated scores suggest depression, pessimism, low self-confidence, indecisiveness, distress, a withdrawn style, and psychomotor retardation.
3 Hy Hysteria	Elevated scale scores are common in clients with specific somatic complaints, who have low insight, are self-centered, emotionally involved, and open to therapy (but have poor follow-through).

(Continued)

TABLE 4.3 (Continued)

Scale	Description
4 *Pd* Psychopathic Deviate	Elevated scale suggests problems incorporating society's values, poor behavioral planning, rebelliousness toward authority, impatience, family conflict, and alienation. These clients are egocentric and outgoing, but fulfill their needs without care for societal expectations. Scale has been known to be elevated in clients who do not show the above described tendencies and are from ethnic minorities.
5 *Mf* Masculinity Femininity	Elevated scores in men suggest sexual issues and concerns, and a lack of stereotypical masculine interests. Low scores in men suggest a very masculine presentation and stereotypical masculine interests. Elevated scores in women suggest a rejection of the female role, and a greater interest in stereotypical masculine interests. Low scores in women suggest the presence of stereotypical feminine interests, and appear more stereotypically feminine. The scale is modestly correlated with level of education.
6 *Pa* Paranoia	Elevated scores suggest psychotic symptoms, disturbed thinking, and paranoia. These clients can be guarded and suspicious, and have issues of trust. Very low scores may also suggest paranoia by wanting to appear extremely nonparanoid. They may appear as moralistic.
7 *Pt* Psychasthenia	Elevated scores suggest distress, turmoil, discomfort. These clients may be introspective, self-doubting, obsessive-compulsive, phobic, or ruminative.
8 *Sc* Schizophrenia	Very high scores (T = 75–90) suggest a psychotic disorder, with confusion and disorganization. T > 90 usually doesn't indicate psychosis, but extreme turmoil. High scores (T = 65–74) suggest unusual thoughts, poor judgment, psychological turmoil, negativity, self-doubt, a schizoidal lifestyle, family discord, or alienation. African Americans and Native Americans tend to score higher than White subjects.
9 *Ma* Hypomania	Very high scores (T > 80) suggest mania or hypomania. Elevated scores suggest overactivity, energy, talkativeness, impulsiveness, a wide range of interests, and socialness. These clients can form superficial relationships and may get bored easily. Low scores suggest low energy and motivation.
0 *Si* Social Introversion	Elevated scores suggest social introversion, insecurity in social situations, lack of desire to be in social situations, lack of confidence; they can be hard to get to know. They have poor social skills and lack social support.

Note: Adapted from Graham (1993), Archer (1997), and Greene (1991).

may have elevations on most of the clinical scales. In this case, it may be that only the most severely elevated scales should be interpreted.

Common Configurations of the Validity Scales (L, F, K)

- *Inverted V* (low L, high F, low K). "Cry for help," "Everything is wrong with me," "I want others to know I feel bad." Tends to create exaggerated clinical scales.
- *V* (high L, low F, high K). "Nothing is wrong with me," "I don't want anyone to know something is wrong." Tends to lower clinical scales.
- *Elevated K.* "I may have some problems, but I'm not crazy," "My problems are none of your business." May lead to fewer clinical scale elevations.

Random Responses

These profiles tend to have an inverted V profile, with the F scale elevated > 100 and the K scale around 50 (Graham, 1993). Scale 8 may also be elevated. However, if only some items are answered randomly, this profile may look different.

Functional Complaints

Malingerers tend to have a sawtooth pattern with elevations on Scales 2–4–6–8, and the validity scales set as an inverted V (Graham, 1993).

SCORING AND INTERPRETATION OF THE CLINICAL SCALES

The 10 Clinical Scales Are Actuarially Based

The 10 clinical scales were originally developed to identify clinical clients with specific disorders. Items, irrespective of content, were included in a scale if they distinguished people with and without the disorder. For example, the original clients with elevations on the *Hs* scale would have diagnoses of hypochondriasis. Today, the 10 original clinical scales are not interpreted as *DSM-IV* diagnoses, and are more suggestive of behavioral patterns or clusters of symptoms that have diagnostic significance.

Interpretation

The primary method of interpreting MMPI-2 scores is to examine the two or three most elevated scale scores. For example, a patient with the highest elevation on Scale 4 and the next highest on Scale 5 would be listed as 4-5. A variety of books provide interpretations of these code-types (Archer, 1997; Graham, 1993; Greene, 1991; Groth-Marnat, 1997), and we have summarized the key features for common two and three point code types in Appendix E. In terms of interpretation, the two highest code types are considered equivalently, regardless of their order (e.g., 4-5 vs. 5-4). These code types are also mentioned in Section II of this text, to assist in diagnosis. A client with multiple elevations (e.g., 2, 3, 7) may need to have multiple profiles examined (e.g., 2-3, 2-7, 3-7). Graham has contended that code types should not be interpreted if there isn't at least a 5 point difference between the lowest scale in the code type and the next highest scale in the pattern, though this has not been adopted by all researchers or clinicians.

Interpreting Scales That Are Not Significantly Elevated

Sometimes, a client will not have any clinically significant scores, though two or three scales will show relatively greater elevations. Some clinicians interpret these profiles by identifying the two-point code type, and then diluting the severity of the description. This most likely occurs in clients who showed significant F or K scale elevations. We suggest extreme caution when commenting on nonsignificant scales, particularly when the validity scales are not elevated. Instead, you may want to consider the profile for further hypothesis generating. Whenever you draw conclusions about a profile that did not reach significance, make sure to mention in the report your rationale and the limitations in doing so.

Content and Supplemental Scales

Numerous additional scales to the MMPI-2 have been derived from the original items. There are (a) 31 subscales derived from the 10 clinical scales; (b) 15 scales, typically referred to as the Content scales; (c) subscales dividing scale item content into subtle and obvious dimensions, and (d) numerous supplementary scales. These are also summarized in Appendix E.

Testing Tip
MMPI-2 Rapid Interpretation

- Check for missing items, indicating invalidity.
- Interpret the validity scales (Table 4.3). If invalid, comment on the validity scale profile, and identify whether it is consistent with your clinical impression.
- Identify the 2-point code type, which are the two highest clinical scale elevations that cluster together (see Appendix E for summary).
- Examine the pattern of individual clinical scales that are significantly elevated or depressed to see if they concur with your clinical impression.
- Examine content and supplementary scales if time permits, particularly MAC-R (alcoholism) (Appendix E).

CLIENT FACTORS

Numerous studies have identified differences on the MMPI-2 based on ethnicity or cultural background, but conclusions are difficult to draw. Medically ill clients are more likely to show elevations on scales sensitive to somatic concerns (Scales 1, 3, 7). It is best to consider ethnic and cultural diversity factors on the MMPI-2 when findings are inconsistent with other clinical data or with your clinical impression.

The MMPI-2 standardization sample had an upper age range of 85 years, though there is little research identifying biases in the MMPI-2 based on age. Graham (1993) reported that older adults were underrepresented in the standardization study. It should be noted that the MMPI-2 can be cumbersome for many older adults to complete, due to its length.

Millon Clinical Multiaxial Inventory-III (MCMI-III)

DESCRIPTION

The Millon Clinical Multiaxial Inventory-III (MCMI-III; Millon, 1994) is used to assess the presence of *DSM-IV* Axis I psychiatric syndromes and Axis II Personality Disorders. Clients must be 18 years of age or older and read at the eighth-grade reading level. There are 24 scales (and four validity scales) divided into four sections: Personality Scales, Severe Personality Patterns, Clinical Syndromes, and Severe Clinical Syndromes. Except for the three validity scales, each scale consists of 13 to 17 items. Because it has only 175 items, it is easier to administer and can be given to clients who refuse the lengthy MMPI-2.

The MCMI-III is based on a personality theory developed by Millon that posits personality to be based on a combination of two primary dimensions: source of personal satisfaction and coping style. The 13 possible permutations correspond closely to the 10 Personality Disorders in the *DSM-IV*.

We are not strong proponents of this measure because of its tendency to overpathologize and because of the lack of validity checks. It's usually given when a client refuses to do an MMPI-2. (See the Testing Tip on page 56.)

Items Were Chosen That Closely Fit DSM-IV Criteria and Fit the Theoretical Rationale for Each Disorder

Unlike the MMPI-2, MCMI-III items were chosen that logically fit with the descriptive and theoretical characteristics of each *DSM-IV* disorder or syndrome. Items also had to meet reliability requirements.

Testing Tip
MCMI-III

When to Use It
- After a clinical interview, you still lack a diagnostic impression of the client.
- An MMPI-2 shows surprising results and you want to confirm the earlier test findings.
- The client won't complete or is unable to complete an MMPI-2.
- *Do not use it with clients who are knowingly noncompliant because the validity checks are not exhaustive, and clients can easily deny symptoms.*

Advantages
- Quick to administer.
- Fits well with *DSM-IV* nomenclature.
- Developed with a theoretical model of personality pathology.

Disadvantages
- Tendency to create false positives and overpathologize.
- Not validated in nonclinical populations (e.g., rehabilitation settings).
- Reliance on a theoretical model with limits in construct validity.
- Tendency to mislabel older adult males as having dependent personality style (Choca & Van Denburg, 1997).
- Scoring service charges a fee for each testing.

The MCMI Theoretical Model Is a Shortcoming

Although the MCMI-III uses a well-described theory to explain personality pathology, it is not clear whether this theory is correct, despite the use of similar diagnostic categories in *DSM-IV*. Research of MCMI personality theory is still in its relative infancy. Yet, there is research establishing the reliability of some of the MCMI-III scales (e.g., Scales CC, D, H), and concurrent validity with similar scales on the MMPI-2. Thus, some of the Personality Disorders identified in the MCMI-III show evidence for their existence.

The MCMI-III Is Standardized Differently Than the MMPI-2

The MCMI-III uses base rates, that is, the actual frequency of the disorder or syndrome in a clinical setting, to identify significant elevations. On the MMPI-2, for every scale, a score is clinically significant if the score is seen in only 7% of the population (T-score > 64). On the MCMI-III, the threshold for clinical significance was set by identifying the specific score that corresponded to the frequency of each disorder or syndrome in a clinic setting. This difference likely has little effect on the interpretation of the scale, provided that the base rate estimates that were used in developing the test were accurate.

Use the MCMI-III in Nonclinical Populations with Caution

The MCMI-III was standardized in clinical populations; giving it to nonpatients has the tendency to overpathologize them. When nonpatients score in the clinically significant range, it may be best to use descriptive labels (e.g., health concerns) rather than diagnostic ones (e.g., Somatoform).

SCORING AND INTERPRETATION

In interpreting the MCMI-III, first check its validity by examining the Modifying Indices. Next, examine the clinical scales. Base rate scores > 75 indicate presence of a disorder or syndrome. Base rate scores > 85 indicate prominence of a disorder or syndrome.

The MCMI-III includes the following scales as listed in Table 4.4 on pages 58–59. They are divided into four groupings: Clinical Personality Patterns, Severe Personality Pathology, Clinical Syndromes, and Severe Syndromes. Note that the personality scales correspond mostly to Axis II disorders, and the syndromes correspond to Axis I disorders. The following interpretive method is based on Choca and Van Denburg (1997).

Examine the Modifying Indices

- *Validity Index, Scale V.* A score of 1 or more is of questionable validity. A score of 2 or more invalidates the profile.
- *Disclosure Index, Scale X.* Very low or high scores invalidate the profile. Moderate scores suggest a desire to be open to disclosing emotional problems.
- *Desirability Index, Scale Y.* Higher scores suggest a desire to want to present oneself in a favorable light.
- *Debasement Index, Scale Z.* Higher scores suggest a tendency to present oneself negatively.

Examine the Personality Scales

- Examine the three highest scales (base rates > 74) among the following eight personality styles scales: Schizoid, Avoidant, Dependent, Histrionic, Narcissistic, Antisocial, Compulsive, and Passive-Aggressive. If numerous elevations are present, be suspicious and consider whether this is due to elevated Scales X or Z. If so, be careful not to overpathologize.
- Examine the remaining personality scales. Consider whether they are clinically significant and consistent with other data.

TABLE 4.4

Millon Clinical Multiaxial Inventory-III (MCMI-III) Scales and Descriptions

Scale	Description
	MODIFYING INDICES (VALIDITY)
V Validity	Three items that are extremely improbable. Endorsement of 2 or more indicates careless, random, or confused responding.
X Disclosure	High scores (>74) indicate openness, ease at endorsing negative items. Very high scores indicate lack of validity. Low scores indicate secretiveness, hesitancy. Very low scores indicate lack of validity.
Y Desirability	High scores indicate a desire to appear favorably; "faking good."
Z Debasement	High scores suggest a desire to appear troubled; "faking bad." May be a cry for help.
	CLINICAL PERSONALITY PATTERNS
1 Schizoid*	Asocial, unemotional, interpersonally disinterested, aloof, overintellectual.
2A Avoidant*	Asocial, desires relationships, but is fearful of them resulting in worry and anguish.
2B Depressive	Unhappy, helpless, passive, dysphoric, brooding, self-critical.
3 Dependent*	Passive, relying on others for guidance or security, behaviorally inconsistent.
4 Histrionic*	Overemotional, attention-seeking, superficially confident, fickle, manipulative.
5 Narcissistic*	Self-absorbed, unempathic, exploitative, entitled, relies on rationalization.
6A Antisocial*	Lack a sense of shame; impulsive, angry, manipulative.
6B Aggressive (Sadistic)	Hostile and abusive, but not publicly antisocial, rigid, dominating.
7 Compulsive*	Perfectionistic, rigid, oppositional, constricted, disciplined.
8A Passive-Aggressive (Negativistic)	Struggle between conforming and oppositional behaviors, stubborn, irritable.
8B Self-Defeating	Self-sacrificing, high shame, place themselves in negative view, doleful.
	SEVERE PERSONALITY PATHOLOGY
S Schizotypal*	Unusual, eccentric, magical thinking, emotionally flat or anxious.
C Borderline*	Emotionally labile, impulsive, need for affection, splitting, regression, black and white thinking; risk of self-injurious behavior or suicide.
P Paranoid*	Marked mistrust, irritability, defensiveness, rigidity, provocative.

TABLE 4.4 (Continued)

Scale	Description
	CLINICAL SYNDROMES
A Anxiety	Suggests generalized anxiety, edginess, obsessions, irritability, turmoil, or specific phobia.
H Somatoform	Suggests broad somatic symptoms, complaints, denial of emotional issues. Tend to have many doctors; check for real medical problems.
N Bipolar Manic	Suggests mania; very high scores suggest psychotic symptoms. Irritability, mood swings, impulsivity, decreased need for sleep.
D Dysthymia	Broadly consistent with *DSM-IV* Dysthymia: chronic low grade depression, social withdrawal.
B Alcohol Dependence	Suggests history of alcoholism, or drinking problems.
T Drug Dependence	Suggests history of drug abuse.
R Posttraumatic Stress Disorder	Consistent with *DSM-IV* Posttraumatic Stress Disorder: nightmares, anxiety, avoidance, hypervigilance.
	SEVERE SYNDROMES
SS Thought Disorder	Suggests thought disorder found in Schizophrenia, Schizophreniform, or Brief Reactive Psychosis. Disorganized, tangential, isolative. Possibly experiencing hallucinations/delusions.
CC Major Depression	Suggests severe depression including vegetative signs. Check for suicidality, substance abuse.
PP Delusional Disorder	Suggests acute paranoia, delusions such as thought control or thought insertion. Frequently hostile, mistrusting.

*Personality Disorder listed in *DSM-IV*. Further descriptions of Personality Patterns and Severe Personality Pathology are located in Chapter 10.
Note: Adapted from Millon (1994).

- Use descriptive information to describe each elevation, rather than merely using diagnostic labels.
- To help identify diagnostic features, examine specific items in each scale.
- If no scale is clinically significant, cautiously examine scales that are near significance. Only if they are consistent with the client's interview should you consider discussing the clinical features in a less severe manner.

Examine the Ten Clinical Scales

- Identify the highest scales(s).
- To help identify diagnostic features, examine specific items in each scale.

Testing Tip
MCMI-III Rapid Interpretation

(Based on Choca & Van Denburg, 1997)

- Examine the Modifying Indices to ensure that the profile has sufficient validity. Note whether the client's approach to the test was consistent with your clinical impression.
- Examine the three highest scales with base rates > 74 (presence) and >84 (prominence) amongst these 8 personality styles: Schizoid, Avoidant, Dependent, Histrionic, Narcissistic, Antisocial, Compulsive, and Passive-Aggressive. If numerous elevations are present, be suspicious.
- Examine the remaining personality scales and clinical syndromes. Consider whether they are clinically significant and consistent with other data.
- Use descriptive information based on each elevation to add to the clinical picture of the client, rather than merely using diagnostic labels.

CLIENT FACTORS

Relative to the MMPI-2, few studies identify differences on the MCMI-III based on ethnicity or cultural background. As with the MMPI-2, it is best to consider ethnic and cultural factors on the MCMI-III when findings are inconsistent with other clinical data or your clinical impression.

We have not identified studies with the MCMI-III examining differences for older adults. The standardization sample included only 6.8% of clients over the age of 55 years. The majority of clients were Caucasian (86.7%).

Rorschach Inkblot Test

OVERVIEW

Description

The Rorschach (Exner, 1991, 1993, 1995b) is a sophisticated projective test of emotional functioning, although it can be considered a test of visuo-perceptual organization, too. It can be given to clients 5 years of age or older. Clients are shown 10 inkblots, of which half are monochromatic, and asked to respond to the general question, "What might this be?"

Based on the projective hypothesis, a client presented with an ambiguous stimulus will project unconscious conflicts and issues, and demonstrate the primary coping style. Because of the test's ambiguity, a resistant client can often provide better clinical data on the Rorschach than on self-report personality questionnaires.

The Rorschach is typically scored with the Comprehensive System, named as such by Exner (1993), because it (a) integrates the earlier scoring methods created by early Rorschach researchers, and (b) provides standardized instructions, interpretation, and norms. It is now the standard in the field. This method is reviewed here and data are presented from the published norms.

During the response "free association" phase, each inkblot is given to the client with minimal instruction and the clinician records the client's verbatim responses. After the inkblots have been shown, the clinician begins the "inquiry" phase by having the client listen to each response and identify the features in the inkblot that led to the response. The responses are coded into numerous variables that suggest cognitive and personality function.

Testing Tip
Rorschach Inkblot Test

When to Use It
- You want more traditional information about character and defense mechanisms.
- The client will not complete a personality questionnaire.
- The client has created an invalid or questionable MCMI-III or MMPI-2.
- Extra time is available.
- Your clinical impression of the client suggests pathology, but it is not detected or described clearly in the personality inventories.
- You need more information to distinguish between reality testing and mood disturbance.
- You own the scoring software that can rapidly generate a narrative report.

Advantages
- Describes the client's ability to relate to others and the environment.
- Indicates defenses, coping styles, and emotional control.

Disadvantages
- Time-consuming to administer, score, and interpret, when hand scoring is used.
- Construct validity remains in question by some researchers.
- Seldom reimbursed for the time needed when hand scoring is used.

A Caveat

The Rorschach is a difficult instrument to administer, score, and interpret. However, with training and good scoring software, it can be a relatively rapid instrument to use. The purpose of this section is to familiarize clinicians with its use and interpretation. Clinicians inexperienced in administering the Rorschach are strongly encouraged to obtain supervision and training. (See Testing Tip on page 61.)

SIMPLIFIED OVERVIEW OF KEY RORSCHACH CONCEPTS

The Number of Responses Made Is Meaningful

Few responses to the inkblots can be due to oppositional behavior, paranoia, depression, low IQ, or being emotionally overwhelmed by the cards. For example, psychotic clients are more likely to be unable to keep from seeing disturbing images, which they try to prevent themselves from saying. Many responses can suggest obsessiveness or mania as well as creativity. Without a minimum number of responses (14), the test is invalid, and a second administration can be performed.

Can You See What the Client Said?

By showing an ambiguous stimulus, the client is required to organize it into something meaningful. A client with problems in reality testing is more likely to go outside the realm of the inkblot, by stating uncommon responses, using bizarre content, or by focusing on secondary elements of the blot (shading, color, texture, etc.). If you have trouble perceiving what the client saw, it may reflect problems in reality testing. This is typically coded using the term "form quality."

Using the Whole Blot Is Better

When the client is able to use the whole blot and make an appropriate response, it suggests the ability to integrate information coherently. When the client comes up with responses based on parts of the blot, it can suggest the tendency to focus on irrelevant details. Using the whole blot all the time, however, can suggest a tendency to avoid looking at any details.

Responses Based on the Blot's Form Are the Best

Most responses in nonclinical samples use the form (shape) of the blot as the basis for a response. Form represents the ability to see things conventionally and realistically. The assumption is that most of a client's responses to the blots should come primarily from form. Even in normal adults, some responses will include elements other than form, such as the color, shading, texture, and perceived depth of the blot. These other elements are thought to reflect emotion to some degree. A relatively large proportion of responses that do not include form suggests emotional turmoil. The exclusive use of form, however, suggests an avoidance in dealing with emotions.

How the Client Talks Matters

Strange verbalizations, strange words, and strange use of wording suggest problems in cognitive processes. To some degree, then, the Rorschach picks up language problems seen in psychosis (e.g., alogia), which are coded as deviant verbalizations.

Coping Styles

Coping styles are indicated in part by color responses and human movement responses. Human movement responses suggest creativity, reasoning, and imagination, in part because movement is a clear projection (the blots, after all, are motionless). The use of color, on the other hand, is thought to suggest emotion. The ratio of human movement to color responses suggests the degree to which the client's problem solving style is more internally based or externally based.

SCORING AND INTERPRETATION: A DETAILED PRIMER

Many codes and scales result from scoring a Rorschach protocol. Some of these are sums or percentages based on elemental aspects of the protocol, whereas other variables are based on the relationships between the variables. The following are key variables that clinicians are likely to interpret when scoring the Rorschach. A score is considered significantly high or low if it is outside the ranges listed. Alternatively, for certain variables, the modal response is used to indicate nonpathological responses.

Number of Responses (R) (M = 22.67, Normal Range = 19–27; Invalid: 14 or less)

Fewer responses suggest depression, defensiveness, oppositional behavior, low energy, or suspiciousness. Many responses suggest mania, a disclosing nature, or expansive mood.

Location

Location identifies whether the client used the whole blot *(W)*, a frequently used part of the blot *(D)*, an infrequently used part *(Dd)*, or the white space *(S)*. Responses are also coded for the quality of the response:

- W responses (Adult M (mean) = 38%, Normal Range = 29%–46%) are considered more integrative, and are seen more in adults than children. More *W* suggests creativity; fewer suggests depression.

- *D* responses (M = 57%, Normal Range = 41%–72%) are more common and considered easier to create. They are more common in clients who are eager to please.
- *Dd* responses (M = 5%, Mode = 0) suggest unusual responding, attention to detail, and can be due to many factors ranging from obsessiveness to psychosis. Most clients give only 0 or 1 *Dd* response per protocol.
- *S* responses (M = 6%, Mode = 1) suggest oppositionality or autonomy and are associated with disorders suggesting alienation. Most adult clients give only 1 *S* response per protocol.

Determinants

What were the features of the blot that led to the client's response? There are several categories: color, movement, shading, texture, depth, and form (shape). Responses are coded based on the presence of one or more of the determinants. A blend occurs when more than one determinant is used. Mean frequencies and acceptable ranges indicated are for nonclient adults (M R = 22.67, SD = 4.23). Table 4.5 describes the determinants.

Form Quality

This variable reflects perceptual accuracy and is coded based on the degree that the response makes sense given the part of the blot used.

Lambda (L)

This index suggests to what extent the client becomes involved and connected to the environment (M = 0.58, Range = .3–.8). It is calculated as the proportion of pure form responses *(F)* to all nonpure F responses (FC, FV, etc.). Low scores suggest overinvolvement with stimuli, resulting in feeling unable to break away from complex situations. High scores suggest underinvolvement and oversimplification. *L* is greater in children.

Pairs (2)

Seeing pairs of objects (M = 8.68, Range = 7–11). High scores suggest egocentricity or narcissism.

Active/Passive Ratio (a:p)

Extent to which movement responses are coded as active or passive (M ratio = 2.4:1.0). When a:p is around 1:1, the client tends to be overly passive. When a:p is around 3:1 or more, the client tends to act too soon.

Populars (P)

The 13 responses that are most commonly made to the inkblots (M = 6.7, Range = 5.02–7.36). High scores suggest a need to conform or be liked; low

TABLE 4.5
Rorschach Comprehensive System Determinants

Category	Code	Mean, Normal Range, and/or Mode	Description
Pure Form	F	M = 7.99, Range = 5–11	Most affect-free response to the blot. High scores suggest overly simple view of the world. Low scores suggest turmoil or psychosis.
Form Dimension	FD	M = 1.34, Mode = 2	Use of nonshading features to denote depth. Indicates degree of appropriate introspection. Low scores suggest lack of introspection.
Chromatic Color			High scores suggest distractability and emotionality. Low numbers suggest emotional restrictiveness. Children show a greater proportion of color responses compared with form.
	C	M = .08, Mode = 0.0	Pure Color. Uncommon. Higher scores suggest affective instability. Low scores suggest depression or emotional overcontrol.
	CF	M = 2.36, Range = 1–4	Predominately color and some form. Low scores suggest depression, or emotional overcontrol.
	FC	M = 4.09, Range = 2–6	Predominately form with some color. High scores suggest good emotional integration. Low scores suggest poor emotional control.
	Cn	M = 0.1, Mode = 0.0	Color Naming. Uncommon. High scores suggest concreteness and severity of pathology.
Achromatic Color	Sum C'	M = 1.53, Mode = 1	Responding to white, black, or grey in the blot. Suggests unhealthy emotional restraint. Seen in somatoform or obsessive-compulsive disorders, and depression.
	C'		Pure achromatic color.
	FC'		Form with some achromatic color.
	CF'		Achromatic color with some form.
Human Movement	M	M = 4.31, Range = 2–6	Suggests thoughtfulness and the presence of internal resources available to deal with information (e.g., ego). Anxious clients score low; bright clients score high.

(Continued)

TABLE 4.5 (Continued)

Category	Code	Mean, Normal Range, and/or Mode	Description
Animal Movement	FM	M = 3.70, Range = 3–5	Suggests a more drive-related way to deal with problems, compared to M, which is more deliberate. High scores suggest impulsivity; low scores suggest repression.
Inanimate Movement	m	M = 1.12, Range = 0–2	Related to situational stress. Suggests conflict and tension.
Shading	Sum Y	M = 0.57, Mode = 0	Suggests awareness of unpleasant emotions, more common in depression. Suggests depression and loss of control.
	Y		Pure shading response.
	FY		Form with some shading.
	YF		Shading with some form.
Texture	Sum T	M = 1.03, Mode = 1	Interpreting the blot to look like a textured surface. Suggests a desire for emotional connection with others. High scores suggest unmet needs of nurturance.
	T		Pure texture.
	FT		Form with some texture.
	TF		Texture with some form.
Vista	Sum V	M = 0.57, Mode = 0	Attributing depth to the inkblot. Suggests very negative self-appraisal, withdrawal and alienation. Seen in suicidal or depressed clients.
	V		Pure vista.
	FV		Form with some vista.
	VF		Vista with some form.

Note: Adapted from Exner (1991, 1993, 1995b).

scores suggest a lack of concern for convention. Inpatient schizophrenics give the lowest number of *P* responses.

Content and Special Scores

These items code for the verbal content of the client's response. Multiple content areas can be coded per response. Although there are many content categories, the ones considered most frequently are listed in Table 4.6.

Special scores are based on the quality of the verbal content of the client's speech and indicate the potential presence of severe psychopathology. They are

TABLE 4.6
Exner Comprehensive System: Commonly Used Content and Special Scores

Item	Description
CONTENT AREAS (CODES BASED ON THE NATURE OF THE CONTENT)	
Human *H* Human Detail *Hd* Mythical Human *(H)* Mythical Human Detail *(Hd)*	Common content. High scores indicate: interest in others, greater self-esteem, and greater treatment potential. Low scores suggest low empathy, poorer treatment prognosis, withdrawal from others.
Animal *A* Animal Detail *Ad* Mythical Animal *(A)* Mythical Animal Detail *(Ad)*	Common content. High number suggests predictable manner of approaching the world. Low scores suggest spontaneity, unconventionality.
Fire *Fi*	Associated with impulsivity and anger.
Explosion *Ex*	Associated with impulsivity and anger.
SPECIAL SCORES (SCORES THAT HAVE DIAGNOSTIC IMPLICATIONS)	
Deviant Verbalization *DV1*, *DV2*	Neologisms or redundancy. Suggests cognitive slippage; high scores suggest psychosis. A few *DV1* responses (Median = 1) are not too serious; *DV2* responses (Mode = 0) suggest greater cognitive mismanagement.
Deviant Responses *DR1, DR2*	Inappropriate phrases or circumstantial statements that have little to do with the response. Presence of *DR1* (Mode = 0) suggests some impulsiveness in ideational expression. *DR2* (Mode = 0) suggests more significant problems in cognitive impulse control.
Contamination *CONTAM*	Violation of reality (Mode = 0). Most serious of the special scorings. Suggests cognitive slippage; high scores suggest psychosis.
Incongruous Combination *INCOM1, INCOM2*	*INCOM* is the least significant sign of slippage (Mode = 0) and a couple in a protocol is not too serious. The presence of *INC2* suggests thought disorder (Mode = 0).
Autistic Logic *ALOG*	Use of unconventional logic. Suggests cognitive slippage (Mode = 0), poor judgment; high scores suggest psychosis.
Perseveration *PSV*	Perseverative speech (Mode = 0). Be alert to organicity.
Fabulized Combination *FABCOM1, FABCOM2*	An unlikely relationship between at least two objects seen in the blot (Mode = 0). High scores suggest disorganized thinking (*FABCOM1*) or impaired reality testing (*FABCOM2*).
Aggression *AG*	Aggressive content. Associated with impulsivity and sociopathy (Mode = 1).
Morbid *MOR*	Morbid or dysphoric content. Associated with severe depression (Mode = 0).
Cooperative Movement *COP*	Content indicating cooperation. Suggests ability to relate to others (M = 2).
Weighted Sum of Special Scores *WSum6*	Indication of disorganized thought content (M = 3).

Note: Adapted from Exner (1991, 1993, 1995b).

> ### Testing Tip
> ### Rorschach Rapid Interpretation
>
> For those readers familiar with the Comprehensive System, the following key variables should be examined in every protocol (Exner, 1993), provided that at least 14 responses were given (and usually if $L < .99$).
>
> | | | |
> |---|---|---|
> | 1. | $SCZI > 3$ | Suggests psychosis. |
> | 2. | $DEPI > 5$ | Suggests depression. |
> | 3. | $D < adjusted\ D$ | Suggests ability to control/tolerate stress is lower than usual. |
> | 4. | CDI is positive | Suggests poor social relationships, poor coping. |
> | 5. | $Adjusted\ D$ is negative | Suggests ineffective functioning, and being overloaded. |
> | 6. | $L > .99$ | Suggests that stimuli are interpreted in an oversimplified way, suggesting defensive problem solving and coping. |
> | 7. | At least 1 reflection | Suggests narcissism and overinflation of self-worth. |
> | 8. | EB is introversive | See Table 4.7. |
> | 9. | EB is extratensive | See Table 4.7. |
> | 10. | $p > a$, by > 1 points | Suggests a more passive role in interpersonal relations. |
> | 11. | HVI is positive | Suggests need to be in a continued state of preparedness; few friends, pre-occupation with personal space. |
>
> Be sure to consider S-Con in clients who are 15 years or older.

summarized in Table 4.6. Some special scores include a severity rating, rated as Level 1 or Level 2. Level 1 responses are less severe than Level 2. Level is notated by a numeric suffix after the abbreviation (e.g., $DV1$).

Higher Level Rorschach Concepts

Although there are many scores based on the specific frequencies of various criteria, there are also summary scores that aggregate and compare these variables further (Table 4.7).

TABLE 4.7
Exner Comprehensive System: Commonly Used Summary Scores

Score	Code	Mean	Description and Interpretation
Form Quality-Form	F+%	M = 0.71	Proportion of good quality F responses (reality testing without emotion). Indicates perceptual accuracy, reality testing, capacity to cope with stress, ability to function with structure. F+% does not consider emotion. F+% < 0.70 suggests psychopathology, intellectual limits.
Extended Form Quality	X+%	M = 0.79	Proportion of good quality responses (reality testing with emotion). Indicates perceptual accuracy when emotion is included. High X+% (> 0 .87) suggests overconventional, perfectionistic style; low X+% (0.71)suggests perceptual distortion.
Distorted Form	X–%	M = 0.07	Proportion of poor responses. Scores >0.2 suggest emotional/ perceptual difficulties, including delusional projections.
Organizational Efficiency	ZD	M = 0.72	Ability to organize and deal with the environment. Scores < −3.0 suggest careless *underincorporating* of information; fast speed, but misses details. Scores > 3.0 suggest *overincorporating*, an overly cautious and thorough style.
Erlebnistypus	EB	Extratensive: M = 1:2 Intratensive: M = 2:1 Ambitent: M = 1:1	Problem-solving style determined by ratio between human movement and chromatic color (sum M: WSumC). *Extratensives* give more color responses, and interact with their environment to solve problems (trial-and-error) and get gratification. *Intratensives* give more human movement responses, are more thoughtful prior to taking action, and get gratification from their internal resources. *Ambitents* show an even level of color and human movement that can lead to inefficient problem solving.
FC: CF+C		M = 1.7:1	Degree to which emotions are controlled. Ratio in children is reversed (e.g., 1:3).
Capacity for Control	D Score	M = 0.07	Relationship between emotional resources (human movement and color) and actual demands (nonhuman movement, achromatic color and shading), computed as a Z-score. Scores > 0 suggest greater capacity to deal with stress, suggesting rigidity and aloofness. Scores ≤ −1 suggests emotional overload.
Affect Ratio	Afr	M = 0.69 Range = .53–.85	Comparison of response frequency of last three color cards to the first seven cards. High scores suggest emotional seeking style; low scores suggest avoidant style.

Note: Adapted from Exner (1991, 1993, 1995b).

Testing Tip
Beck Depression Inventory-II
───────────

When to Use It
- You need a quick index of the client's current mood.
- You want to identify whether the client has major depression.

Advantages
- Quick to administer, score, and understand.
- Useful for identifying treatment effects.

Disadvantages
- Easy for clients to exaggerate responses or malinger.
- Hard for older adults to complete due to item design.

Special Indices

Each index lists several scoring criteria, based on a series of variables. If enough criteria are present, the index is considered positive. Like all cutoff scores, clinicians should use caution before concluding that a disorder is present.

S-Con   *Suicide Potential.* Identifies approximately 75% of suicidal clients. Applicable only to clients > 14 years of age.

SCZI   *Schizophrenia.* Clients who score positive are more likely to have disordered thinking consistent with schizophrenia.

DEPI   *Depression.* Clients who score positive are experiencing distress commonly found in depression.

CDI   *Coping Deficit.* Clients who score positive have problems in coping and social relationships.

HVI   *Hypervigilance.* Client may feel the need to be in a continued state of preparedness; they have few friends and a preoccupation with personal space.

OBS   *Obsessive Style.* Clients who score positive are likely to be obsessive, not necessarily diagnosed with Obsessive Compulsive Disorder.

CLIENT FACTORS

Eighty-one percent of the normative sample used for the Comprehensive System were White subjects, whereas only 12% were African American, 6% were Hispanic, and 1% were Asian. When used with non-English-speaking clients from countries other than the United States, caution is strongly warranted (Howes & DeBlassie, 1989). As with other tests, culture should be considered a factor in interpretation.

The normative sample used for the Comprehensive System included only 19 clients over the age of 65 years, constituting 3% of the sample. Although it is not clear whether there are biases as a result, age differences are not typically reported in the literature. However, it is important to ensure that older adults' responses aren't affected by any perceptual difficulties with vision or hearing.

Beck Depression Inventory-II (BDI-II)

DESCRIPTION

The 1996 revision of the BDI-II (Beck, Steer, & Brown, 1996) is a 21-item self-report inventory of the key symptoms of depression. Its reliability and validity are well-established. Clients are asked to consider each item based on the past two weeks. Each item has a title (e.g., concentration difficulty) and several responses ranging in severity (e.g., I can concentrate as well as ever, I find I can't concentrate on anything). Higher scores indicate greater severity.

SCORING AND INTERPRETATION

The BDI-II items are summed to create a total score. This score is compared with a standardization sample as well as with a series of cut score guidelines. In addition, client's specific responses to items can be examined to aid in identifying prominent mood symptoms (e.g., suicidal ideation).

The BDI-II standardization sample ($N = 500$) had a mean age of 37.2 years ($SD = 15.9$; Range = 13–86). There were a majority of women (63%) and White subjects (91%). Scores above 13 points suggest depression.

CLIENT FACTORS

Earlier versions of the BDI have been translated into numerous languages. The BDI-II items are harder for older adults to complete because each item has four or more choices. It may be easier to read the questionnaire to the client. The BDI-II, because it includes somatic items of depression, is more likely to result in higher scores in medically ill clients. Nevertheless, somatic symptoms of depression do occur in the elderly, and with clinical judgment, you should be able to distinguish the client's physical symptoms from mood.

Testing Tip
Rapid Approach to Adult Assessment

Assessment does not have to be lengthy and cumbersome; many clients are straightforward to diagnose and understand. The following plan of action integrates the material in this chapter:

1. Consult with your referral source to get a diagnostic impression and reason for the referral. (Knowing why you are seeing the client focuses you in terms of tests to select and questions to answer.)
2. Consult Section II to identify critical issues involved in the referral question, including essential features of potential disorders and appropriate measures.
3. Have the following on hand at all times: Intake, consent, and release forms, BDI-II, MMPI-2, MCMI-III, and WAIS-III forms.
4. Review medical records, interview client, consult with collateral sources (family, spouses, nursing staff).
5. Testing Decisions:

    Do cognitive testing only if it is warranted by the referral question.

    Very gross global measure of IQ: (a) NART reading test, or (b) Barona formula.

    Gross global measure of IQ: (a) WAIS-III VIQ subtests, or (b) WAIS-III PIQ subtests.

    If you require comprehensive data, do a prorated WAIS-III (9 subtests).

    Do personality/emotional testing only if it is warranted by the referral question.

    If capable, have client complete MMPI-2 and BDI-II.

    Consider MCMI-III if client won't/can't do MMPI-2.

    Consider the Rorschach if (a) you are trained and familiar with it, (b) you have the time or the interpretive software, (c) pathology was not detected by self-report measures, and (d) you need further information on personality and coping.

    Screen for cognitive functioning only if it is warranted by the referral question (see Chapter 11).
6. Use the tables in this chapter to help interpret test results.

    Use Section II to see if test findings are consistent with potential diagnoses.

    Use Chapter 12 to help integrate and understand test findings.
7. Immediately communicate findings to your referral source as they appear.
8. Dictate/write report with guidelines in Chapter 12.
9. Provide feedback to client and relevant others.

CHAPTER 5

Adolescent and Child Assessment

Common Assessment Instruments

THE FOCUS OF THIS CHAPTER is on child and adolescent assessment. As in the previous chapter, we summarize the primary assessment instruments used today. In many cases, these are adapted from the measures given to adults, and in some cases identical interpretive strategies can be used. In addition, measures specific to child and adolescent clients are discussed.

Wechsler Intelligence Scale for Children-III (WISC-III)

DESCRIPTION

Like the WAIS-III, the WISC-III (Wechsler, 1991) is a comprehensive measure of verbal and nonverbal intellectual function. The WISC-III can be administered to children from 6 to 16 years, 11 months of age and is widely used. It is nearly identical to the WAIS-III, so refer back to Chapter 4 if you need assistance in conceptualizing, scoring, or interpreting WISC-III scores.

Like the WAIS-III, the WISC-III computes FIQ, VIQ, and PIQ scores with a mean of 100 and a standard deviation of 15. There are 13 subtests, of which two are considered optional. Although both the WISC-III and WAIS-III have four index scores, the WAIS-III Working Memory Index is called Freedom from Distractibility in the WISC-III.

Subtest Differences in the WISC-III Compared with the WAIS-III

There are some minor differences in the subtests given in the WISC-III.

- Digit Symbol-Coding is replaced by a subtest called Coding. Part A is for younger children and consists of placing a mark inside a symbol. Part B is for older children, and is similar to the Digit Symbol-Coding subtest

---

Testing Tip
WPPSI-R and WISC-III

When to Use It
- Identification of client's intellectual function.
- Determination of client's cognitive strengths and weaknesses.
- Determining impact of emotional or psychiatric issues on cognitive function.
- To assess for eligibility of special local services.

Advantages
- Provides comprehensive picture of cognitive abilities and related clinical factors.
- Widely used in school systems, and well understood by referring sources.
- Considerable research database on its relationship with measures of academic achievement.
- Can administer abbreviated versions, depending on referral source.
- Well-researched, solid psychometric properties.

Disadvantages
- Full testing can be time consuming.
- Materials are somewhat bulky.

---

on the WAIS-III. Both can be interpreted identically to Digit Symbol-Coding.

- Letter-Number Sequencing and Matrix Reasoning are not given in the WISC-III.
- WISC-III includes a supplemental test called Mazes. It assesses psychomotor speed and planning ability. Clients are asked to draw their way out of a maze. It has a low correlation with PIQ and VIQ, which makes it appear to be a less useful measure of intellectual function. We agree with Kaufman (1994) that its use should be avoided.
- There is latitude over which subtests to give. You can substitute Symbol Search for Coding, provided that you calculate PIQ, FIQ, and VIQ using the appropriate tables (reported in *Psychological Assessment*; Reynolds, Sanchez, & Willson, 1996; 8, 378–382). Symbol Search is considered a measure of mental processing, whereas Coding is considered a measure of psychomotor speed. Symbol Search correlates higher with PIQ and FIQ, but you may need Coding as a measure of psychomotor speed.
- Digit Span is not required to compute IQ scores, but we recommend it as a good measure of attention span and auditory recall.

SCORING AND INTERPRETATION

Of the 14 specific subtests on the WAIS-III described in Table 4.2, 12 are subtests common to the WISC-III and were developed to assess the same abilities. Thus, the same descriptors and interpretations can be applied. Use the steps outlined in Chapter 4 to interpret WISC-III data.

CHOOSING BETWEEN THE WISC-III AND WAIS-III

Both tests can be administered to clients who are 16 years of age. Here are several guidelines for choosing the appropriate test.

Use the WISC-III for:

- *Potential Learning Disorder.* The WISC-III was standardized using the same sample as the WIAT (a test of academic achievement described in this chapter). You can compare discrepancies between the two tests to identify academic strengths and weaknesses.
- *Children who will be upset by failure.* The WAIS-III items are harder than the WISC-III, resulting in more failed responses.

Use the WAIS-III for:

- *A more accurate assessment of IQ scores.* The WAIS-III was standardized most recently, resulting in the best estimate of intellectual function.
- *When you have less time.* The greater difficulty of WAIS-III items increases the chance that you will complete subtests more rapidly due to scoring cessation rules.
- *Longitudinal assessment.* Clients that you know will receive future assessments will have the same baseline instrument.

CLIENT FACTORS

Ethnic and Cultural Diversity

The WISC-III was standardized with a large sample of children and adolescents who were stratified and selected to closely resemble U.S. Census data ($N = 2200$). Yet, many subtests are influenced by educational quality, exposure to the U.S. education system, level of acculturation, and degree of English comprehension and fluency. As with the WAIS-III, caution is recommended when assessing and interpreting the test results of minorities or persons with disabilities.

Wechsler Preschool and Primary Scale of
Intelligence-Revised (WPPSI-R)

DESCRIPTION

The WPPSI-R (Wechsler, 1989) can be administered to children from 3 years of age to 7 years, 3 months. Like the WISC-III, the WPPSI-R computes FIQ, VIQ, and PIQ scores, with a mean of 100 and a standard deviation of 15. There are subtest scale scores, but no factor index scores.

WPPSI-R versus WAIS-III and WISC-III

The 12 WPPSI-R subtests are common to the WISC-III, except for Animal Pegs, Geometric Design, and Sentences. Unlike the WAIS-III, Digit Span, Digit Symbol-Coding, Symbol Search, Letter-Number Sequencing, and Matrix Reasoning are not included.

- *Animal Pegs.* This test is similar to Digit Symbol-Coding, except that the client matches 4 colored pegs to 4 pictures of animals. As with Digit Symbol-Coding, the test measures eye-hand coordination, psychomotor speed, concentration, and visual memory. It is sensitive to anxiety and motivation level.
- *Geometric Design.* This untimed test requires the client to copy a series of designs with a pencil. It tests visuomotor perception, organization, and coordination. It can help identify whether any problems that occur on Animal Pegs are due to visuomotor speed as opposed to coordination. It can also detect level of motivation. Scoring can be cumbersome, however.
- *Sentences.* This optional subtest assesses the client's ability to repeat sentences of increasing length. It is analogous to Digit Span, but its greater reliance on verbal material means it also taps verbal comprehension and verbal expression. Scoring can be cumbersome.

SCORING AND INTERPRETATION

The WPPSI-R can be interpreted similarly to the WAIS-III; Table 4.1 and Chapter 4 offer interpretive data.

CHOOSING BETWEEN THE WISC-III AND WPPSI-R

Both tests can be administered to clients who are between 6 and 7.3 years of age. Here are several guidelines for choosing the appropriate test.

Use the WISC-III for:

- *Potential Learning Disorder.* The WISC-III was standardized using the same sample as the WIAT.
- *A more accurate assessment of IQ scores.* The WISC-III was standardized more recently than the WPPSI-R, resulting in the best estimate of intellectual function.
- *When you have less time.* The greater difficulty of WISC-III items increases the chance that you will complete subtests more rapidly due to scoring cessation rules.

Use the WPPSI-R for:

- *Children who will be upset by failure.* The WISC-III items are harder than the WPPSI-III, resulting in more failed responses.

In addition, Kaufman (1994) noted that the WPPSI-R has an (a) overreliance on speed, (b) increased ceiling effects, and (c) lower reliability than the WISC-III.

CLIENT FACTORS

Ethnic and Cultural Diversity

Like other Wechsler scales, the WPPSI-R was standardized with a large sample of children, stratified and selected to closely resemble U.S. Census data. It is influenced by culture and ethnicity in a similar fashion.

Tests of Academic Achievement

A common referral question for children or adolescents is whether there is a learning disability. Learning Disorders are usually identified by a discrepancy between ability and achievement, as assessed by achievement and intelligence tests. This difference is usually defined as at least 1.5–2.5 standard deviations or two grade levels, depending on the school district. A detailed discussion of specific learning difficulties and cognitive difficulties is provided in Chapter 11. However, the need for an academic assessment of the child is not limited to these disorders.

Wechsler Individual Achievement Test (WIAT)

DESCRIPTION

The WIAT (Psychological Corporation, 1992) is an achievement test that can be administered to clients from 5 to 19 years of age. It consists of eight subtests that result in four Composite Scores (Reading, Mathematic, Language, and Writing). In addition, there is the WIAT Screener, which includes three of the eight subtests (Basic Reading, Mathematics Reasoning, Spelling), and can be given in about 15 minutes. Scores have a mean of 100 and a standard deviation of 15.

Subtest Organization

The eight WIAT subtests are described in Table 5.1.

SCORING AND INTERPRETATION

Table 5.1 provides descriptive and interpretive data on the eight WIAT subtests. Interpreting WIAT scales is done similarly to Wechsler scales. First, note relative strengths and weaknesses of the individual scales and the four Composite Standard Scores. Second, examine absolute levels of performance. Finally, compare the WIAT scales to an intelligence test to identify significant discrepancies between achievement and intelligence (usually 1.5–2.5 *SD*).

Testing Tip
WIAT
───────────────────

When to Use It
- Identification of client's academic achievement.
- Determination of client's academic strengths and weaknesses.
- To assess Special Needs requirement or Regional Center Programs.

Advantages
- Standardized with the same sample as the WISC-III.
- Provides clear picture of academic abilities.
- Widely used.
- Can administer screening version, depending on referral source.
- Evidence for solid psychometric properties.

Disadvantages
- Shows ceiling effects for gifted children and floor effects for mentally retarded children.

TABLE 5.1
Subtests of the WIAT

Subtest	Interpretation
READING	
Basic Reading* *Client is asked to pronounce a list of letters and words.*	Assesses word reading and decoding skill. Can identify Dyslexia-related errors.
Reading Comprehension *Client reads short passages and is asked questions about the content.*	Assesses ability to read, interpret, and make inferences based on a text. Also taps attention to detail, comprehension of sequences, and logic.
MATHEMATICS	
Mathematics Reasoning* *Client is given age appropriate applied word problems involving mathematical concepts.*	Assesses ability to apply mathematical concepts to everyday problems (e.g., use of decimals, fractions, geometry).
Numerical Operations *Client is asked to solve age appropriate math problems (basic arithmetic, fractions, decimals, algebra).*	Assesses age-appropriate and specific mathematical abilities.
LANGUAGE	
Listening Comprehension *Client listens to short passages and is asked questions about the content.*	Assesses reception and comprehension of speech, ability to make inferences.
Oral Expression *Client is asked to describe objects and scenes, provide directions, and give the steps involved in doing specific tasks.*	Assesses ability to communicate orally. Also assesses ability to speak in a logical and clear format.
WRITING	
Spelling* *Client is asked to spell words.*	Assesses ability to encode and spell. Can identify Dyslexia related errors.
Written Expression *Client is asked to write freely about a topic.*	Assesses ability to develop and communicate ideas, to write logically, to use correct grammar.

*Subtest included in WIAT Screener.

Note: Content adapted from The Psychological Corporation (1992).

Comparing WIAT Scores with IQ Scores

The WIAT Ability-Achievement Discrepancy Analysis box allows you to compare WIAT scores to Wechsler IQ scores (e.g., WPPSI-R, WISC-III, or WAIS-III). These scores are needed when diagnosing Learning Disorders or determining eligibility for special community services. There are two methods of calculating differences: Simple and Predicted-Actual. We prefer the Predicted-Actual method because it is a statistically better technique to compare the scores. Recall that a score must be statistically significant and have occurred infrequently in the standardization sample.

Interpreting WIAT Subtest Differences

- *Intact Reading Comprehension versus Low Basic Reading.* Low Basic Reading might be due to poor school attendance (leading to gaps in basic skills) or Dyslexia. Intact Reading Comprehension suggests the child may be using context to compensate for problems in phonological decoding.
- *Intact Basic Reading versus Low Reading Comprehension.* This can possibly occur due to short-term memory problems, or non-phonological language problems.
- *Intact Mathematics Reasoning versus Low Numerical Operations.* Similar to above, low Numerical Operations may be due to forgetting basic skills because of disrupted or poor school attendance. Intact Mathematics Reasoning suggests adequate reasoning ability to work with mathematical concepts.
- *Reading Comprehension versus Listening Comprehension.* When Reading Comprehension and Listening Comprehension are low, this can suggest an overall pervasive language problem. When Listening Comprehension is intact and Reading Comprehension is low, this points to Dyslexia.

CLIENT FACTORS

Ethnic and Cultural Diversity

The WIAT was standardized identically to the WISC-III.

Woodcock-Johnson Psycho-Educational Battery-Revised (WJ-R)

DESCRIPTION

The WJ-R (Woodcock & Mather, 1989) is a widely used measure of academic achievement. It can be administered to individuals ages 2.5 through 95 years. It tests cognitive functioning (21 subtests, 14 optional) and achievement (18 subtests, 9 optional). Typically, only the achievement subtests are given because the

Wechsler scales are more commonly used to assess cognitive function, and because the WJ-R underestimates intellectual function. Because the WJ-R is a complicated test to administer, we advise that clinicians interested in using this test complete the training as described in the administration manual.

Subtest Organization

The 18 achievement subtests are grouped into four clusters and are described in Table 5.2 (on page 82). Computerized scoring is available. The four clusters are Reading, Mathematics, Written Language, and Knowledge.

Scoring and Interpretation

Some of the subtests are cumbersome to score and interpret, and can take a relatively long time to administer (compared with the WIAT). Table 5.2 provides descriptive data on the 18 WJ-R subtests. WJ-R scales can be scored in a variety of ways. Many tests are scored using *W* scores, which have a mean of 500 and are interpreted as the average score of the average fifth grader. Tests also can be reported using standard scores with a mean of 100 and a standard deviation of 15, or using percentile ranks.

Interpreting WJ-R scales is done similarly to Wechsler scales, in that you note relative strengths and weaknesses of the individual scales and the four

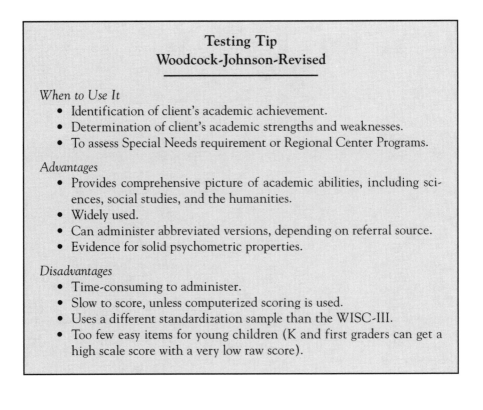

Testing Tip
Woodcock-Johnson-Revised

When to Use It
- Identification of client's academic achievement.
- Determination of client's academic strengths and weaknesses.
- To assess Special Needs requirement or Regional Center Programs.

Advantages
- Provides comprehensive picture of academic abilities, including sciences, social studies, and the humanities.
- Widely used.
- Can administer abbreviated versions, depending on referral source.
- Evidence for solid psychometric properties.

Disadvantages
- Time-consuming to administer.
- Slow to score, unless computerized scoring is used.
- Uses a different standardization sample than the WISC-III.
- Too few easy items for young children (K and first graders can get a high scale score with a very low raw score).

TABLE 5.2
Subtests of the Woodcock-Johnson Psycho-Educational Battery-Revised (WJ-R)

Subtest	Description
	READING
Letter-Word Identification	Assesses ability to identify specific letters and specific words within texts. Recognition skills are minimized on this test.
Passage Comprehension	Assesses ability to read and comprehend a short text and identify a key word that is missing.
Word Attack*	Assesses ability to use phonics and structural analysis to pronounce nonsense words.
Reading Vocabulary*	Assesses ability to pronounce words and give their definitions.
	MATHEMATICS
Calculation	Assesses ability to perform mathematical calculations, using written traditional math problems.
Applied Problems	Assesses ability to use mathematics to solve applied practical word problems.
Quantitative Concepts*	Assess ability to verbally express comprehension of mathematical concepts and mathematical vocabulary.
	WRITTEN LANGUAGE
Dictation	Assesses knowledge of letter forms, spelling, punctuation, capitalization, and word usage, as tested with a dictation task.
Writing Samples	Assesses writing ability under different circumstances.
Proofing*	Assesses ability to identify and correct mistakes in typed passages.
Writing Fluency*	Assesses speed in creating and writing simple sentences.
Punctuation and Capitalization*	Assesses ability to punctuate and capitalize correctly, as well as to detect errors in punctuation and capitalization.
Spelling*	Assesses ability to spell correctly and detect spelling errors in sample texts.
Usage*	Assesses ability to write grammatically and detect grammatical errors in written passages.
Handwriting*	Assesses legibility of client's handwriting.
	KNOWLEDGE
Sciences	Assesses scientific knowledge. An orally administered test.
Social Studies	Assesses social studies knowledge. An orally administered test.
Humanities	Assesses humanities knowledge. An orally administered test.

*Supplemental subtests.

Note: Content adapted from Woodcock and Mather (1989).

clusters. Next, examine absolute levels of performance. Difference scores between ability and achievement also can be examined.

CLIENT FACTORS

Ethnic and Cultural Diversity

The WJ-R was standardized on 6,359 subjects between the ages of 2 and 90+. Subjects were selected to match 1980 census data. The sample included 14% African American, 8% Hispanic, 2% Asian, and 1% Native American subjects.

Older Adults

Although the WJ-R is standardized for use in older adults, it is not commonly used.

Wide Range Achievement Test-3 (WRAT-3)

DESCRIPTION

The WRAT-3 (Wilkinson, 1993) has been one of the most frequently used measures of academic achievement in clinical practice because it can be rapidly administered to clients aged 5–75 years. It has three subtests: Spelling, Math, and Reading. These subtests are similar to the WIAT Screener.

Despite its wide use, we recommend the WIAT Screener over the WRAT-3 because it was costandardized with the WISC-III, has better psychometric properties, and if a more comprehensive assessment is needed, it takes only a little more effort to perform the remainder of the WIAT. Do not use the WRAT-3 for diagnosis.

Testing Tip
Choosing an Achievement Test

WIAT	When you need to make a clear comparison with the WISC-III.
WJ-R	When you want the broadest sampling of academic achievement, including knowledge of science, social studies, and the humanities.
WIAT Screener or WRAT-3	When you need a very quick screening.

Adaptive Rating Scales: The Vineland

DESCRIPTION

Adaptive rating scales are most often used in identifying problems in adaptive function for diagnosis of Mental Retardation or a Pervasive Developmental Disorder. The Vineland Adaptive Rating Scales (Sparrow, Balla, & Cicchetti, 1984) come in three versions: a semistructured interview (20–60 minutes), expanded form (60–90 minutes), and a classroom questionnaire for teachers to complete (20 minutes). It can be used with clients of all ages. Scores are standardized (Mean = 100; $SD = 15$), and also can be expressed in terms of the equivalent age of functioning. The Vineland scales are combined into Subdomains, Domains, and an Adaptive Behavior Composite score.

Domain	Subdomain
Communication	Receptive: comprehension, listening, following instructions.
	Expressive: initiative to talk, use of interactive speech, speech skills.
	Written: initiative to read, reading and writing skills.
Daily Living Skills	Personal: eating, toileting, dressing, bathing, grooming, health care.
	Domestic: housekeeping, chores, clothing care.
	Community: safety, telephone and money skills, time and dates, job skills.
Socialization	Interpersonal Relationships: responding socially, social communication, friendship, thoughtfulness, dating.
	Play and Leisure Time: hobbies, TV and radio.
	Coping Skills: manners, following rules, apologizing, keeping secrets, responsibility.
Motor Skills	Gross: sitting, walking, running, play activity.
	Fine: manipulating objects, drawing, using scissors.

SCORING AND INTERPRETATION

The Vineland can be hand or computer scored. Scores can be interpreted as percentiles and stanines.

CLIENT FACTORS

The Vineland was standardized on a sample of 3,000 subjects ranging from 0 to 18 years, based on 1990 U.S. Census estimates.

EMOTIONAL MEASURES

Factors other than intelligence impact performance, the most significant being emotional and motivational issues. If your referral question requires an emotional assessment of the child or adolescent, several tests are available.

The Minnesota Multiphasic Personality Inventory-A (MMPI-A)

DESCRIPTION

The MMPI-A (Butcher & Williams, 1992) is a 478-item true-false questionnaire that can be administered to clients between the ages of 14 and 18 years with a sixth-grade reading level. Items were specifically developed that are relevant to adolescents. Although you may consider giving it to very mature 12- or 13-year-old clients, keep in mind that during the standardization of the test, most 13-year-old clients had difficulty completing it.

Differences between the MMPI-2 and MMPI-A

The client's responses are scored and interpreted in a manner similar to that discussed for the adult version (MMPI-2), with the following exceptions:

- *MMPI-A gray zone.* MMPI-A scores that fall within this band ($T = 60–65$) are regarded as marginal or transitional, and may be interpreted if they are consistent with the overall presentation.
- *Two new infrequency scales: F1 and F2.* F1 includes items in the first half of the booklet, and F2 includes the items from the remainder of the booklet, similarly to MMPI-2 *(Fb).*
- *K scale.* Although there is a K scale, it is not used to correct scores on the clinical scales.
- *Interpretation of Scale 5.* This scale is interpreted somewhat differently. In addition to the descriptors in Table 4.3, high Scale 5 in males may suggest passivity in interpersonal relationships and comfort in expressing

---

Testing Tip
MMPI-A

When to Use It
- To assess emotional functioning.
- To clarify coexisting diagnoses.
- To obtain information regarding the patient's level of impulsivity.

Advantages
- Items appropriate for adolescents and specific adolescent content scales.
- Contemporary adolescent norms.
- Good psychometric properties.
- Well-known by most clinicians.

Disadvantages
- Not as widely researched as MMPI-2.
- Lengthy to complete.
- Reading and comprehension requirements high.
- Impact of lower cutoff scores unclear.
- MMPI-A profile potentially unstable.

---

feelings. High Scale 5 in females may suggest assertiveness, competitiveness, and greater behavioral and school problems.

- *Content and supplementary scales.* The MMPI-A includes new content and supplementary scales. Descriptions of these scales are presented in Appendix E.

SCORING AND INTERPRETATION

Like the MMPI-2, interpreting MMPI-A scores involves examining the validity scales, followed by an interpretation of the clinical scales. Chapter 4, along with Table 4.3, can be used for assistance.

2-Point Code Types

Archer (1992, 1997) recommends cautious interpretation of code types (Appendix D), and only if they are separated from the other clinical scales by $T = 5$ points. Others (Graham, 1993) prefer not to use them at all, although recent research validates the use of certain code types in adolescents (e.g., 4–9; Pena, Megargee, & Brody, 1996).

> **Testing Tip**
> **MMPI-A Rapid Interpretation Method**
>
> ----
>
> • Check for missing items, indicating invalidity.
> • Interpret the validity scales (Table 4.3). If invalid, comment on the
>   validity scale profile, and identify if it is consistent with your clinical
>   impression.
> • Identify and interpret significantly elevated clinical scales.
> • Examine the 2-point or 3-point code type elevations (see Appen-
>   dix D).
>
>   Interpret code types if they are greater than 5 T-score points
>   above other clinical scales.
>
>   Cautiously examine consistent low scales.
>
> • Examine significant adolescent-specific content scales (Appendix E).

Low Scores

There remains controversy over the interpretation of low scores (*T* < 45). We
caution against interpreting low scores and recommend that you do so only
when they provide information consistent with several other findings.

Following analysis of the clinical scales, the significant adolescent-specific
content and supplementary scales are examined and incorporated into the
interpretation.

CLIENT FACTORS

Ethnic and Cultural Diversity

The 1,620 adolescents that were part of the normative standardization sample
were chosen to match current census data. Seventy-six percent of the sample was
Caucasian, 12% were African American, 2% were Hispanic, 10% were listed as
"other." A sample of 713 subjects made up the clinical sample.

Millon Adolescent Clinical Inventory (MACI)

DESCRIPTION

The MACI (Millon, 1993), a 160-item true-false questionnaire, was developed
to assess adolescent psychopathology. It can be administered to clients ages
13–19 years, who read at a sixth-grade level. It takes approximately 30 minutes

---

Testing Tip
MACI

When to Use It
- You lack a diagnostic impression of the client, and other tests have failed to help you.
- An MMPI-A shows surprising results and you want to confirm the earlier test findings.
- The client won't complete an MMPI-A.
- You want to know the adolescent's perception of current problems.
- There is a concern about an underlying Personality Disorder.
- *Do not use it with clients who are knowingly noncompliant because the validity checks are not exhaustive, and clients can easily deny symptoms.*

Advantages
- Quick to administer.
- Specifically developed for use with adolescents.
- Developed with a theoretical model of personality pathology.
- Adolescent prevalence data was used to establish scale cutoff points.

Disadvantages
- Very limited research database, limited interpretation information, small standardization sample.
- Reliance on a theoretical model with limits in its construct validity.
- Not validated in nonclinical populations.
- Use of lower base rate cutoffs in interpretation needs to be validated.

---

to complete. Although it's based on Millon's theory of personality, it is structured and interpreted differently than the MCMI-III.

There is very little published research on the MACI, apart from that reported in the test manual. Consequently, although the test has potentially useful scales, its reliability and validity has not been as robustly established as other scales reported in this chapter. Use it solely as a secondary measure of psychopathology, or when alternative measures are unavailable. Table 5.3 describes the scales.

MACI versus MCMI-III

There are several differences between the MACI and the MCMI-III:

- The MACI Reliability scale (VV) replaces the MCMI-III Validity scale (V). It measures how well the client attended to the test.
- The MACI does not include the Paranoid (P) and Schizotypal (S) Severe Personality Pathology scales.

TABLE 5.3
MACI Scales and Descriptions

Scale	Description/Interpretation
CLINICAL PERSONALITY PATTERNS	
1 Introversive	Asocial, unemotional, interpersonally disinterested, listless, distant.
2A Inhibited	Asocial, desires relationships, but is fearful of rejection resulting in worry.
2B Doleful	Unhappy, helpless, passive, dysphoric, low self-esteem.
3 Submissive	Passive, clingy, needy, relying on others for guidance or security.
4 Dramatizing	Overemotional, attention-seeking, superficially confident.
5 Egotistic	Self-absorbed, unempathic, exploitative.
6A Unruly	Lacks a sense of shame or empathy, impulsive; angry, manipulative.
6B Forceful	Hostile and abusive, but not publicly antisocial; blunt.
7 Conforming	Perfectionistic, rigid, oppositional, overcontrolled.
8A Oppositional	Struggle between conforming and oppositional behaviors; discontented.
8B Self-Demeaning	Self-sacrificing, high shame, places self in negative view.
9 Borderline Tendency	Emotionally labile, impulsive, need for affection, splitting, regression, black & white thinking; risk of self-injurious behavior or suicide.
EXPRESSED CONCERNS	
A Identity Diffusion	Confused, directionless, unfocused, unclear.
B Self-Devaluation	Low self-esteem, self-critical.
C Body Disapproval	Poor body image, dissatisfied with social appeal.
D Sexual Discomfort	Fears expression of sexuality, in conflict over sex.
E Peer Insecurity	Sadness, rejection by peers, withdrawal, isolation.
F Social Insensitivity	Cool, indifferent, lacking empathy.
G Family Discord	Conflict and tension in family life.
H Childhood Abuse	Shame, disgust at being victim of abuse.

(Continued)

TABLE 5.3 (Continued)

Scale	Description/Interpretation
	CLINICAL SYNDROMES
AA Eating Dysfunction	Anorexic or bulimic traits.
BB Substance Abuse	Proneness to maladaptive alcohol or substance abuse.
CC Delinquency	Predisposition to being involved in violating others' rights.
DD Impulsive Propensity	Poor control, acts out with minimal provocation.
EE Anxious Feelings	Anxious, apprehensive, and fretful.
FF Depressive Affect	Guilt, low self-esteem, and lack of energy.
GG Suicidal Tendency	Suicidal ideation and plans, hopeless, feels unwanted.

Note: Adapted from Millon (1993).

- The Personality Pattern Scales have all been renamed with less patholog-ical terms (e.g., Doleful vs. Depressive), but use the same codes (e.g., 2B).
- There are eight new scales, called Expressed Concerns. They assess feel-ings and attitudes that tend to concern troubled adolescents.
- The Clinical Syndromes have been extensively changed. The Severe Syndromes have been removed. These seven scales relate to problems or issues that frequently require therapeutic intervention.

SCORING AND INTERPRETATION

The scoring of the MACI is identical to the MCMI-III. A base rate score > 74 indicates the presence of a trait, and a score > 84 indicates the prominence of a disorder or problem. Scores between 60 and 75 should be interpreted cautiously. Expressed Concerns that have a base rate < 35 indicate a strength.

To interpret the MACI, first examine the four Modifying Indices. Once the profile has been determined to be valid, the clinical information can be inter-preted. Next, separately identify significant elevations for the Personality Patterns, Expressed Concerns and Clinical Syndromes. Significant elevations may be de-scribed as problematic, present, or prominent. You may need to examine item con-tent to get a more specific picture of the client.

CLIENT FACTORS

The MACI normative group includes a total of 579 adolescents; 74% of sub-jects were Caucasian, 7% were African American, 6% were Hispanic, 3% were

Native American, less than 1% were Asian, and 5% were listed as "other" or didn't report it.

Rorschach Inkblot Test

DESCRIPTION

The Rorschach is a frequently used measure of emotional functioning administered to children and adolescents. It can be used with children 5 years of age and older. Review Chapter 4 for a detailed description on the use of this test.

SCORING AND INTERPRETATION

When interpreting child or adolescent protocols, use the separate tables provided in most of the Exner manuals. There are notable differences between adult and child Rorschach responses, due to the influence of development on the cognitive and emotional processes assessed by the test. First, the *S-Con* index is invalid for clients ≤ 14 years of age. In particular, as the client ages (Exner, 1995a):

- *R* (Response length) increases.
- In terms of location, *W* decreases while *D* increases.
- Developmental quality improves.
- Human movement responses increase.
- Chromatic color responses (*C, Cn, CF*) decrease as *FC* increases.
- Vista responses (*V*) increase slightly with age.
- *FD* responses increase.
- Adolescents give more P responses than children.
- Special scores decrease.
- Lambda (*L*), Affective Ratio (*Afr*), and Egocentricity Index $((3r + (2))/r)$ decrease.
- Introtensive frequency increases gradually.
- Animal content decreases.

Thus, younger children's responses may be dominated at first by form and color, but with age comes greater complexity, reflecting their increased emotional and cognitive resources, and an increased awareness of the complexity of their world. Moreover, children's responses can sound disordered and odd. This is not an indication of early psychosis, but instead reflects the child's developmental level.

Children's Depression Inventory (CDI)

DESCRIPTION

The CDI (Kovacs, 1992) is a 27-item self-rating scale of depression for children between the ages of 7 and 17 who read at a first-grade reading level. It takes about 15 minutes to complete. It is similar in structure to the BDI-II, with each item requiring the client to choose one of three answers.

SCORING AND INTERPRETATION

A total score and five factor scores are computed: Negative Mood, Interpersonal Problems, Ineffectiveness, Anhedonia, Negative Self-Esteem.

APPERCEPTION TESTS

Apperception tests are projective measures of interpersonal relationships and emotional functioning. They all involve showing the child or adolescent a series of cards with pictures, and asking the client to tell a story based on what is seen. In general, the number and type of cards administered depends on the particular test and the person's age and gender. The clinician usually records verbatim the client's responses. Responses may be interpreted intuitively, or with a formal scoring system, though reliability and validity are reduced when a scoring system is not used. Thought disorder and psychosis are usually detectable.

Thematic Apperception Test (TAT) and Children's Apperception Test (CAT)

DESCRIPTION

The TAT (Morgan & Murray, 1935) consists of 30 black-and-white pictures and one blank card and can be given to subjects over the age of 10 years. It is customary to give 8 to 12 cards, with the cards selected by the examiner based on the age, sex, and issues of the client. Clinicians interested in more sophisticated use of the TAT should consult an excellent text by Bellak and Abrams (1997).

The CAT (Bellak & Abrams, 1997) is used with very young children, ages 3 to 10 years. It consists of 10 black-and-white cards featuring animals. It is designed to explore the child's drives and relationships with persons important in his or her life.

SCORING AND INTERPRETATION

The most common method of interpreting the CAT and TAT is to examine the client's stories for recurrent themes and generate diagnostic hypotheses. Themes are often related to core issues and the nature of the child's interpersonal relationships. In addition, psychosis and thought disorder are usually identifiable based on the level of disorganization and confusion seen in the story content.

Robert's Apperception Test for Children (RATC)

DESCRIPTION

The RATC (McArthur & Roberts, 1982) is for clients 6 to 15 years of age. It consists of 27 cards depicting realistic drawings of children and adults in everyday situations. Depending on the child's gender, 16 cards are administered in a standardized manner. It takes approximately 20 to 30 minutes to administer.

SCORING AND INTERPRETATION

Although the RATC is simple to give, it is time consuming to score and interpret because the responses to each story are coded onto a set of 14 standardized scales, based on their frequency. T-scores between 40 and 60 represent the normal range, and T-scores > 60 indicate statistically significant responses. Many clinicians ignore the formalized scoring system and listen for themes, coping ability, problem-solving approaches, and possible thought disorder.

RATC Scales

The RATC scales are divided into three parts: (1) Adaptive scales code for adaptive function; (2) Clinical scales code for clinical symptoms; and (3) Indicators to reflect the validity of the test:

Adaptive Scales

Reliance on Others	Seeks help, asks for permission, asks for objects.
Support Others	Helps others, gives love, understanding, advice, or permission.

Adaptive Scales (*Continued*)

Support Child	Child advocates for self, shows assertiveness, feels happy, pleased.
Limit Setting	Appropriate limit setting, discipline.
Problem Identification	Adaptive ability to identify problems.
Problem Resolution	Shows age-appropriate problem resolution.

Clinical Scales

Anxiety	Fear, apprehension, self-doubt.
Aggression	Anger, attacking, destruction, hatred.
Depression	Sadness, crying, giving up.
Rejection	Physical separation, unmet needs, divorce, discrimination, jealousy.
Unresolved	No resolution to story or Maladaptive Outcome coded.

Indicator (Validity) Scales:

Atypical Response	Unfiltered primary process thinking, extreme deviation from typical themes, illogical, child abuse, suicide, dangerousness.
Maladaptive Outcome	Outcome that contributes to the problem, is socially unacceptable, etc.
Refusal	Refusal to respond.

Supplementary Scales

The RATC also includes three supplementary scales: Ego Functioning, Aggression, and Levels of Projection. These variables are coded by tallying their quality for each story, on an 8-point scale.

Interpersonal Matrix

This matrix is used to display the number of responses for each scale, based on who is involved. Thus, responses can be seen in terms of specific family members, friends, or others.

Interpretation

There are two ways of scoring the RATC. First, one may consider scoring it according to the manual. The manual suggests the method for interpreting the RATC, given in the Testing Tip at the bottom of page 95.

Testing Tip
RATC

When to Use It
- You want more information about the client's view of interpersonal relationships or problem-solving style.
- Client fails to complete objective measures.
- Client showed difficulty in being able to create organized stories from the CAT or TAT.
- You want a measure of client's coping mechanisms.
- You want to assess change over time.

Advantages
- Describes the child or adolescent's ability to relate to others.
- Specifically designed for children and adolescents.
- Can be used with nonclinical groups.
- Includes minority children in stimuli.
- Stimuli represent everyday interpersonal situations.
- Acceptable psychometric properties.
- Standardized administration and scoring systems.

Disadvantages
- Time-consuming scoring.
- Relatively new, limited research and clinical database.
- Small and limited normative data.
- Needs additional validity studies.
- Added structure of the test tends to make more disordered clients appear healthier.

Testing Tip
RATC Interpretation

- Identify significantly high or low profile scales and indicators.
- Compare mean scores of adaptive and clinical scales to determine global level of psychological functioning.
- Examine scatter within clinical and adaptive scales.
- Complete and interpret Interpersonal Matrix.
- Examine protocol for themes, defenses, and so on.
- Integrate quantitative and qualitative information.

Testing Tip
Choosing an Apperception Test
_____

You are concerned about psychosis:

> The TAT and CAT are more likely to detect psychosis than the RATC because of their unstructured format.

You are concerned about response biases:

> Choose the TAT or CAT. The themes in the RATC are more obvious to children than the ones in the TAT or CAT.

You want a psychometrically sound assessment of the child's interpersonal relationships:

> Choose the RATC. It is well standardized.

When to give multiple tests:

> The RATC provides children an easier route in creating stories due to the structure inherent in the situations portrayed on the cards. The TAT and CAT, on the other hand, show ambiguous situations. Consequently, it may be useful to determine to what extent a child can make use of the structure on the RATC, and to what extent a child is unable to manage cognitively and emotionally with the ambiguity of the TAT and CAT. Some children can manage to tell a coherent story on the RATC, but not on the TAT. If you were to give only one of these tests, you might miss this difficulty.

Alternatively, clinicians can score the RATC by making clinical judgments based on the content of the response. Children whose stories are largely removed from the images on the cards may be showing signs of oppositionality or thought disorder. Most clinicians note when the child avoids a critical element of a card; often that part is upsetting. On the other hand, some children alter the situation shown in the card to create a fantasy ending that mirrors their own wishes.

CLIENT FACTORS

The RATC was standardized with a sample of 200 clinical and 200 nonclinical children ages 6 to 15 years. Ethnicities were not reported. The RATC manual mentions that the test has been given to samples of children of different ethnicities and cultures, finding few differences.

PROJECTIVE DRAWINGS

Projective drawing tests are popular for use with children because they are non-threatening. The child is asked to draw, with minimal feedback from the examiner. The drawings are then analyzed either using a scoring system or with attention to particular features. Scoring systems focus on a range of characteristics, including graphomotor qualities, the extent to which the drawings are atypical, and omissions. The majority of scoring systems have very poor psychometrics properties. A better one is the Draw-A-Person: Screening Procedure for Emotional Disturbance (DAP: SPED; Naglieri, McNeish, & Bardos, 1991). On this test, the child is asked to draw a man, woman, and self. Coding is performed on 55 items, and is time consuming. However, it shows relatively good reliability and validity (Trevisan, 1996).

Alternative measures include (a) Kinetic Family Drawing (KFD; Knoff, 1985; the child is asked to draw a picture of his or her family doing something), and (b) the House-Tree-Person (HTP; Buck, 1966; the child is asked to draw a house, tree, and person on one sheet of paper). Use these tests, if you have the time, either to build rapport or as a supplement to more robust measures.

PARENT AND TEACHER RATING SCALES

Rating scales provide a fast method for quantifying the client's behavior. Their major limitation is that they can be easily affected by social desirability and halo effects. Thus, they can make inferior-quality information appear more legitimate.

Anser System Rating Scales

DESCRIPTION

The Anser (Aggregate Neurobehavioral Student Health and Educational Review) scales (Levine, 1981, 1985, 1988) are a set of lengthy and comprehensive questionnaires for parents and teachers. There are several forms:

Form 1P	Ages 3–5	Parent Questionnaire
Form 2P	Ages 6–11	Parent Questionnaire
Form 3P	Ages 12+	Parent Questionnaire
Form 1S	Ages 3–5	Teacher Questionnaire
Form 2S	Ages 6–11	Teacher Questionnaire
Form 3S	Ages 12+	Teacher Questionnaire
Form 4	Ages 9+	Student Self-Administered Questionnaire

The parent forms identify previous and current treatments, possible pregnancy problems, newborn infant problems, health problems, behavioral problems, developmental history, educational milestones, family history, skills and abilities, specific interests, attentional function, behavioral and mood symptoms, and strengths.

The teacher forms identify previous and current treatments, academic skills, motor function, language, visuo-perception, memory, temporal-sequential skills, organization, assets, attentional function, and behavioral symptoms.

The advantage to the Anser forms is that they provide an extremely detailed set of information that can help with the selection of tests and interpretation of interview data. For example, the parent forms include detailed items of possible pregnancy problems (e.g., presence of bleeding during the last three months of pregnancy). They can be given prior to meeting the parents or teacher, and can be used to set the framework for your interview. A scoring system is available.

Conners' Rating Scales

DESCRIPTION

The Conners' scales (Conners, 1997) are a recent revision of widely used 4-point rating scales for judging child behavior. They can be used with children from ages 3 to 17 years, and are quick to complete and score. The rater is asked to judge the frequency of each item on a 4-point scale ("not at all" to "very much"). Data are standardized by age and gender. Items are tallied and converted to T-scores (Mean = 50, SD = 10). T-scores > 69 indicate problems.

*Conners' Parent Rating Scale–Revised Short
Form (CPRS-R:S)*

The CPRS-R:S is a 27-item scale. Items are loaded onto four factors: Oppositional, Cognitive Problems, Hyperactivity, and ADHD Index. An 80-item version (CPRS-R:L) also exists that has 10 factors.

*Conners' Teacher Rating Scale–Revised Short
Form (CTRS-R:S)*

The CTRS-R:S has 28 items that load onto the same four factors as the CPRS-R:S. Like the CPRS, there is also a long form, the CTRS-R:L (59 items).

CLIENT FACTORS

These scales have been standardized with a sample of approximately 2,000 parents.

Achenbach Rating Forms

DESCRIPTION

The Achenbach forms (1991, 1992, 1997) are widely used for assessing children's competencies and identifying behavioral and emotional problems. Unlike the Conners' scales, Achenbach forms seem to focus more on symptoms, include positive attributes, and are considered broad-band measures. They are also more time-consuming to complete and score than the Conners'. Each form includes a Behavior Problems scale (with 112 or 113 items). Items are rated on a 3-point scale, ranging from "not true" to "very true." Items are tallied and converted to T-scores (Mean = 50, SD = 10). T-scores > 69 indicate problems. The items are further divided into eight subscales. Data are standardized by age and gender, using a sample of 2,000 clinic and nonclinic clients. Computer scoring is available.

Behavior Problem Subscales

There are eight subscales, called narrow-band syndromes. Three of them are used to create an Internalizing scale, and two are used for an Externalizing scale.

- Internalizing
    Withdrawn
    Somatic Complaints
    Anxious Depressed
- Externalizing
    Delinquent Behavior
    Aggressive Behavior
- Other
    Social Problems
    Thought Problems
    Attention Problems

CHILD BEHAVIOR CHECKLIST (CBCL)

The CBCL/4–18 is given to parents with children from 4 to 18 years of age. There is also a CBCL/2–3 for children ages 2 to 3. In addition to the Behavior Problems scales, there are items assessing social competencies.

YOUTH SELF-REPORT (YSR)

The YSR can be given to children who are 11 to 18 years of age. It is structurally similar to the CBCL.

TEACHER'S REPORT FORM (TRF)

The TRF includes the Behavior Problems items, but does not have ratings of social competencies or behaviors that occur outside school settings.

Home Situations (HSQ) and School
Situations Questionnaires (SSQ)

These scales (Barkley, 1987, 1995) can be used in place of the Conners' scales,
and are primarily used in the diagnosis of Attention-Deficit Hyperactivity Disorder. However, the norms are limited to children between the ages of 6 and 12.
They are shorter and easier to complete than the Conners' scales, but are not as
widely used. We find the added comprehensiveness of the Conners' scales useful
given the slight increase in time needed to complete them.

The HSQ has 16 items and the SSQ has 8. Four scores can be derived from
the HSQ: Number of Problem Settings, Mean Severity, Compliance Situations,
Leisure Situations. The SSQ only includes Number of Problem Settings and Mean
Severity.

Summary

Choosing child and adolescent assessments is harder than for adults because of
the sample's wide developmental range. Table 5.4 should help you to decide
which tests fit within your client's age range. The Testing Tip on page 102 summarizes our approach to rapid assessment.

TABLE 5.4
Age Ranges for Child and Adolescent Assessments

Test Name	2	3	4	5	6	7	8	9	10	11	12	13	14	15	16	17	18	19	→
INTELLECTUAL FUNCTION																			
WAIS-III														X	X	X	X	X	
WISC-III					X	X	X	X	X	X	X	X	X	X	X	X			
WPPSI-R		X	X	X	X	X													
ACADEMIC ACHIEVEMENT																			
WIAT					X	X	X	X	X	X	X	X	X	X	X	X	X		
WJ-R	X	X	X	X	X	X	X	X	X	X	X	X	X	X	X	X	X	X	X
WRAT-3					X	X	X	X	X	X	X	X	X	X	X	X	X	X	X
PERSONALITY AND EMOTIONAL FUNCTIONING																			
MMPI-A													X	X	X	X	X		
MACI												X	X	X	X	X	X	X	
RORSCHACH				X	X	X	X	X	X	X	X	X	X	X	X	X	X	X	X
CDI						X	X	X	X	X	X	X	X	X	X	X			
APPERCEPTION TESTS																			
TAT									X	X	X	X	X	X	X	X	X	X	X
CAT		X	X	X	X	X	X	X	X										
RATC					X	X	X	X	X	X	X	X	X	X					
RATING SCALES																			
Anser		X	X	X	X	X	X	X	X	X	X	X	X	X	X	X	X	X	X
Conners		X	X	X	X	X	X	X	X	X	X	X	X	X	X	X			
CBCL/2–3	X	X																	
CBCL/4–18			X	X	X	X	X	X	X	X	X	X	X	X	X	X			
YSR										X	X	X	X	X	X	X	X	X	
HSQ					X	X	X	X	X	X	X								
SSQ						X	X	X	X	X	X	X							

Testing Tip
Rapid Approach to Child/Adolescent Assessment

1. Consult with your referral source to get a diagnostic impression and reason for the referral.
2. Consult Section II to identify critical issues, referral questions, essential features, and appropriate tests for each diagnosis.
3. Obtain consent for testing; clarify custody and confidentiality.
4. Have informants complete intake questionnaire or rating scales (e.g., Anser scales) prior to intake.
5. Obtain releases of information for all third parties.
6. Have the following on hand at all times: intake, consent and release forms, abuse reporting forms, WISC-III or WPPSI-R, MMPI-A, apperception tests.
7. Interview parent and child or adolescent and obtain collateral information.
8. Testing Decisions:

   Do cognitive testing only if it is warranted by the referral question. Suggested choices are:

   Gross measure of IQ: (a) Wechsler VIQ, (b) Wechsler PIQ.
   Prorated Wechsler scale.

   Do emotional testing only if it is warranted by the referral question:

   Consider Rorschach if (a) you are trained to give it and test it, and (b) you have time or the software to score and interpret it.

   Have patients who are old enough complete MMPI-A.

   Consider MACI if patient won't/can't do MMPI-A.

   Screen for Learning Disorder only if warranted by the referral question:

   Obtain School Educational and Attendance Record.

   Administer WIAT Screener, followed by WIAT.

   Use WJ-R if you need broader sampling of data.

   Consider problem-specific measures (see Chapters 6–10).

   Administer Parent or Teacher Rating Scales.

9. Immediately communicate findings to your referral source as they come in.
10. Dictate/write report using Chapter 12 guidelines. Be sensitive to referral-specific formats.
11. Provide feedback to parent and child or adolescent and include it with releases to relevant others.

DIFFERENTIAL DIAGNOSIS: PRACTICAL ISSUES

DSM-IV Seldom Fits What You See in Reality

SELDOM DO CLIENTS MEET DIAGNOSTIC CRITERIA in the neat and organized manner presented in the *DSM-IV*. As a result, clinicians are often faced with diagnosing someone using the wastebasket NOS (not otherwise specified) category, which is used when clients meet some, but not all, symptom criteria for a specific disorder. Alternatively, other clinicians take a less rigid approach, diagnosing a client when they meet largely all the criteria.

Most Referring Sources Don't Need an Exact Diagnosis

Most referring sources are not so rigid that they require you to come up with the exact diagnosis specified in the *DSM-IV*. In general, they want more information and assurance that test results confirm their impressions, and desire recommendations for treatment. Thus, your expertise should include a broad familiarity of each disorder.

When a Diagnosis Is Required, Be Careful

When you render a diagnosis, you expose yourself to legal liabilities. For example, an incorrect diagnosis of mental retardation might send a child unnecessarily into special education programs and underestimating a client's depression is dangerous, particularly when suicide is a possibility.

Diagnostic Codes and Treatment

For each *DSM-IV* disorder listed, we have included corresponding ICD codes. In some cases, codes will appear with the letter *x* substituted for a number. This occurs when the code can be modified based on such factors as chronicity or severity. Treatment recommendations and test findings found throughout this section are based on our clinical experience, as well as from several excellent manuals (e.g., Busse & Blazer, 1996; Choca & Van Denburg, 1997; Graham, 1993; Greene, 1991; Groth-Marnat, 1997; Jongsma & Peterson, 1995; Jongsma, Peterson, & McInnis, 1996; Levine, 1994; Lewis, 1996; Maxmen & Ward, 1995; Meyer & Deitsch, 1996; Schneider, Reynolds, Lebowitz, & Friedhoff, 1994). They can be used as a starting point for the recommendations section of an assessment report.

Diagnostic Differentials

At the end of each chapter, we have included common diagnostic differentials and the key features to help you tease apart similar disorders.

CHAPTER 6

Mood: Depression, Anxiety, Somatoform, and Related Disorders

Practical Considerations

WHY THESE DISORDERS ARE GROUPED TOGETHER

FREQUENTLY, WHEN REFERRING CLINICIANS ask for an assessment of a client, they will tell you that the client has symptoms of depression, somatic complaints, and nervousness. Most clients don't have all three diagnoses, but because Mood Disorders, Anxiety Disorders, and Somatoform Disorders share overlapping features, it's up to you to figure out what diagnosis (and sometimes diagnoses) best accounts for the cluster of symptoms. Thus, a client with panic attacks also may be depressed, but complains of multiple somatic problems. Table 6.1 summarizes the key descriptive features of each disorder. Table 6.2 presents the key test findings. Treatment recommendations are presented with each disorder, and additional recommendations for children and older adults are listed at the end of the chapter.

Testing Tip
Rapid Assessment of Mood-Related Disorders

For most clients, an efficient assessment might include:

Children	RATC, Children's Depression Inventory, Rorschach
Adolescents	MMPI-A (preferred) or MACI, Children's Depression Inventory
Adults	MMPI-2 (preferred) or MCMI-III, BDI-II
Elderly	MMPI-2 (preferred) or MCMI-III, BDI-II

TABLE 6.1
Key Descriptive Features of Mood-Related Disorders

Disorder/Syndrome	Behavioral	Emotional	Interpersonal
Major Depression	Psychomotor retardation/agitation; weight changes; sleep changes; fatigue	Depressed mood; worthlessness; poor concentration; suicidal thoughts; anhedonia	Diminished interest in activities; social impairment/occupational impairment; isolation/withdrawal
Bipolar Disorder (Manic)	Decreased sleep; talkative; self-destructive; amusing; impulsive	Elevated, expansive, irritable mood; inflated self-esteem/grandiosity; racing thoughts	Selfish; disinterest in other's opinions; need for attention; demanding
Panic Disorder without Agoraphobia	Anxious; hypervigilant	Concern over recurring panic attacks; shame	Intellectual; marital conflict
Panic Disorder with Agoraphobia	Avoidance of places that feel unsafe; prone to stay away from crowds; hypervigilant	Concern over recurring panic attacks; shame; depression	Need to have trusted companions when venturing out; marital problems
Phobia (Social or Otherwise)	Avoidance of phobic stimuli	Depression about phobia; shame about phobia	Anxious; embarrassed easily
Obsessive-Compulsive Disorder	Compulsions; rituals	Embarrassment about symptoms; anxiety when attempting not to do compulsions; depression	Failure to marry
Posttraumatic Stress Disorder/Acute Stress Disorder	Avoidance of stimuli associated with prior trauma; sleep disturbance; flashbacks	Emotional nonresponsiveness or irritability; hypervigilance; depression	Sense of foreshortened future; lower functioning
Generalized Anxiety Disorder	Anxiety complaints	Worry; anxiety; tension; depression	Not reassured easily
Somatization Disorder	Numerous somatic complaints; frequent visits to M.D.; resistant to nonphysiological explanations; dramatic style	Depression; anxiety	External stresses in life (family, marital)
Conversion Disorder	Primary physiological symptom that cannot be explained	Indifference to symptom; emotionally unsophisticated	External stress related, unsophisticated relationships
Pain Disorder	Pain symptoms without physiological basis; resistant to nonphysiological explanations	Depression; anxiety	"Sick role"
Hypochondriasis	Fear that symptoms are due to a major illness; resistant to nonphysiological explanations	Depression; anxiety	Preoccupied with illness
Body Dysmorphic Disorder	Mirror checking; hiding of "ugly" part; visits to dermatologist/plastic surgeon	Unrealistic worry about appearance or minor defects (not weight related); depression; anxiety	Noted self-concern

TABLE 6.2

Key Diagnostic Test Findings for Mood-Related Disorders

Disorder/ Syndrome	WAIS-III/WISC-III	MMPI-2/ MMPI-A	MCMI-III	Rorschach
Major Depression	PIQ < VIQ Subtests: Lower scores on Digit Span, Digit Symbol-Coding (Coding), Arithmetic Factors: Lower scores on Working Memory (Freedom from Distractibility) and Processing Speed "I don't know" responses	Profiles: 2-7, 2-4, 2-3, 2-8 (depression with psychotic features) Content: DEP	D, CC, A, 1, 2, 3, 8A, 8b	Positive *DEPI* index Higher *V, C′, S, D, MOR* Lower *R* Check *S-CON*
Bipolar Disorder (Manic)	Subtests: Higher scores on timed tests (e.g., Digit Symbol-Coding (Coding)) Lower scores on Block Design, Picture Arrangement, Matrix Reasoning	Elevations: 9, 6, 8, and/or 4, low Scale 2	N, T, 4, 5, 6A, SS	Ambitent style More deviant responses Poorer form quality
Panic Disorder with/without Agoraphobia	If anxious during testing: PIQ < VIQ Subtests: Lower scores on Digit Span, Arithmetic, Digit Symbol-Coding (Coding), Block Design, Symbol Search	Profiles: 2-8, 1-3-7, 3-9 Elevations: 7, 1, 3, and/or 2 Content: ANX, LSE, A	A, D, H sometimes: 2, 3, 8A, 8B	
Social Phobia	See Panic Disorder	Profiles: 1-4 Slight elevations: F, 0, 3, and/or 2	A, D, H sometimes: 2	
Specific Phobia	See Panic Disorder	Slight elevations: F, K, 2, 3, and/or 7 FRS, PHO	A, D, H	
Obsessive-Compulsive Disorder	VIQ > PIQ Subtests: Higher scores on Similarities, Vocabulary, Comprehension Lower scores on: Digit Symbol-Coding, Block Design, Symbol Search	Profiles: 7, 7-8, 7-2, 2-7-8 Content: HEA, OBS	D, H, 7	Positive OBS index Higher *R* (>33), *W, Dd, C′, F+%, X+%,* (2AB + (*Art* + *Ay*))
Posttraumatic Stress Disorder/ Acute Stress Disorder	If anxious during testing: PIQ < VIQ Subtests: Lower scores on Digit Span, Arithmetic, Digit Symbol-Coding (Coding), Block Design, Symbol Search	Profiles: F-2-8, 7-2, 8-2-7, 1-9 Content: PK	R, 8A, 2A	Extratensive style Low *Afr*, high *L*
Generalized Anxiety Disorder	See Panic Disorder	Elevations: 2, 3, and/or 7, sometimes with 9, 8, or F	A, H	Low FC, high FM

(Continued)

TABLE 6.2 (Continued)

Disorder/ Syndrome	WAIS-III/WISC-III	MMPI-2/ MMPI-A	MCMI-III	Rorschach
Somatization Disorder	No specific findings	Elevations: 1, 2, 3, and/or 7 Profiles: 1-2, 1-2-8	H, A	More popular responses, lower M
Conversion Disorder	No specific findings	Profiles: conver- sion V (1-3), 2-1-7, 3-9	No specific findings	Positive CDI index
Pain Disorder	No specific findings	Elevations: 1, and/or 2	Possibly H, A, D	No specific findings
Hypochondriasis	Similar to OCD	Profiles: 1-3, 2-1, possibly with K, 6, 7	H, A, D	Similar to OCD findings
Body Dysmor- phic Disorder	No specific findings	Elevations: 4 possibly	Possibly 5	No specific findings

Cognitive assessment should occur only when the referral question includes the need to ascertain and predict cognitive function (e.g., generalized anxiety affecting reasoning; depression affecting memory). If rapport is sufficient, the MCMI-III (or MACI) can be used as an alternate test to the MMPI-2, if the client will not complete the MMPI-2 or MMPI-A (or if there is a concern about personality function). Finally, we recommend giving the Rorschach Inkblot Test only when the examiner has (a) facility with both scoring and interpretation, (b) time to give it, and (c) the self-report measures were uninformative.

MEDICAL CONDITIONS/MEDICATION

Keep in mind that these disorders and syndromes are often only considered present if it is established that they are not due to the physiological effects of a medication or treatment or an underlying medical problem.

For the most part, sedating medications have modest effects, usually lowering a client's performance by one standard deviation. When they do affect function in this way, it is usually in concert with the combined effects of physical illness (e.g., post-surgery).

SUICIDE ASSESSMENT

Clients with mood symptoms are more at risk for suicidal ideation. This should always be considered in evaluating a client's mood. Severely depressed clients are less likely to be suicidal due to their vegetative state. As the depression lifts, the risk of suicidal gestures increases. Suicide risk factors are discussed in Chapter 9.

Mood Disorder Syndromes

THE BOTTOM LINE ON MOOD DISORDERS

Mood Disorder diagnoses are based on the presence of two syndromes: depression or mania. All of the *DSM-IV* categories that compose the Mood Disorders are based on combinations of these two syndromes, though it may be in less severe forms (e.g., hypomania).

ELDERLY CLIENTS

Depression is more frequent in older adults, but the presentation can vary (Schneider et al., 1994). Elderly clients are more likely to have suffered the loss of loved ones. They are more likely to deny depressed mood. Yet, physical problems can appear in the same way as depression's vegetative symptoms creating difficulties in making a diagnosis. Older adults are more likely to complain about memory problems when feeling depressed.

DEPRESSIVE EPISODE

A depressive episode is present when the client reports or appears to have depressed mood, and/or anhedonia. The *DSM-IV* specifies a two-week period. Unlike everyday mood fluctuations, if untreated, the episode of melancholia or anhedonia can last for weeks or longer. Depressive symptoms include feelings of worthlessness, inappropriate guilt, and loss of energy. As severity increases, vegetative symptoms occur, including marked change in appetite (up or down), marked change in sleep (up or down), and psychomotor agitation or retardation. Suicidal thoughts or actions also may be present. A depressive episode often leads to loss of functioning in the client's job or social life.

MANIC EPISODE

Manic episodes are present when the client appears to be excited and agitated, with a very elevated mood. These clients often appear amusing, which is a useful clue to notice. Their speech jumps from topic to topic, but is usually understandable (unlike psychosis). Often, mania is accompanied by impulsive or grandiose thinking and actions that otherwise wouldn't occur (e.g., spending binges, wanting direct contact with celebrities). Insight is apparently lost, and medication compliance suffers. Manic clients often become easily irritated when their impulses are kept in check. You are most likely to see them in inpatient settings because of the profound loss of functioning. Manic clients can develop delusions and sometimes are misdiagnosed with psychotic disorders. Left untreated, an episode can last from weeks to months.

HYPOMANIC EPISODE

A hypomanic episode is a less severe form of a manic episode. In theory, it does not result in significant impairment in social or occupational function.

MIXED EPISODE

In a mixed episode, a client meets criteria for both a depressive and manic episode.

Mood Disorder Diagnoses in DSM-IV

Mood disorder diagnoses are based on the presence of one of the mood syndromes. The diagnosis is based on whether the client:

1. Is experiencing a depressive or manic episode.
2. Has repeated episodes.
3. Cycles between depression and mania.
4. Has subthreshold depression or mania.

MAJOR DEPRESSIVE DISORDER (296.xx)

Essential Features

The client is experiencing a major depressive episode, which can range in severity from mild to severe, with or without psychotic features. This is also called unipolar depression. The DSM-IV distinguishes between a client having a single episode (296.2x) versus those with a history of repeated episodes (296.3x). The client cannot have experienced a manic or hypomanic episode.

Diagnosis

Most of the time, a clinical interview should be sufficient to diagnose depression. For clients who are more guarded, or for clients where you need to judge the severity of the symptoms, we have provided typical test results on each of the major tests.

Older Adults

Depression may be one of the most common psychiatric disorders in the elderly, in part due to increased negative life events associated with aging. Major

---

Testing Tip
Test Results Associated with Depression

- On the WAIS-III, the classic pattern is to find PIQ < VIQ or PSI < VCI. Psychomotor retardation, and low effort can lead to lower scores on measures of attention and processing (Digit Span, Arithmetic, and Digit Symbol-Coding; Working Memory, Processing Speed), whereas tasks assessing formal learning are unaffected (Vocabulary). Responses suggesting a lack of motivation are more common (e.g., "I don't know," 1-point responses, refusal to continue).
- On the MMPI-2/MMPI-A, most likely elevations will include Scale 2 (Depression), in concert with Scales 7 (Psychasthenia), 4 (Psychopathic Deviate), 3 (Hysteria), or 8 (Schizophrenia; elevated 8 suggests Schizoaffective Disorder, greater agitation, and possible suicidality). Low Scale 9 (Mania) suggests motor retardation. A 1-9 profile suggests a masked depression, and a 2-0 profile suggests chronic depression and a greater risk of suicide. The DEP and LSE content scale may be elevated.
- On the MCMI-III, elevations may occur on Scales D (Dysthymia), and CC (Major Depression), as well as A (Anxiety), 1 (Schizoid), 2B (Depressive), 3 (Dependent), 8B (Self-Defeating), and 8A (Passive-Aggressive).
- On the BDI-II, clients with Major Depressive Disorder are likely to score >14 points. Also make sure to check Item 9 to assess for suicidal risk.
- On the Rorschach, depression is usually present when there is a positive *DEPI* index. Depression is also exhibited by higher Lambda *(L)*, more Vista *(Sum V)*, achromatic color *(SumC')*, space *(S)*, Shading *(Sum Y)*, or Morbid content *(MOR)*, and fewer depth *(FD)* responses than average. You may also see lower *a:p* (active to passive ratio), lower F+%, X+%, and fewer FC and CF responses. Always check S-CON to evaluate risk of suicide.

depression appears in approximately 11% of older adults in hospitals, and 12% in long-term care settings. Older adults may present with memory or cognitive problems, rather than depression, and may not endorse the presence of dysphoria. Some present with somatic complaints. Older adults are at greater risk of suicide (Chapter 11 provides a detailed discussion on differentiating depression from dementia in the elderly).

Children/Adolescents

Rates of depression in children have been identified at approximately 1% for preschoolers, 2% for school-age children, and 5% for adolescents, making it common among children seen in psychiatric settings. Children are more likely to show irritability, somatization, and social withdrawal than dysphoria. In addition, depression is more likely to co-occur with Disruptive Behavior Disorders than in isolation. It is common for young children to deny depression when asked, partially because of unfamiliarity with what depression means. Adolescents with depression present similarly to adults, but are more prone to act out with behavioral problems than to appear grossly dysphoric.

On the WISC-III and MMPI-A, depressed children are likely to show the same decreases in performance as adults. On the MACI, elevations may occur on scale GG (Suicidal Tendency), 2B (Doleful), B (Self Devaluation), and FF (Depressive Affect). On the Children's Depression Inventory, scores should fall in the depressed range. On the Roberts Apperception Test for Children, elevations should occur on the Depression scale and possibly on other clinical scales. On the Rorschach, depressed children show similar responses to adults, but tend to show more morbid content (MOR), more vista responses (V), fewer reflections or pairs, and fewer overall responses.

Recommendations

If testing indicates a diagnosis of depression, the following treatment recommendations may be appropriate.

- *Psychotherapy* (cognitive-behavioral, interpersonal, etc.) aimed at:
    Confronting negative thinking and cognitive distortions.
    Identifying and addressing stressors contributing to depression.
    Improving coping.
    Improving client's ability to express and work through painful feelings.
    Increasing activity and self-esteem.
- *Antidepressant* medication evaluation.
- *Therapy* to address and reduce risk of suicide.
- *Electroconvulsive therapy (ECT)* for intractable depression.
- *Potential referrals:* Psychiatrist, couples or family therapist, support group for parents.

DYSTHYMIC DISORDER (300.4)

Essential Features

Stereotypically, Dysthymic Disorder clients appear to always be depressed, with what seems to be a chronic low-grade depression. On closer inspection, they do not meet criteria for a depressive episode, but show depressive symptoms for at least two years. This diagnosis is only given if the client's symptoms are not better accounted for by a diagnosis of Major Depressive Disorder. Also, dysthymic clients can have depressive episodes, which would later change the diagnosis to Major Depressive Disorder (also called double depression).

Diagnosis

Clinically, dysthymia is easy to distinguish from depression because of the client's higher level of functioning and brighter mood. Most of the time, a clinical interview should be sufficient to diagnose it. For clients who are more guarded, or for whom you must judge symptom severity, we have provided typical test results on each of the major tests. In principle, dysthymia creates similar test results as depression, but to a lesser magnitude. It's unlikely to find extreme psychomotor retardation and amotivation in dysthymia.

Older Adults

Dysthymia is found in approximately 25% of older adults in hospital settings. Similar findings should occur as with Major Depression, but at a less severe level. Recall that older adults are at greater risk of suicide.

Testing Tip
Test Results Associated with Dysthymia

- On the WAIS-III, you may see similar results as in Major Depression, but with lesser severity.
- On the MMPI-2, Scale 2 (Depression) is usually elevated along with Scales 3 (Hysteria) or 7 (Psychasthenia). Some dysthymic clients will show elevations on Scales 4 (Psychopathic Deviate) and 6 (Paranoia), Scales 9 (Mania) and 6, or 9 and 8 (Schizophrenia). The DEP content scale may also be elevated.
- On the MCMI-III, elevations may be on Scales 2A (Avoidant), 2B (Depressive), D (Dysthymia), or 8A (Passive-Aggressive). Very low scores are expected on Scale 7 (Compulsive).
- On the BDI-II, scores should be less severe.
- On the Rorschach, responses are less likely to show a positive *DEPI* index than if diagnosed with Major Depression.

Children/Adolescents

Findings should be similar to those that occur with Major Depressive Disorder, but at a less severe level.

Recommendations

See Major Depressive Disorder.

BIPOLAR DISORDER I (296.xx) OR II (296.89)

Essential Features

Clients who meet criteria for mania are always diagnosed with Bipolar Disorder. Subcategorizations specify whether the client only has manic episodes, or more commonly, cycles between manic and depressive episodes. Many of these clients have sufficient insight to be able to describe the cycling that occurs. Bipolar I Disorder is diagnosed when the patient cycles between manic episodes and depressive ones. Bipolar II Disorder is diagnosed when the patient cycles between depression and hypomania.

Diagnosis

In most circumstances, you will not be the first clinician to diagnose mania in these clients. You will be most likely to test them on an inpatient basis, often because of poor medication compliance. On occasion, the referral will be to identify whether the patient is psychotic or manic. Again, a good clinical interview and history should help solve this as much as testing. When testing occurs, it is usually to help in identifying factors that moderate treatment, or to assess for successful treatment (see the Testing Tip on the next page for typical test results).

Older Adults

Similar findings should occur, as mania does not remit with age; older adults are at greater risk of suicide.

Children/Adolescents

Younger children with mania are more likely to have labile, explosive, or erratic symptoms, rather than persistent ones. Irritability and belligerence are more common than euphoria. Reckless behavior is consistent with the child's developmental level (e.g., dangerous play, school failure). These children often have significant behavioral problems and comorbidity with ADHD or Conduct Disorder. The extremes of Bipolar Disorder don't become obvious until puberty. These children typically see their symptoms as signs of "craziness" and will minimize them, unless the clinician treads with sensitivity.

> ## Testing Tip
> ## Test Results Associated with Bipolar Disorder
>
> - On the WAIS-III, manic clients may perform better on timed measures (e.g., Digit Symbol). Frequent or persistent verbalizations may result in higher scores on Comprehension, Vocabulary, and Similarities. Impatience and decreased checking of one's own performance may result in lower scores on Block Design, Picture Arrangement, or Matrix Reasoning.
> - On the MMPI-2 or MMPI-A, in manic episodes, look for high scores on Scales 9 (Mania), 6 (Paranoia), 8 (Schizophrenia), and 4 (Psychopathic Deviate), and a low score on Scale 2 (Depression). When client is depressed, see Major Depression, on page 110, for test findings.
> - On the MCMI-III, in manic or hypomanic episodes, expect elevated Scale N (Bipolar: Manic), as well as T (Drug Dependence), 4 (Histrionic), 5 (Narcissistic), 6A (Antisocial), or moderately high SS (Thought Disorder). When depressed, see Major Depressive Disorder for test findings.
> - On the Rorschach, the Comprehensive System does not specifically describe the constellation of responses found in Bipolar Disorder, when the client is manic. Nevertheless, manic clients are likely more prone to give a higher number of responses, more C and M responses, and more blends. An Ambitent style may be consistent with mania. Manic clients may be more likely to have deviant responses and poorer form quality.

Recommendations

If testing indicates a diagnosis of mania, the following treatment recommendations may be appropriate.

- *Medication* to treat mania.
- *Medication* for depressed periods.
- *Psychotherapy* (cognitive-behavioral, interpersonal, etc.) aimed at:

    Improving medication compliance.

    Identifying factors precipitating mania.

    Improving self-esteem associated with having Bipolar Disorder.

    Reducing odds that client terminates treatment.

- *Therapy* to address and reduce risk of suicide.
- *Potential referrals:* Psychiatrist, couples therapy, family therapy, support group.

CYCLOTHYMIC DISORDER (301.13)

Essential Features

Like clients with dysthymia, those with cyclothymia alternate between depression and mania, but usually do not meet criteria for either. It is considered a less severe form of Bipolar Disorder, and is seen in 1% of clients.

Diagnosis

Cyclothymia should be relatively easy to distinguish from Bipolar Disorder due to the client's greater level of functioning. A good clinical interview and history should be sufficient to render a diagnosis. When testing is requested, it is usually for identifying strengths and weaknesses, or the level of disease severity. Test results should be similar to Major Depression or Mania, but at a significantly lower level of severity.

Recommendations

See Bipolar Disorder, but keep in mind the greater functioning of the client.

Anxiety Disorders

PANIC DISORDER WITH/WITHOUT AGORAPHOBIA (300.01 OR 300.21)

Panic Attacks

Panic attacks are brief periods of extreme anxiety caused by the inadvertent triggering of the body's emergency response. *DSM-IV* lists 13 symptoms (e.g., sweating, panting, or fearing going crazy). Most clients describe a period lasting a few minutes which feels more frightening than anything else ever experienced. Panic attacks are often connected with social situations, resulting in many clients fearing having a panic attack in public. They occur in about 1.5% to 3.5% of adults, and more commonly in women. Depression frequently co-occurs.

Agoraphobia

Agoraphobia is the fear of being in public areas that are perceived as unsafe, with no hope for escape. Agoraphobia is only diagnosed if the client actively avoids these "unsafe areas." Many clients who have panic attacks develop Agoraphobia (approx. 50%).

Diagnosis

Although many of these clients can be diagnosed without testing, some of them will not talk openly about the extent of their symptoms. In this case, an MMPI-2 or other personality test can be revealing (see the following Testing Tip for typical test results).

Testing Tip
Test Results Associated with Panic Disorder

- On the WAIS-III, PIQ may be lower than VIQ. These clients may show signs of anxiety on testing, although Panic Disorder does not predispose the client to be anxious in all situations. Anxiety may reduce scores on Digit Span, Arithmetic, Digit Symbol-Coding, Block Design (seen by hand tremor, concern over timing), and Symbol Search.
- On the MMPI-2/MMPI-A, elevations may occur on Scales 7 (Psychasthenia), 1 (Hypochondriasis), and 3 (Hysteria), often in combination with Scale 2 (Depression). Profiles with 2-8, 1-3-7, or 3-9 are also possible. The ANX (Anxiety) scale and A supplemental scale may be elevated, as is sometimes LSE.
- On the MCMI-III, elevations are common on Scales A (Anxiety), D (Dysthymia), and H (Somatoform), with elevations sometimes on 2B (Depressive), 3 (Dependent), 8A (Passive-Aggressive), or 8B (Self-defeating).

Older Adults

There is little research suggesting differences in the presentation of Panic Disorder in the elderly, though in general, they are more likely to deny symptoms compared with adults. This disorder is less prevalent in older adults.

Children/Adolescents

Panic Disorder is less common in children, with the onset occurring in early adolescence.

Recommendations

If testing indicates a diagnosis of Panic Disorder, the following treatment recommendations may be appropriate.

- *Medication* during depressed periods.
- *Medication* treatment for anxiety (on a short-term basis).
- *Psychotherapy* (systematic desensitization, cognitive-behavioral, interpersonal, stress inoculation) aimed at:

    Reducing panic attacks and decreasing isolation.

    Exposing patient to feared stimuli to reduce anxiety.

    Teaching relaxation training and breathing exercises.

    Teaching cognitive techniques to combat maladaptive thinking (e.g., catastrophizing).

Working on issues of self-esteem associated with having panic symptoms.

Working on issues regarding psychological dependence on anxiolytic medications.

SOCIAL PHOBIA (300.23)

Social Phobia is the fear of being judged or negatively evaluated, and being embarrassed. Its onset is usually during adolescence. Agoraphobia, on the other hand, is usually not bound to performance, but in leaving safe places. Exposure to the fearful social situation leads to anxiety and sometimes to panic attacks. The client realizes that the fear is unreasonable or excessive. Avoidance often occurs. The fear affects the client's routine. Depressive symptoms can co-occur.

Diagnosis

Although some of these clients can be diagnosed without testing, others will not talk openly about the extent of their symptoms. In this case, an MMPI-2 or other personality test can be very revealing (see Testing Tip for typical test results).

Older Adults

Specific information is not available about the presence of Social Phobia in the elderly, though the disorder does continue into older adulthood.

Testing Tip
Test Results Associated with Social Phobia

- On the WAIS-III, clients may be more likely to show signs of anxiety on testing, although Social Phobia does not predispose the client to be anxious in all situations. Anxiety, if present, may reduce scores on Digit Span, Arithmetic, Digit Symbol-Coding, Block Design (seen by hand tremor, concern over timing), and Symbol Search. PIQ may be lower than VIQ.
- On the MMPI-2 or MMPI-A, the profile is usually normal, with slight elevations on Scales F (Infrequency) suggesting distress, 0 (Social Introversion) suggesting isolation, 3 (Hysteria) suggesting worry, or 2 (Depression), and slightly lower Scale 9 (Mania). A 1-4 profile may occur. Acute distress may lead to an elevation on Scale 7 (Psychasthenia).
- On the MCMI-III, elevations on Scales A (Anxiety), D (Depression), and H (Somatoform) are more common, with an elevation sometimes on Scale 2B (Depressive).

Children/Adolescents

In young children, Social Phobia often appears as a failure to achieve at an expected level of social functioning, rather than as a decline. When the disorder appears in adolescence, decline may be observed. Children with Social Phobia may cry, cling to familiar others, or have tantrums. They may appear shy in new situations, avoid group play, and stay at the perimeter of social situations. Children cannot often avoid the situations arousing fear, which may make it hard for them to identify the cause of their anxiety. Classroom performance, refusal to attend school, or failure to attend dances or other events may occur. To diagnose the disorder, the social anxiety should occur in peer settings, not just with adults, and the child should be able to demonstrate social ability in the first place. Also consider that cultural factors may affect the child's symptom presentation.

Recommendations

If testing indicates a diagnosis of Social Phobia, the following treatment recommendations may be appropriate.

- *Psychotherapy* (group therapy, systematic desensitization, cognitive-behavioral, interpersonal, etc.) aimed at:

  Exposing client to social situations and reducing fear (e.g., stress inoculation).

  Teaching cognitive techniques to combat maladaptive thinking patterns.

  Working on issues of self-esteem associated with having Social Phobia.

  Dealing with issues of psychological dependence on medications.
- *Medication* during depressed periods.
- *Medication* treatment for severe anxiety (on a short-term basis).

SPECIFIC PHOBIA (300.29)

Essential Features

Excessive or unreasonable fears of anything other than participating in social situations or leaving safe places are called specific phobias. Most simple phobias that start in childhood disappear before adulthood.

Diagnosis

These clients are seldom referred for diagnostic testing because the patient merely has to state the existence of an irrational fear to get a diagnosis. Yet, clients with Avoidant, Borderline, or Schizotypal Personality Disorders are more likely to show phobias, suggesting that testing is useful in identifying other psychopathology or emotional factors that might benefit from treatment (see Testing Tip below for typical test results).

Older Adults

There is not significant research information about the presence of Specific Phobia in the elderly, though the disorder is known to occur in older adults.

Children/Adolescents

Specific Phobia occurs in 2%–9% of children. Children with Specific Phobia typically do not appreciate that their fears are excessive and will rarely report worry about the phobia. Symptoms are more likely to be crying, clinging, or tantrums. Significant impairment must be present for a diagnosis to occur (e.g., fear of playing baseball results in avoidance of all social play).

Recommendations

If testing indicates a diagnosis of Specific Phobia, the following treatment recommendations may be appropriate.

Testing Tip
Test Results Associated with Specific Phobia

- On the WAIS-III, PIQ may be lower than VIQ. These clients may be more likely to show signs of anxiety on testing, although Specific Phobia does not predispose the client to be anxious in all situations. Anxiety may reduce scores on Digit Span, Arithmetic, Digit Symbol-Coding, Block Design (seen by hand tremor, concern over timing), and Symbol Search.
- On the MMPI-2 or MMPI-A, the profile should appear essentially normal, though the FRS (Fears) and PHO (Phobia) content scales tend to be high. The F (Infrequency) and K (Defensiveness) validity scales may be slightly elevated due to distress and embarrassment about the phobia. Elevations may occur on Scales 2 (Depression), 3 (Hysteria), and 7 (Psychasthenia). If the client fears having a panic attack, however, Scales 8 (Schizophrenia) or 6 (Paranoia) may also be elevated.
- On the MCMI-III, elevations on Scales A (Anxiety), D (Dysthymia), and H (Somatoform) may occur, depending on the extent of confrontation with the feared stimulus.

- *Psychotherapy* (systematic desensitization, cognitive-behavioral, interpersonal, etc.) aimed at:

  Working to have client confront feared situations or stimuli.

  Working on issues of self-esteem associated with having a phobia.

OBSESSIVE-COMPULSIVE DISORDER (OCD) (300.3)

Essential Features

According to *DSM-IV*, OCD is characterized by obsessions or compulsions, whereas Obsessive-Compulsive Personality Disorder involves obsessional attention to detail and rigidity. Prevalence rates for OCD range around 2%, with most clients showing symptoms as early as 6 years, and a median age around 23 years.

The client usually realizes that the obsessions or compulsions are excessive or unreasonable. OCD symptoms cause marked distress and interfere with the client's functioning. Higher-functioning clients can show complete remission of symptoms in response to cognitive-behavioral treatment.

These symptoms are usually ego-dystonic and embarrassing so you may need to ask direct questions verifying their presence. The most common subtypes are clients who need to wash (fearing contamination), check (needing to check numerous times), doubt (fear catastrophes if all is not perfect), count and arrange (magical thinking and superstitions that guide actions), and hoard (keeping items to avoid catastrophe). OCD can vary in its severity.

Testing Tip
Obsessions and Compulsions

Obsessions have these characteristics:

1. Distressing, recurrent and persistent thoughts, impulses, or images.
2. These thoughts are beyond real world problems.
3. The client tries to ignore or neutralize them with other thoughts or actions.
4. The client realizes that the thoughts are caused by the mind.

Compulsions are:

1. Repetitive behaviors or mental acts that the client feels driven to do in response to the obsession.
2. The behaviors or mental acts that are aimed at preventing distress associated with the action.

Diagnosis

These clients may need to be tested for several reasons. First, the client may not admit to OCD during an interview, but will admit to it on testing. Cognitive testing may also reveal obsessive behaviors. Second, testing helps to identify the severity of the illness, other comorbid disorders, and factors relevant to treatment. Clients with OCD often develop Major Depressive Disorder (see Testing Tip for typical test results).

Older Adults

Older adults with OCD show similar symptom severity as adults, though disease onset occurred later (Kohn et al., 1997).

Children/Adolescents

In children, parents or teachers are usually aware of OCD symptoms prior to the child, which suggests that the symptoms are ego-syntonic. OCD usually does not affect school and extracurricular performance to the same extent as other disorders. However, OCD symptoms are often seen at home. Prevalence studies are lacking in this age range. Children typically find their symptoms signs of "craziness" and will minimize them, unless the clinician treads with sensitivity.

Recommendations

If testing indicates a diagnosis of OCD, the following treatment recommendations may be appropriate.

- *Psychotherapy* (systematic desensitization, cognitive-behavioral, interpersonal, etc.) aimed at:

    Stopping compulsions (via behavioral and cognitive-behavioral, exposure therapy, response prevention).

    Addressing relevant psychological conflicts.

    Working on issues of self-esteem associated with having OCD.

    Developing alternative ways to cope with anxiety.

- *Medication* treatment for reducing obsessions and compulsions.
- *Medication* for concurrent depression.

POSTTRAUMATIC STRESS DISORDER (PTSD) (309.81)

Essential Features

PTSD is a disorder resulting from the client being exposed to events involving threatened death or injury to self or someone else. Its prevalence rate is a function of the frequency of the traumatic events in the community.

Testing Tip
Test Results Associated with Obsessive-Compulsive Disorder
────────────────

- On the WAIS-III, OCD can be difficult to distinguish from Obsessive-Compulsive Personality Disorder. In general, clients with OCD are *less* likely to show an obsessive cognitive style than clients with the Personality Disorder because OCD can affect the client in a more isolated manner. OCD clients may have a higher FIQ, with VIQ > PIQ. A meticulous, detail-oriented approach can result in correct responses but a loss of speed for bonus points. Elaborate responses may result in increased scores on Similarities, Vocabulary, and Comprehension. Obsessiveness may also result in (a) trivial details being named missing in Picture Completion, (b) overly perfectionistic copying or scanning in Digit Symbol-Coding or Symbol Search, or (c) slow times on Block Design due to precisely aligning the pieces.
- On the MMPI-2/MMPI-A, elevations are most common on Scale 7 (Psychasthenia) alone, or with Scales 8 (Schizophrenia) or 2 (Depression); 2-7-8 profiles are common. The HEA (Health Concerns) and OBS (Obsessive Concerns) content scale is higher in clients with health concerns.
- On the MCMI-III, elevations are most common on scales D (Dysthymia) and H (Somatoform), which are often higher than Scale A (Anxiety). Scale 7 (Compulsive) may be elevated.
- On the Rorschach, clients with OCD are more likely to give many responses (> 33), a higher number of W (Whole) or *Dd* (Uncommon Detail) responses, more C' (Achromatic Color) and have a higher F+% (reality testing without emotion) or X+% (reality testing with emotion). OBS (Obsessive Style Index) may also be positive, which suggests an obsessive concern for details, but not necessarily OCD. The intellectualization index may also be higher (2AB + (Art + Ay)).

The trauma should be sufficiently severe to cause a reaction of intense horror, fear, or helplessness. Subsequently, the client may have disturbing recollections or dreams of the events. The client may relive the experience (a flashback) or alternatively block it out of awareness. Anxiety and physiological reactivity may occur when reminders of the events are present. In addition, PTSD includes avoidance of stimuli associated with the traumatic event, or a numbing of general responsiveness. This can be seen as detachment, emotional restriction, or a sense of a foreshortened future. Increased arousal may also occur (e.g., sleep problems, irritability, concentration problems). *DSM-IV* requires the disturbance to last for at least a month. Onset of PTSD symptoms may be delayed for months or years after the event (e.g., later awareness of child abuse).

Testing Tip
Precipitates of Posttraumatic Stress Disorder

- Disasters.
- Large-scale transportation accidents.
- Emergency workers exposed to trauma.
- War.
- Rape.
- Sexual assault.
- Spouse or partner battery.
- Torture or imprisonment.
- Child or elder abuse.

Clients with delayed PTSD are more likely to have depression or alcoholism, and the prognosis for treatment is more negative.

Acute Stress Disorder (308.3) is a variant of PTSD that lasts for no more than 4 weeks, with similar symptoms as PTSD.

Diagnosis

Diagnosis of PTSD in adults due to earlier child abuse may occur (Briere, 1997). In addition, some adults may incorrectly believe that they were victims of child abuse. In either case, you should keep in mind that there can be serious legal repercussions in working with victims of trauma. Specific recommendations for the assessment of abused clients are found in Chapter 9.

The client may see the assessment process as part of the trauma, so establishing rapport and setting appropriate pacing is more important than usual. Sensitivity in having the client discuss the trauma is warranted, perhaps by telling the client in advance about the stress of the assessment process. Be prepared for state-mandated reporting responsibilities associated with the trauma. Also consider that malingering may co-occur, so assess for secondary gains (e.g., monetary gains) associated with establishing the presence of PTSD (see Testing Tip for typical test results).

Older Adults

PTSD can occur at any age. There is not research identifying differences of presentation in older adults.

Children/Adolescents

Expect that anxiety symptoms will be age appropriate. Children may relive the trauma in dreams or through play. Parents and teachers should be interviewed to

---

Testing Tip
Test Results Associated with Posttraumatic Stress Disorder
───────────────────

- On the WAIS-III, clients may be more likely to show signs of anxiety on testing, although PTSD does not predispose the client to be anxious in all situations.
- On the MMPI-2 or MMPI-A, the most stereotypical PTSD profile is the F-2-8 profile, with the 7-2, 8-2-7, or 1-9/9-1 profiles occurring, too. The PK content scale may also help identify PTSD, though it was validated primarily in veteran samples.
- On the MCMI-III, elevations may occur on Scales R (PTSD), 8A (Passive-Aggressive), or 2A (Avoidant). Elevations on Scales A (Anxiety), D (Dysthymia), B (Alcohol Dependence), T (Drug Dependence), 1 (Schizoid), 3 (Dependent), 6A (Antisocial), 8B (Self-defeating), X (Disclosure), and Z (Debasement) have also been associated with PTSD. Note that the R (PTSD) scale does not have items that completely correspond with *DSM-IV* criteria and has not been extensively validated in PTSD clients.
- On the Rorschach, there is limited information regarding PTSD response styles. There is some evidence that PTSD clients will be extratensive, low *Afr*, and high Lambda. Content suggestive of trauma (e.g., morbid, aggressive) may also be a sign of thought disorder and should be ruled out, prior to considering PTSD.
- The Traumatic Symptom Inventory (TSI; Briere, 1995) is a 100-item, standardized scale for clients over the age of 18. It includes 3 validity scales and 10 clinical scales. It may be a helpful additional measure of PTSD symptoms. The Trauma Symptom Checklist for Children (Briere, 1996) is a downward extension of the TSI for children between the ages of 8 and 16.

see whether the client's affect has changed (this is usually difficult for children to describe). Projective measures may be best for younger children. Due to numerous legal issues, do not perform assessments of children who have been abused without sufficient expertise. Issues pertaining to child abuse are discussed in Chapter 9.

Recommendations

If testing indicates a diagnosis of PTSD, the following treatment recommendations may be appropriate.

- *Psychotherapy* (systematic desensitization, cognitive-behavioral, interpersonal, etc.) aimed at:

Creating the ability for client to talk openly about the traumatic situation.

Treating phobic response that developed secondary to the traumatic situation.

Providing stress inoculation training.

Working through victimization issues and prevention of future victimization.

Developing further coping responses (e.g., methods of grieving, methods of initiating help from others).

- *Medication* during depressed periods.
- *Referral* to a support group.

GENERALIZED ANXIETY DISORDER (GAD) (300.02)

GAD clients are chronic worriers, who receive the diagnosis if they have had significant worry symptoms for 6 months. Their worry affects their social and occupational functioning. It affects approximately 5% of the population for some time in their lives. Women are more likely to have the disorder. Comorbidity with depression is common at all ages.

Diagnosis

These clients are likely to have symptoms of anxiety and depression, and may be self-referred. In doing a diagnostic workup, you may find that some clients get diagnosed with a Personality Disorder or Mood Disorder, rather than GAD (see Testing Tip for typical test results).

Older Adults

Older adults are more likely to show symptoms of both GAD and depression, making diagnosis challenging. The BDI-II and MMPI-2 may be useful.

Children/Adolescents

In older children, GAD may present as concerns over school performance or athletics, even when others are not evaluating them. Worries may also be about catastrophic events. On the WISC-III, similar findings as in adults are expected. On the MACI, elevations may occur on Scale B (Self-Devaluation), E (Peer Insecurity), EE (Anxious Feelings), or FF (Depressive Affect). It seems to occur more commonly in families where achievement is stressed or in families where the parents consistently yield to the child's demands. Also rule out the influence of caffeine.

Testing Tip
Test Results Associated with Generalized Anxiety Disorder

- On the WAIS-III, anxiety may reduce scores on Digit Span, Arithmetic, Digit Symbol-Coding, Block Design (seen by hand tremor, concern over timing), and Symbol Search. PIQ may be lower than VIQ.
- On the MMPI-2 or MMPI-A, elevations are likely on Scales 2 (Depression), 3 (Hysteria), and 7 (Psychasthenia), and sometimes on Scales 9 (Mania), 8 (Schizophrenia) and/or F (Infrequency).
- On the MCMI-III, elevations on Scales A (Anxiety), and H (Somatoform) are most common, with possible elevations on Scales D (Dysthymia), 2A (Avoidant), 8A (Passive-Aggressive), or S (Schizotypal).
- On the Rorschach, low FC (form with color) or high FM (form with movement) can indicate anxiety.

Recommendations

If testing indicates a diagnosis of GAD, the following treatment recommendations may be appropriate.

- *Psychotherapy* (cognitive-behavioral, interpersonal) aimed at:

    Teaching cognitive techniques to combat maladaptive thinking.

    Developing relaxation techniques.

    Addressing any underlying depression.

    Improving client's anxiety coping skills.

    Identifying areas of conflict in the client's life.

    Improving time management.

- *Medication* during depressed periods.

SEPARATION ANXIETY DISORDER (309.21)

Essential Features

Children with this disorder (< 18 years) show anxiety symptoms when separated from parents or loved ones. This disorder occurs most commonly around age 11. The children fear dreadful things occurring to their parents. Many aren't seen in clinics until they stop going to school. Anxiety symptoms might be used by the client to prevent having the parents leave. The disorder is believed to be due, in part, to parents who have difficulty in allowing the client to be alone and master the separation experience. If not treated completely, anxiety symptoms can continue into adulthood, sometimes as Panic Disorder. Children who have genuinely had to deal with separation from loved ones (e.g., emigrants) should not be given this diagnosis.

Diagnosis

There aren't specific test signs for Separation Anxiety Disorder, though it would be expected that anxiety symptoms would be present, similarly to GAD. This disorder has specific clinical features that typically render it unnecessary to test for the purpose of identifying the disorder. Testing can be useful to help better characterize (a) the dynamics of the parent-child interaction, and (b) the client's interpersonal and emotional functioning.

Recommendations

- *Psychotherapy* (cognitive-behavioral, systems, interpersonal) aimed at:

    Allowing child to be separated from parents (primary goal).

    Using transitional objects to aid in separations.

    Working on parents' anxiety about the child being alone.

    Having separation periods that increase at a gradual pace.

Somatoform Disorders

PRACTICAL CONSIDERATIONS

Rule Out Physiological Explanations for the Symptoms

Prior to diagnosing a Somatoform Disorder, you should be positive that a physiological cause does not account for the symptoms. Refer the client to appropriate physicians and/or check medical records.

Clients with Somatoform Disorders Complain about Other Doctors

These clients have often had bad experiences with physicians. Either the doctor has confronted them too harshly, resulting in rejection, or the client is put through numerous tests without adequate explanation.

Psychological Factors and Their Role in Somatoform Disorder

Psychological factors are required to affect the presentation of physical symptoms. The client's reactions must be out of proportion to the illness. A client with stress-related diarrhea should not automatically be diagnosed with a Somatoform Disorder.

- *Distinguishing Somatoform Disorders from disorders involving somatic complaints.* Clients with Somatoform Disorders are not faking deliberately. They are genuinely experiencing symptoms. Other disorders may include somatic symptoms that are being feigned by the client. These include Factitious Disorder, Antisocial Personality Disorder, and Malingering.
- *Clients are not always forthcoming about prior medical treatment.* Get releases so you can learn about the client from other clinicians.
- *Be cautious of legal entanglements.* Some clients have such strong convictions regarding their complaints that your impression may be very upsetting. In addition, some somaticizing clients file lawsuits against those who may be associated with the cause of the somatic symptoms. Statements you make that minimize the legitimacy of the client's claims can be the impetus for a lawsuit against you.

SOMATIZATION DISORDER (300.81)

Essential Features

This disorder often appears in adolescence, and is more common in females than males. Lifetime prevalence rates range from 0.1% to 2.0%, whereas its frequency among psychiatric clients is 1% to 6%. These clients have a long history of somatic complaints that aren't explainable by a medical condition; if there is a medical condition, it cannot explain the severity of the complaints. Unlike most people, these clients seek medical care whenever there is a symptom, and can expect or seek out tests and treatments to follow. Their way of describing their symptoms can appear dramatic. Symptoms also can vary in terms of severity. For *DSM-IV*, they must have a specific constellation of complaints: four pain symptoms, two gastrointestinal symptoms, one sexual symptom, and one pseudoneurological symptom. Keep in mind that a client who meets most of these criteria should not be considered free of psychopathology. Undifferentiated Somatoform Disorder (300.81) is similar to Somatization Disorder, but requires the presence of only one symptom.

Diagnosis

Clients with Somatization Disorder are at greater risk for a Mood or Anxiety Disorder. If they are self-referred, it will likely be due to mood symptoms. In some cases, these clients are referred by physicians who want you to establish a Somatoform Disorder. When this occurs, the clients may be particularly defensive and irritated. In addition, clients with PTSD can sometimes show similar symptoms, suggesting that an evaluation for trauma be considered (see Testing Tip on page 130 for typical test results).

Testing Tip
Test Results Associated with Somatization Disorder

- On the MMPI-2 or MMPI-A, elevations on Scales 1 (Hypochondriasis), 2 (Depression), 3 (Hysteria), and possibly 7 (Psychasthenia) are most common. An elevation on Scales 1, 2, and 8 (Schizophrenia) might reflect odd somatic complaints. Clients with elevations on Scales 1 and 2 can have Somatization Disorder with depressive symptoms.
- On the MCMI-III, elevations on Scale H (Somatoform) are to be expected, as might be Scale A (Anxiety). Depression might lead to elevation on Scale CC (Major Depression).
- On the Rorschach, these clients are prone to giving more popular responses, fewer M (Human Movement) responses, and possibly *Hd*, *An*, or *Bl* content responses.

Older Adults

There is not significant research information on this disorder in the elderly.

Children/Adolescents

There is little research on this specific disorder in children, though adults with Somatization Disorder were frequently ill as children. Somatization can affect academic and social functioning, in part due to frequent absences. These children may have difficulty keeping friendships, may be overly dependent on parents, and have low self-esteem. On the MACI, you may see elevation on Scale C (Body Disapproval). On the Achenbach scales, you may see an elevation on the Somatic Complaints scale or the Internalizing scale.

Recommendations

If testing indicates a diagnosis of Somatization Disorder, the following treatment recommendations may be appropriate.

- *Psychotherapy* (supportive, interpersonal) aimed at:

    Helping client improve level of functioning.

    Working to identify stressors in client's life that might be ignored due to focus on somatic symptoms.

    Working with the client to develop better coping responses and increase self-esteem.

    Providing reassurance and education.

    Developing better coordination between treating clinicians.

- *Medication* during depressed periods.

CONVERSION DISORDER (300.11)

Essential Features

This disorder often appears in adolescence or early adulthood. It is fairly uncommon in the general population, whereas its frequency among psychiatric clients is 1%–3%. These clients usually have a primary symptom that cannot be due to a physiological cause (e.g., false pregnancy, blindness, paralysis); unlike Somatization Disorder, these clients tend to minimize the problem ("la belle indifference"). Conversion symptoms appear rapidly. Often the symptom disappears prior to treatment. One assumption behind this disorder is that it is a primitive defense reflecting marked stress.

Diagnosis

These clients usually are less defensive than clients with Somatization Disorder due to their lower level of insight. They are usually referred by physicians. Clients with PTSD can sometimes show similar symptoms, suggesting that your evaluation consider potential traumas (see Testing Tip for typical test results).

Older Adults

There is little information on this disorder in the elderly. However, it is essential to rule out physiological explanations for the symptoms.

Children/Adolescents

Conversion Disorder is a common Somatoform Disorder in children. It may be associated with severe stressors (e.g., child abuse; family troubles, unresolved

---

Testing Tip
Test Results Associated with Conversion Disorder

- On the WAIS-III, there are not specific findings related to this disorder.
- On the MMPI-2, some clients with Conversion Disorder (as well as people with a genuine physical illness) show an elevation on Scales 1 (Hypochondriasis) and 3 (Hysteria), with a low score on Scale 2 (the conversion V). Others have found the 2-1-7 and 3-9 profiles in this disorder. HEA may also be elevated.
- On the MCMI-III, elevations on Scale H (Somatoform) are less likely because the client usually has only one complaint.
- On the Rorschach, there are not specific findings related to this disorder, though a pattern suggesting ineffective coping might appear.

grief). On the Achenbach scales, you may see an elevation on the Somatic Complaints scale or the Internalizing scale.

Recommendations

If testing indicates a diagnosis of Conversion Disorder, the following treatment recommendations may be appropriate.

- *Psychotherapy* (supportive, interpersonal) aimed at:

  Helping client improve level of functioning.

  Working to identify stressors in client's life that might be ignored due to focus on somatic symptoms.

  Improving coping skills.

- *Medication* during depressed periods.

PAIN DISORDER (307.xx)

Essential Features

This disorder often appears in adolescence and is more common in females than males. These clients suffer from pain, rather than from multiple medical problems. If there is a medical condition, it cannot explain the severity of the pain.

Diagnosis

Clients who seek treatment for chronic pain may instead have Major Depressive Disorder. Thus, they are often referred for mood symptoms (see Testing Tip for typical test results).

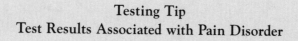

Testing Tip
Test Results Associated with Pain Disorder

- On the WAIS-III, there are not specific findings related to this disorder.
- On the MMPI-2, specific patterns are not found among pain disorder clients, though elevations on Scales 1 (Hypochondriasis) and 2 (Depression) might occur. An elevation on HEA is also common.
- On the MCMI-III, elevations on Scale H (Somatoform), A (Anxiety), or D (Dysthymia) may occur.
- On the Rorschach, there are not specific test findings.

Older Adults

Pain is more frequent in older adults, often due to degenerative conditions. Keep in mind that psychological factors must play a part in the pain symptoms for a diagnosis in *DSM-IV*. Older adults are underrepresented in pain clinics, possibly due to tolerance of pain as a part of aging.

Children/Adolescents

Children tend to show abdominal pain, headaches, or limb pain. Most children with recurrent abdominal pain (which can occur between ages 9 and 12 years) do not have an organic illness. Headache appears earlier, around the age of 7 years. Children with Pain Disorder may come from families where somatic complaints are more common. On the Achenbach scales, you may see an elevation on the Somatic Complaints scale or the Internalizing scale.

Recommendations

If testing indicates a diagnosis of Pain Disorder, the following treatment recommendations may be appropriate.

- *Psychotherapy* (supportive, interpersonal) aimed at:

    Helping client improve level of functioning.

    Working to identify stressors in client's life that might be ignored due to focus on somatic symptoms.

    Increasing quality of life and independence, taking focus off pain.
- *Medication* during depressed periods.
- *Medical evaluation* to ensure pain is being correctly treated.

HYPOCHONDRIASIS (300.7)

Essential Features

Whereas Somatization Disorder clients complain about the suffering that comes from their symptoms, clients with Hypochondriasis fear that their symptoms are due to a serious illness. It usually appears in early adulthood. Symptoms rarely disappear entirely; when it affects social or occupational functioning, it is due to unnecessary doctor or hospital visits. These clients may have low self-esteem.

Diagnosis

A clue to Hypochondriasis: clients with this disorder react poorly when told that there is nothing wrong with them. In addition, there are often multiple caregivers or physicians, and most of them are kept from talking to one another. Comorbidity exists with depression, which is often the reason for an assessment (see Testing Tip on the following page for typical test results).

Testing Tip
Test Results Associated with Hypochondriasis

- On the WAIS-III, clients with Hypochondriasis may appear similar to obsessive clients, with higher VIQ scores.
- On the MMPI-2 or MMPI-A, elevations on Scales 3 (Hysteria) and 1 (Hypochondriasis), or 2 (Depression) and 1 are common. Elevations on Scales K, 6 (Paranoia) and 7 (Psychasthenia) can occur, due to defensiveness.
- On the Rorschach, the client may show similar signs to OCD, due to excessive concern over health.

Older Adults

This disorder rarely develops for the first time in the elderly; it usually has a long history.

Children/Adolescents

Hypochondriasis is associated with past medical illness; identify relevant medical history in the client and relatives. Hypochondriasis is often found in children who received the most affection when they were ill. On the Achenbach scales, you may see an elevation on the Somatic Complaints scale or the Internalizing scale.

Recommendations

If testing indicates a diagnosis of Hypochondriasis, the following treatment recommendations may be appropriate.

- *Psychotherapy* (cognitive-behavioral, interpersonal, etc.) aimed at:

  Encouraging the client to talk about interpersonal events that might be precipitants of the somatic complaints.

  Working with the primary care physician to develop a fixed weekly visit schedule for approximately 10 weeks, which is then systematically lengthened. The client should be told in advance that visits are of a fixed length.

  Addressing and treating underlying depression.
- *Medication* during depressed periods.

Expect more anger and resistance from these clients because they believe the goal of the therapist is to show that the symptoms are psychologically based.

BODY DYSMORPHIC DISORDER (300.7)

Essential Features

Clients with Body Dysmorphic Disorder (BDD) have overconcern for imagined physical defects or marked concern for minor ones (e.g., my nose sticks out). It usually appears in adolescence, and may affect 1%–2% of adults, and 12% of clinic clients. Unlike nonclients, these individuals spend significant amounts of time mirror checking, mirror avoiding, or doing other obsessive rituals. Due to embarrassment, these clients will seldom share their feelings with anyone except physicians or plastic surgeons. Most see dermatologists or other physicians to try to correct the problem. Some will wear clothing to hide the perceived defect from view. The belief is not a delusion; clients should be able to acknowledge that they may be exaggerating their concerns.

Diagnosis

This diagnosis should not be made for people whose concern isn't excessive. Most of these clients will have Major Depression. Some will have Social Phobia. Many clients with OCD (approximately 23%) have concurrent BDD (Phillips, 1996) (see Testing Tip for typical test results).

Older Adults

There is little research on this disorder in the elderly. It continues into older adulthood and may worsen with age.

Children/Adolescents

Although most clients show BDD in adolescence, be careful not to diagnose this disorder in adolescents who show age-appropriate overconcern for appearance. Elevations may occur on MACI Scale C (Body Disapproval).

Recommendations

If testing indicates a diagnosis of BDD, the following treatment recommendations may be appropriate.

Testing Tip
Test Results Associated with Body Dysmorphic Disorder

- There is little evidence for specific test findings for this disorder.
- Due to inflated self-concern, these clients may show an elevation on Scale 4 (Psychopathic Deviate) on the MMPI-2 or MMPI-A, and elevations on Scale 5 (Narcissistic) of the MCMI-III.

- *Psychotherapy* (cognitive-behavioral, interpersonal, etc.) aimed at:

  Using cognitive-behavioral techniques to help reduce obsessive behaviors and challenge beliefs about appearance.

  Using graduated exposure to help the client participate more in the social situations that produce obsessive worries.

- *Clients with BDD are resistant to psychological interventions.* One approach is to work proactively with dermatologists or physicians who see the client's concerns as excessive.
- *Medication* during depressed periods.
- *Participation of the family in treatment (spouse, parents (with children))* to help educate them about the disorder, and to help teach them methods that reinforce cessation of the symptoms.

Treatment Recommendations for Children and Older Adults

We now describe specific treatment recommendations for children and older adults who have mood-related symptoms. These recommendations should be considered along with those described for specific disorders.

Children and Adolescents
- Improve academic performance (e.g., educational therapist, tutor).
- Improve peer relationships.
- Participation of family in treatment (e.g., family therapy, couples therapy):

  To address family contribution.

  To increase support.

  To help with setting limits.

  To educate family.

- Consult with school to increase socialization.

Older Adults
- Decrease social isolation.
- Encourage family involvement in treatment.
- Increase social activities.
- Rule out medical problems that can account for symptoms.

Differential Diagnosis

Several of the most frequent or prominent differential diagnoses are discussed in this section.

MOOD DISORDERS VERSUS SOMATOFORM DISORDERS

Mood Disorders can co-occur with Somatoform Disorders. However, if the somatic symptoms are better accounted for by the Mood Disorder, then a Mood Disorder diagnosis should be given. If the somatic symptoms continue in the absence of mood symptoms, you can be more confident of a Somatoform Disorder. If the mood symptoms continue in the absence of somatic symptoms, you can be more confident of a Mood Disorder. Depression is likely to occur with all Somatoform Disorders except for Conversion Disorder. For example, 60% of clients with depression have pain symptoms, and 87% of clients with Pain Disorder have depression.

ANXIETY DISORDERS VERSUS MOOD DISORDERS

Depressive symptoms can occur with many Anxiety Disorders, frequently due to frustration and dysphoria from the unintended anxiety symptoms. As with Somatoform Disorders, the way to identify the primary disorder is to establish whether the mood or anxiety symptoms occur separately.

BIPOLAR DISORDER (MANIC) VERSUS PSYCHOSIS

Occasionally, you will be referred a client whose referral source wants to know whether the client is psychotic or manic. Here are some ways of narrowing your options:

- *Get a good history.* Read the chart, and attempt to talk to the client's relatives or friends (with consent). Premorbid differences should be identifiable. Unless the client is under 18 years old, you should be able to detect telltale manic signs. Most clients with psychotic disorders do not show as clear a remission from symptoms as manic clients, so listen for ups and downs.
- *Check the medication history.* Has the client been treated successfully with lithium, valproic acid (Depakote), or carbamazepine (Tegretol), the most common treatments for Bipolar Disorder? Use of neuroleptics, on the other hand, is far less predictive of a diagnosis because many clients are given them to control behavior in general.
- *If the client is delusional, check the content.* Psychotic clients are more likely than manic clients to have delusions associated with thought broadcasting (believing that their thoughts can be heard by others) or delusions of reference (believing that messages are being sent directly to them from the TV). Manic clients, on the other hand, have delusions

that are grandiose, but somewhat possible. For example, a manic client might be convinced that a celebrity wants to know him. The other type of delusions seen in manic clients involve foolish ventures (e.g., the client wastes money to build a hotel on top of his home).

IN CHILDREN: BIPOLAR DISORDER VERSUS ADHD, CONDUCT DISORDER, OR SCHIZOPHRENIA

As with adults, mania in children can be misdiagnosed as Schizophrenia due to the presence of delusions. However, schizophrenic children have a more insidious onset of symptoms and are less engaging, whereas manic children have pressured speech and irritability.

Children with ADHD or mania can exhibit distractibility, irritability, hyperactivity, agitation, and restless sleep. ADHD symptoms are usually identified by preschool, whereas symptoms of mania occur later in life. Restless sleep in ADHD is usually pervasive, whereas in mania it is only during the manic episode.

Mania also overlaps with Conduct Disorder with shared antisocial and provocative behaviors (e.g., aggression, school failure, sexually inappropriate behaviors). Children with Conduct Disorder are more hurtful and vindictive, lacking remorse; whereas manic children are more mischievous. Children with Conduct Disorder do not show symptoms of pressured speech or flight of ideas. Note that Bipolar Disorder, ADHD, and Conduct Disorder can co-occur, too.

OBSESSIVE-COMPULSIVE DISORDER VERSUS OBSESSIVE-COMPULSIVE PERSONALITY DISORDER

The distinction between OCD and Obsessive-Compulsive Personality Disorder is often one of severity. OCD can be far more debilitating. The Personality Disorder is a personality style; the obsessive-compulsive behaviors are more ego-syntonic and the client will retain more adaptive features. A client with OCD has specific behaviors and obsessions; whereas a client with the Personality Disorder is rigid and orderly in many situations.

DISTINGUISHING SOMATOFORM DISORDERS

Somatization Disorder clients have multiple medical complaints, and have had them for years. Hypochondriasis Disorder clients have few complaints, but fear having a terrible illness. Conversion Disorder clients have a strange medical symptom with rapid onset and sometimes show indifference to its occurrence (e.g., paralysis).

CHAPTER 7

Behavior: Attention-Deficit and Disruptive Behavior Disorders

---

Why These Disorders Are Grouped Together

Behavioral symptoms are the most common reason for referral of children and adolescents for treatment. In practice, you are most likely to see child clients with one of the three *DSM-IV* Disruptive Behavior Disorders: Attention-Deficit/Hyperactivity Disorder (ADHD), Conduct Disorder, or Oppositional Defiant Disorder. While these disorders are typically seen in childhood and adolescence, more recent research indicates that they may persist into adulthood. These disorders occur more frequently in males than females (ratios range from 2:1 to 10:1).

Tables 7.1 and 7.2 review the essential features of these disorders in terms of their behavioral, emotional/cognitive, and interpersonal components, and summarize test findings.

Practical Considerations

SOME OF THESE BEHAVIORS ARE DEVELOPMENTALLY APPROPRIATE

Overactivity is characteristic of early childhood, especially for preschoolers and boys ages 6 to 12 years. Diffuse activity, varied attention span, and a defiant attitude are common. Similarly, oppositional behavior in adolescence is often associated with age-appropriate individuation.

Comorbidity

The most common disorders to coexist with behavioral disorders are Learning, Mood, and Anxiety Disorders. Conduct Disorder and Oppositional Defiant Disorder are often associated with a higher risk of substance-related diagnosis.

TABLE 7.1
Essential Features of Behavioral Disorders

Disorder/Syndrome	Behavioral	Emotional/Cognitive	Interpersonal
Attention-Deficit/Hyperactivity Disorder	Impulsiveness, distractibility; careless mistakes; poor listening; lacking persistence; forgetfulness or impatience; low frustration tolerance; poor impulse control; on the go; accident prone; passive-aggressive	Mood lability; demoralization; poor self-esteem; temper tantrums; immaturity; dysphoria; inattention; poor concentration	Rejection by peers; poor interpersonal skills; conflict with parents; school failure or dropout; negative interactions; reputation with authority; difficulty turn taking
Conduct Disorder	Aggressive and cruel; reckless and risk taking; being tough; causing deliberate destruction; violating rules; being truant and running away	Lacking empathy; callous and hostile; lacking guilt or remorse; having low self-esteem	Bullying; harming others/animals; problems with authority; exploitativeness; power relationships
Oppositional Defiant Disorder	Hostile or defiant; losing temper; disobedient; arguing and throwing tantrums; limit testing; being passive-aggressive	Angry or resentful; having low self-esteem; showing depression; showing mood lability; blameful	Conflict with family; conflict with authority; frequent arguments; provocation of others; power struggles; vindictiveness or spite

An assessment of Conduct Disorder should routinely involve an assessment for ADHD. Fifty percent of children with ADHD experience social problems, 25% are at risk of developing a Learning Disorder, and many have been held back a grade by high school. These clients tend to be more accident prone, and more frequently involved in risk-taking behaviors. Multiple diagnoses also suggest the need for more intense and earlier intervention, and may suggest a poorer prognosis.

Absence of Symptoms

Don't be surprised that these clients may initially appear well behaved, indicating the importance of multiple informants and cross-situational assessment. In ADHD, inattention may be absent in novel, challenging, or one-to-one situations, and is more likely to occur with repetitive tasks in group settings. Medication may also help to reduce symptoms. It is important to clarify to parents that lack of symptoms during an evaluation is common, thus minimizing any guilt or anger while facilitating rapport.

Cross-Situational Evaluation and Multi-informant Approach

The behaviors common among these disorders can differ in severity across situations. These clients rarely demonstrate significant disruption in all settings or in the same setting consistently, although the *DSM-IV* requires functional impairment in at least two settings. It is also common for these clients to minimize the significance of their behavior, particularly those with Conduct Disorder. Multi-informant, multifaceted, cross-situational assessment helps overcome these challenges.

Rapport

The establishment of rapport can be more difficult with these clients. You may need to take frequent breaks or divide the assessment over several sessions. In addition, the child's low frustration tolerance and increased risk of making errors require greater support and encouragement. Use of behavioral rewards and consequences can be advantageous.

History and Parent Interview

In addition to a standard history, it is necessary to include an assessment of parenting style. Ineffective parenting and/or a chaotic home environment can produce a distractible, inattentive, and disorganized child. The assessment can include an evaluation of the family structure, the limits parents set, the level of stability, and so on. This data is particularly useful when the child seems to respond well in a school environment (due to its structure), but not at home.

Given the symptom overlap between these disorders and Learning Disorders, academic history can help clarify whether problems are secondary to learning difficulties, truancy problems, or difficulty with authority figures. A detailed history of peer relationships can aid in the diagnosis of Conduct Disorder, where the presence of peer rejection in elementary school contributes to the formation of a deviant peer group.

Recommended Battery

When selecting tests, it is important to appreciate the heterogeneity of these clients. As the client becomes older, there needs to be an increased focus on social and academic problems. This may warrant using measures more sensitive to social skills, academic skills, and social behavior for older children. The typical strategy for assessment of these disorders is to administer a battery of tests supplemented by specific measures that may include rating scales completed by significant others (e.g., Conners' Scales).

TABLE 7.2
Key Test Findings for Behavioral Disorders

Disorder/Syndrome	WAIS-III/ WISC-III	MMPI-A	MACI
Attention Deficit/ Hyperactivity Disorder	VIQ < PIQ Lower Arithmetic, Digit Span, Digit Symbol-Coding Lower Freedom from Distractibility (Working Memory)	Elevations: 7 Content: A, A-lse, A-sch, A-fam	Elevations: B, G
Conduct Disorder	VIQ < PIQ Lower Information, Vocabulary, Arithmetic Compare Picture Arrangement to Comprehension	Profiles: 4-9 Elevations: 4, 9 Content: MAC-R, A-con, A-sch, A-trt	Elevations: 6A, G, CC, BB, DD
Oppositional Defiant Disorder	VIQ < PIQ Higher Comprehension Lower Picture Arrangement, Information, Vocabulary, Arithmetic (if academic problems exist)	Elevations: 4 Content: MAC-R, A-ang, A-fam, A-sch, A-lse	Elevations: 8A, G, DD

Common Behavioral Disorders

ATTENTION-DEFICIT/HYPERACTIVITY DISORDER (314)

Essential Features

Children with this disorder present with poor sustained attention, overactivity, and poor impulse control. As a result, they appear disorganized, careless, distracted, impatient, unable to pay attention or to stick to one activity, and are always on the move. They have difficulty following instructions, act impulsively, have difficulty learning from experience and exhibit a low frustration tolerance. Because they often respond well to structure, the role of parenting in the client's symptom picture should be considered, especially when noncompliance is prevalent.

Clients with ADHD have a higher likelihood of having experienced child abuse, in part because their behaviors often frustrate caregivers. In addition, clients with Anxiety Disorders can present with ADHD-like symptoms due to severe anxiety leading to irritability and distractibility. ADHD clients are also more likely to have a Learning Disorder, or Oppositional Defiant or Conduct Disorder.

The *DSM-IV* describes three types: predominantly inattentive (314.00), predominantly hyperactive-impulsive (314.01), and combined (inattentive and

Rorschach	TAT/ RATC	Conners'	Achenbach
EB > EA C + CF > FC Higher FM, A, S Lower R	Distracted Themes: Difficulty focusing, family conflict	Elevated indices: Hyperactivity, Hyperactive Impulsive, ADHD Index	Attention Problems, Aggressive Behavior, Externalizing, Social Problems, Anxious/Depressed
Higher C, CF, A, L, Per, AG, S Lower R, F+%	Themes: Anger, entitlement, manipulation, authority problems, punishment, lack of empathy	Elevated indices: Conduct Problems, Learning Problem	Externalizing, Delinquent Behavior, Aggressive Behavior
Higher S, C, CF, AG, Fi, Ex Lower R, W%	Themes: Resistant, angry, rebellious	Elevated indices: Oppositional	Aggressive Behavior Delinquent Behavior Externalizing

hyperactive-impulsive 314.01). These distinctions are not simple to make. The *DSM-IV* requires at least six symptoms of inattention or six symptoms of hyperactivity/impulsivity in at least two situations (e.g., home and school) for at least 6 months. Children who meet criteria in only one situation do not have ADHD, but instead are likely having conflict in that particular area. Symptoms must be present before the age of 7 years, however, it is difficult to diagnose children younger than 4 or 5 years of age because their behavior is more variable. Yet, 50% of documented cases showed symptoms before age 4.

Other causes of inattention to rule out include: (a) high intelligence in an under-stimulating academic environment, (b) difficulty with planning secondary to a chaotic home environment, (c) ineffective parenting, (d) family conflict, or (e) an underlying Learning Disorder that is contributing to behavioral symptoms at school.

Adolescents and Adults

As the child ages, behavioral symptoms may be overshadowed by poor self-esteem and interpersonal difficulties. However, distractibility often endures through adolescence. Research suggests that some adults retain ADHD symptoms. In general, children with both ADHD and Conduct Disorder tend to have a more

---

Testing Tip
Rapid Assessment of Behavioral Disorders

Cognitive or Academic Assessment

1. Wechsler scale to assess intellectual function.
2. WIAT for academic function (the WJ-R or WRAT-III may also be used; see Testing Tip in Chapter 5 for guidance).

Emotional Function Assessment

For children   Rorschach (for children ages 5 or older).

                          RATC or TAT to assess interpersonal and familial inter-
                          actions.

For adolescents   MMPI-A (preferred) or MACI.
                          RATC or TAT.

Rating Scales

For children   Achenbach or Conners' parent and teacher rating scales.

For adolescents   Achenbach or Conners' parent and teacher rating scales.

For adults   Brown Attention-Deficit Disorder Scales (Brown, 1996).

---

negative outcome. These clients often are unable to hold a job, their work histories usually include emotional outbursts, and they show problems with autonomy.

Diagnosis

Typical test results of clients with Attention-Deficit/Hyperactivity Disorder are
shown for each of the major tests.

Adults

In general, adult clients with ADHD show similar WAIS-III performance to child
clients, but with reduced effects due to added maturity. It is also important to
consider that cognitive deficits, if found, may be due to chronic substance abuse.
There should also be a clear history of ADHD in childhood. On the MMPI-2,
there may be elevations on Scales 4, 6, 8, and 9, suggesting feelings of alienation,
resentment, difficulties with authorities, agitation, distractibility, and excess energy. Adults with ADHD may also present with a 4–9 profile, suggesting difficulties with employment and interpersonal relationships, and the need to consider
substance related disorders. A 2–4 profile may occur, especially if the client is
discontented or depressed.

In addition to these scales, the Brown Attention-Deficit Disorder (ADD)
Scales (Brown, 1996) may be used for assessing ADHD. Unlike other rating
scales, the Brown has been standardized for adult use.

Testing Tip
Test Results Associated with
Attention-Deficit/Hyperactivity Disorder

- In children, on the Wechsler scale, there is often a significant VIQ-PIQ difference with greater PIQ scores. Both poor attention and the ability to stay on task may affect formal learning and hence depress scores on VIQ or create subtest scatter. Only some clients show a low score on the Freedom from Distractibility Index (Working Memory on WAIS-III) because the novel testing situation can mask problems in impulsivity and inattention. Clients are more likely to experience deficits on tasks of attention and concentration (Digit Span, Arithmetic, Coding (Digit Symbol-Coding on the WAIS-III) or sometimes on subtests of academic learning (Information, Vocabulary, Arithmetic). In general, these clients tend to do better at concrete tasks rather than abstract tests.
- On measures of academic function (WIAT, WJ-R, WRAT-3), some clients may score below average, due to ADHD affecting academic performance. There is no ADHD stereotypical profile.
- On the MMPI-A, they may present with an elevated Scale 7 suggesting tension, and difficulties coping, and elevated content Scales A (Anxiety), A-lse (Low Self-Esteem), A-fam (Family Problems), and A-sch (School Problems).
- On the MACI, there may be elevations on Scale B (self-devaluation), and G (family discord).
- On the Rorschach, clients may show resistance (high S, low R) or have anger leading to difficulty with cognitive organization. In addition clients may appear as externalizers who have difficulty controlling their attention (*EB* > *EA*, high *FM*, high *A*) or show impulsivity (*C* + *CF* > *FC*). *ZD* suggests underincorporating.
- Apperception tests can appear disorganized, with unfocused thoughts. Frequently, there are themes of difficulty focusing and becoming distracted. Interpersonal conflicts are common. On the RATC, low scores on Limit Setting, and high scores on Indicator scales may occur.
- The Achenbach scales (CBCL, TRF) may indicate elevations on Attention Problems, Aggressive Behavior, Social Problems, and Externalizing scales. For adolescents, there are higher scores on Anxiety-Depression, Withdrawal, Aggressive Behavior, Anxiety-Depression, and Somatic Complaints and lower scores on Social Competence.
- The Conners' scales should show elevations on the ADHD Index and Hyperactive-Impulsive scales.

Recommendations

If testing indicates a diagnosis of Attention-Deficit/Hyperactivity Disorder, the following treatment recommendations may be appropriate.

- *Psychotherapy* (behavioral, cognitive-behavioral, interpersonal, family) aimed at:

    Improving client's coping, problem solving, and social skills.

    Increasing client's self-esteem.

    Addressing interpersonal issues associated with ADHD (fewer conflicts with friends, family).

    Reducing client's secondary depression, anxiety, or anger management where appropriate.

- *Medication* evaluation to help reduce ADHD symptoms.

- *Family therapy* aimed at:

    Identifying and decreasing family conflict contributing to symptoms.

    Parenting skills to help parents develop more clear ways of instructing and communicating.

    Addressing consequences of behaviors. Alerting parents to possible child abuse.

    Educating family about ADHD.

    Developing an organizational system that parents can use to help client stay on task and complete assignments.

    Developing home- and school-based behavioral interventions to increase positive behaviors.

- *Psychoeducational evaluation:* Goal to develop strategies to compensate for deficits.

    Develop individualized study plan and feedback system between parent, school, and therapist.

    Increase client's studying skills to improve school performance (educational psychologist).

- *Potential referrals:* Psychiatrist, neuropsychologist (to assess for potential Learning Disorder), educational psychologist, tutor, IEP (individualized education program), parenting group, CHADD (Children and Adults with Attention Deficit Disorders—a nationwide support organization).

CONDUCT DISORDER (312.8)

Essential Features

Children or adolescents with Conduct Disorder show little regard or concern for the rights of others and engage in violations of major societal norms. These clients are almost exclusively referred by authority figures: parents, teachers, or the justice system. Symptoms may appear as early as age 5 or 6 and it is rare that the onset is after 16 years. Use caution when making this diagnosis due to the prognostic implications, the stigma, and self-fulfilling nature of the diagnosis. Conduct Disorder may be diagnosed in adult clients provided they fail to meet criteria for Antisocial Personality Disorder.

Essential features include a persistent pattern of violating basic rights of others and/or major societal rules. The *DSM-IV* distinguishes Conduct Disorder in terms of age of onset (before or after 10 years) and severity. Earlier onset suggests more severe pathology and prognosis. The *DSM-IV* also clusters symptoms into four groupings: (a) aggressiveness (e.g., harm or threat of harm to others or animals), (b) property destruction (e.g., fire setting), (c) deceitfulness or theft (e.g., lying, stealing), and (d) rule violation (e.g., running away, truancy).

Less severe symptoms appear first, and some clients are first diagnosed with Oppositional Defiant Disorder. Often these children have problems with trust and attachment from infancy. As they age, problem behaviors at school and with peers occur. Alienation can lead to their joining a "bad" peer group and engaging in antisocial acts. Adolescents with Conduct Disorder are often referred for assessment secondary to misbehavior. They can have blatant disregard for others. They may also have ADHD.

Frequently, clients with Conduct Disorder demonstrate cognitive deficits particularly in social problem solving and processing skills. The disorder's etiology is associated with two factors: (a) inconsistent, inadequate parental supervision, neglect or abuse, frequent changes in caregivers, lack of involvement in the child's activity, and the use of harsh discipline, and (b) genetic factors.

Adults

The adult version of this disorder is Antisocial Personality Disorder, which is reviewed in Chapter 10.

Diagnosis

Rapport is difficult to establish because of issues with trust and honesty or the client's inappropriate behavior. Be cautious of superficial rapport and being manipulated into a false sense of security. These clients typically tend to minimize the significance of their behavior. Their parents often lack accurate knowledge due to inadequate supervision. Make sure to evaluate for an underlying Substance Related Disorder (see Testing Tip on page 148 for typical test results).

Recommendations

If testing indicates a diagnosis of Conduct Disorder, the following treatment recommendations may be appropriate.

Testing Tip
Test Results Associated with Conduct Disorder

- On the Wechsler scales, these clients may show lower scores on tests sensitive to academic learning (Information, Vocabulary, Arithmetic). Undersocialized clients, who appear more aggressive, show PIQ > VIQ and significant subtest scatter. A comparison of Comprehension (social knowledge) to Picture Arrangement (applied social knowledge) can identify if social problems are due to a lack of knowledge or instead due to failure in application. Clients who do well on both tests may be particularly manipulative, if corroborating history shows conduct symptoms. Content on VIQ subtests should be examined to identify situational factors. Lowered scores on Similarities or Comprehension may also occur.

- On the MMPI-A, a 4-9 profile is common (Pena et al., 1996). If Scale 6 (Paranoia) is elevated, there may be suspiciousness, whereas if 6 is in the normal range they may appear naive. Elevated Scale 8 (Schizophrenia) suggests alienation. Elevation on Scale 2 (Depression) may be a good prognostic indicator, suggesting awareness and discomfort with their behavior. Check for additional elevations on MAC-R, A-con (Conduct Problems), A-sch (School Problems), and A-trt (Negative Treatment Indicators).

- On the MACI, there may be elevations on Scales 6A (Unruly), as well as F (Social Insensitivity), G (Family Discord), CC (Delinquent Predisposition), BB (Substance Abuse Proneness), and DD (Impulsive Propensity).

- On the Rorschach, these individuals may appear resistant or defensive (low R, high L, high S). If cooperative, there may be evidence of impulsivity, aggression, and an egocentric approach to the environment (C + CF > FC, High Per, High A and AG). They may also reject the cards.

- Apperception tests (RATC, TAT) may indicate themes of material gain, a lack of empathy, and manipulative interpersonal relationships. The hero may be angry and entitled. The stories may be aggressive and involve conflict with authorities.

- On the Achenbach (CBCL) there may be elevations on Externalizing, Delinquent Behavior, Aggressive Behavior, and Conduct Problem.

- On the Conners' scales, there may be elevations on Oppositional, and possibly Cognitive Problems scales.

- *Psychotherapy* (behavioral, cognitive behavioral, and family) aimed at:

    Attempting to build trust with client through consistent behavior and clear limit setting.

    Building moral reasoning and empathy.

    Confronting antisocial behavior and pointing out its effects.

    Working with client to take responsibility for behaviors.

    Implementing self-control strategies.

- *Establishment of therapeutic rapport and trust.* Clarification of legal involvement.
- *Consideration of whether client requires to be placed out of home.*
- *Family therapy* aimed at:

    Identifying family issues contributing to client's behavior.

    Encouraging family to allow client to face legal consequences.

    Assisting family in setting up well-defined rules and boundaries.

    Educating family about the client's disorder.

- *Treat coexisting Substance Related Disorder.*
- *Medication evaluation* for coexisting depression or other disorders.
- *Potential referrals:* Parent training, parent support group, vocational program, charity groups, team sports, group homes.

OPPOSITIONAL DEFIANT DISORDER (313.81)

Essential Features

Oppositional Defiant Disorder is characterized by a negative, hostile attitude toward authority figures and acting-out behavior that creates a disruption in the social environment. These clients can be disobedient, argumentative, bad tempered, spiteful, noncompliant, and deliberately annoying. They persistently test limits, ignore requests, fail to accept responsibility, blame others for their mistakes, and lack insight. Behaviors may only be expressed at home or targeted at one parent. The *DSM-IV* requires a duration of at least 6 months. Naturally, clients with these symptoms are frequently referred for assessment.

Oppositional symptoms seem to be affected by harsh and inconsistent discipline, resulting in power struggles that further exacerbate existing parent-child difficulties. An examination of parenting styles should be considered as part of the evaluation. While one should be cautious about diagnosing children with either common transient preschooler oppositional behaviors or a Parent-Child Relationship Problem (V61.20), the symptoms of this diagnosis are usually evident before age 8. Symptoms often appear gradually. A significant number of these clients develop Conduct Disorder.

Diagnosis

The symptom overlap with Conduct Disorder requires you to differentiate both diagnoses at the onset. Always evaluate for potential child abuse. The key in differentiating these disorders is that Oppositional Defiant Disorder has an earlier onset and better prognosis, and is more amenable to treatment than Conduct Disorder. Conduct Disorder, on the other hand, usually presents with a greater number and intensity of problems (see Testing Tip for typical test results).

Recommendations

If testing indicates a diagnosis of Oppositional Defiant Disorder, the following treatment recommendations may be appropriate.

Testing Tip
Test Results Associated with Oppositional Defiant Disorder

- On the Wechsler scales, impulsivity, minimal effort, lack of motivation, and low frustration tolerance may adversely affect scores. PIQ may be greater than VIQ, due to dislike of verbal subtests, or a tendency to provide numerous brief 1-point answers to 2-point items. While these clients may demonstrate adequate Comprehension scores, suggesting an awareness of social judgment, lower scores on Picture Arrangement may occur due to issues with authority figures, defiance, and anger. If oppositional behaviors have affected school performance, low scores on Information, Vocabulary, and Arithmetic may appear. Lowered scores on Similarities or Comprehension may also occur.
- On the MMPI-A, there may be elevations on Scale 4 (Psychopathic Deviate), reflecting difficulties with authority figures and anger. There may also be significant scores on MAC-R, A-ang (Anger), A-fam (Family Discord), A-sch (School Problems), and A-lse (Low Self-Esteem).
- On the MACI, they may have elevations on Scale 8A (Oppositional), G (Family Discord), and DD (Impulsive Propensity).
- On the Rorschach, resistant and oppositional symptoms may result with a protocol suggesting a defensive, minimal-participation approach (low *R*, high *L*, and high *S*) and difficulty modulating affect and impulses (High *C*, *AG*, *Fi* (Fire)).
- On apperception tests (RATC, TAT), stories may involve authorities, aggression, and punishment. There may be themes of resistance, rebellion, and punishment.
- On the Achenbach forms, clients may score significantly high on Aggressive Behaviors, Delinquent Behaviors, or Externalizing scales. On the Conners,' elevations may occur on the Oppositional scale.

- *Psychotherapy* (behavioral, cognitive-behavioral, and family) aimed at:

  Working to develop client's trust.

  Developing ways for client to verbalize negative feelings, rather than acting out.

  Helping client learn association between feelings and negative behaviors.

  Improving client's coping and problem-solving skills.

  Treating associated depression.

- *Family therapy* aimed at:

  Working with parents to clarify acceptable behaviors.

  Identifying and addressing underlying family conflicts.

  Considering use of behavioral contracts or time-out.

  Parenting skills; be alert to child abuse.

- *School Intervention* aimed at:

  Coordinating treatment with school.

  Improving academic performance.

- *Potential referrals:* Social skills, youth organizations, sports or arts programs, parent effectiveness training groups, study skills training.

Differential Diagnosis

ADHD VERSUS OPPOSITIONAL DEFIANT DISORDER

ADHD clients have problems on cognitive tasks, secondary to distractibility and problems with attention and concentration. They appear impulsive and anxious, and have difficulty dealing with basic needs and planning. Oppositional Defiant Disorder clients have difficulty with cognitive tasks because of their negative attitude and noncompliance with schoolwork. They appear defiant, resistant, angry, and emotional, with ongoing family problems. In ADHD, the behavior reflects problems with attention. ADHD clients often avoid school and school assignments because of the potential for failure. In Oppositional Defiant Disorder, on the other hand, the behavior reflects a refusal to comply with demands.

ADHD VERSUS CONDUCT DISORDER

Both disorders may present with impulsivity and hyperactivity. However, ADHD children do not present with the violation of social norms, disregard for others, and lack of empathy that characterize Conduct Disorder. Aggression and defiance are not a consequence of ADHD; rather, they are a consequence of negative parent-child interactions that can occur in families with ADHD children.

As a result, there is significant comorbidity between ADHD and Oppositional Defiant Disorders.

OPPOSITIONAL DEFIANT VERSUS CONDUCT DISORDER VERSUS PARENT-CHILD RELATIONAL PROBLEM (V61.20)

Defiance of authority is common to both Oppositional Defiant Disorder and Conduct Disorder. However, Oppositional Defiant Disorder does not include the more serious pattern of violating major social norms or basic rights of others. If both criteria are met, Conduct Disorder takes precedence. Adolescents with Conduct Disorder often have difficulties on cognitive tasks that involve school learning. They are angry, entitled, manipulative, impulsive, and tend to act out and become involved in drugs. Parent-Child Relational Problem is a milder form of interpersonal difficulties than is seen in either disorder.

DISRUPTIVE BEHAVIOR DISORDERS VERSUS MOOD DISORDERS

Disruptive behaviors can be the result of a Mood Disorder such as Depression or Mania. However, in the latter cases, the disruptive behaviors coincide with mood episodes, and other mood symptoms should occur. Clients with a Disruptive Behavior Disorder may also have a concurrent Anxiety Disorder.

ADHD VERSUS ANXIETY

Individuals with both disorders experience tension, distractibility, anxiety, and the tendency to act impulsively with agitation. In Anxiety Disorders, *DSM-IV* requires that the onset of inattention occur later than age 7, and that there is no school history of inattention, hyperactivity, or school disruption. However, you may see clients with marked anxiety who *do* have school problems. Don't let *DSM-IV* prevent you from drawing appropriate conclusions, if you suspect that both factors play a role.

EXCEPTIONS TO THE RULE

Children with these disorders form a heterogeneous group and these behaviors may vary considerably with the context and the nature of the relationship with the examiner, and amount of rapport that has been established.

CHAPTER 8

Reality Testing: Schizophrenia and Psychotic Disorders

Psychosis Primer

WHY THESE DISORDERS ARE CLUSTERED TOGETHER

THESE DISORDERS are grouped together because they are most frequently considered when you are asked to evaluate the client for psychosis. We have included the disorders within Schizophrenia and Other Psychotic Disorders, Mood Disorders with Psychotic Features, and pertinent Personality Disorders.

The classical hallmarks of psychosis include thought disorder, hallucinations, and delusions. Disordered thinking is often evidenced by problems with speaking. This might include loose associations or derailment (changing topics in a way that doesn't make sense), clang associations (changing topics based on the way words rhyme), or alogia (reduction in the production or content of spontaneous speech). Psychosis can also include negative symptoms such as amotivation and anhedonia.

Most hallucinations are auditory and are usually experienced by the client as unpleasant. Some hear hypercritical voices that make negative comments all the time. Common hallucinations include hearing voices or sounds coming from the TV or radio. Common delusions are often persecutory, and may involve federal agencies, conspiracies, or UFOs.

PRACTICAL CONSIDERATIONS/INTERVIEWING

Medication

These clients are often taking antipsychotics, antidepressants, anticonvulsants, or medications to counteract side effects, and all can affect test performance.

153

Thus a medication history that details side effects, the client's perception of the impact of the medication, and the level of medication compliance should be collected. Chronic or paranoid patients who are unable or unwilling to provide this information may require you to contact the prescribing physician(s).

Comorbidity

These clients, prior to their first major psychotic symptoms often show signs of disturbance. Some appear as odd, peculiar, and passive, showing difficulty socializing and seeming uninvolved. Others appear aggressive, showing inappropriate behavior in classroom settings. As a result, many of these clients will show prior diagnoses of a Learning Disorder, Pervasive Developmental Disorder, or Disruptive Behavior Disorder. The most frequent coexisting diagnoses are Mood Disorders and Alcohol and Substance-Related Disorders.

These clients may also have a Personality Disorder. When a client presents with both psychotic symptoms and a Personality Disorder, keep in mind that the personality problems may compound the person's difficulties and lead to a poorer prognosis.

Psychosis may be of such prominence that it dominates the client's symptom presentation and masks underlying cognitive impairments such as Mental Retardation or a Learning Disorder. Get a detailed history, especially from collateral sources, to identify past academic-related difficulties.

Risk Factors and Suicide

Clients with these diagnoses have a high suicide risk (up to 10 times more likely than normals) that needs to be continually monitored and assessed. They are at risk for acting self-destructively. If they experience demand or command hallucinations (hallucinations that tell the client to do things), you should assess how much control the client has over them.

High comorbidity with Mood Disorders and Substance-Related Disorders increases these clients' risk for suicide, particularly at the point when the psychotic symptoms abate. Many psychotic clients become depressed as they deal with the realities associated with their disorder. Chapter 9 reviews suicide assessment and prevention.

Psychotic Symptoms Affect Assessments

Establishing rapport and conducting an assessment while someone is actively hallucinating or delusional is extremely difficult. When a client is untestable for these reasons, you should immediately consider a psychotic disorder. Auditory hallucinations impair concentration and attention. Delusional content may create unwillingness to complete tests. Paranoid delusions may prohibit any evaluation. If possible, we recommend waiting until the client has been stabilized on medications prior to the evaluation. Otherwise, you may need to tailor your evaluation to the client's level of functioning. Any test modifications should be addressed in the psychological report.

Lack of Collateral Contact and Support

Clients with chronic psychosis are often isolated, disengaged from their families, and have few relationships with significant others. Obtaining a sense of premorbid functioning or what resources are available can be difficult.

Trust and Rapport with Paranoid Patients

If the client is paranoid, the following guidelines may be helpful:

- Be consistent. If the testing is scheduled for a particular time, try not to be late or change it. Paranoid clients often misinterpret change.
- Clarify confidentiality and obtain informed consent.
- Do not confront or collude with the delusions.
- Avoid intellectualization and cognitive games.

Premorbid Factors and Prognosis

The Testing Tip below highlights factors associated with a better or poorer prognosis.

Testing Tip
Predicting Prognosis in Psychotic Patients

Good Prognostic Indicators	Poor Prognostic Indicators
Positive symptoms—hallucinations or delusions.	Negative symptoms—anhedonia or flat affect.
Late, sudden onset.	Early, slow onset.
Family history of Mood Disorders.	Family history of Schizophrenia.
Good premorbid functioning.	Poor premorbid functioning.
Married or stable relationship.	Single or rejected by peers.
Higher SES; no cognitive deficits.	Low IQ scores.
Brief first hospitalization; no ECT.	Birth and prenatal problems.
	Multiple hospitalizations.

TABLE 8.1
Key Descriptive Features of Psychotic Disorders

Disorder/Syndrome	Behavioral	Emotional/ Cognitive	Interpersonal
Schizophrenia Undifferentiated (295.90)	Disorganized, catatonic behavior; bizarre behavior; stupor, rigidity, posturing, avolition; apathy, immaturity; regressiveness	Hallucinations, delusions, flat affect; disorganized thinking, loose associations, anhedonia; disorganized/poverty of speech, tangential speech; loss of sense of self	Downward drift; not married; isolative, withdrawn, limited social contact; high expressed emotion in families
Disorganized Type (295.10)	Disorganized behavior, impairment in daily living skills, grimacing, mannerisms, odd behavior	Flat or inappropriate affect; disorganized speech	Lack of goal orientation; occupational impairment; insidious onset; impaired interpersonal relationships; extreme social withdrawal
Catatonic Type (295.20)	Psychomotor disturbance; motoric immobility; waxy flexibility; stupor or excitement; excessive motor activity; peculiar voluntary movements; extreme negativism; bizarre postures, prominent grimaces, mimicry; automatic obedience	Mutism, echolalia, or echopraxia	Withdrawal; interpersonal discomfort
Paranoid Type (295.30)	Argumentative; absence of catatonic or disorganized behavior	Persecutory or grandiose delusions; hallucinations; anger	Aloofness; patronizing, stilted, or extremely intense relationships
Residual Type (295.60)	Eccentric behavior; absence of disorganized behavior	Flat affect; poverty of speech; mildly disorganized speech; odd beliefs, nonprominent delusions, nonprominent hallucinations	Withdrawal; limited social supports
Schizophreniform Disorder (295.40)	Similar to 295.90 with shorter duration	As 295.90, emotional turmoil, very upset	As above, 295.90
Brief Psychotic Disorder (298.8)	Grossly disorganized or catatonic behavior; sudden onset; overwhelming confusion; bizarre behavior	Disorganized speech, derailment, incoherence; delusions, hallucinations; emotional turmoil, rapid shifts	Withdrawal; return to premorbid level; may be no impairment
Schizoaffective Disorder (295.70)	Psychomotor retardation or agitation, bizarre behavior	Depression, anxiety	Isolation
Delusional Disorder (297.1)	Behavior that is *not* odd or bizarre, irritable, violent behavior, litigious behavior, legal difficulties	One or more nonbizarre delusions; nonprominent, auditory or visual hallucinations; tactile or olfactory hallucinations	Variable; apart from impact of delusions not markedly impaired or severe interpersonal and occupational impairment due to delusion
Shared Psychotic Disorder (297.3)	Aside from delusion, behavior that is *not* odd or bizarre	Delusion shared with inducer; bizarre or nonbizarre delusions	Close relationship with inducer; social isolation

156

Psychosis in the Elderly

Older adults are more likely to show increased suspiciousness, delusions, and paranoia as they age. These symptoms, however, may be due to the onset of a dementia, especially in older adults seen at long-term care facilities. The symptoms may also be due to medication. Nondemented older clients who show these symptoms are more likely to be socially isolated. In clients who do not have a prior history of a psychotic disorder, we recommend a cognitive assessment as recommended in Chapter 11 as part of the evaluation.

Delusions and Hallucinations as Functional Complaints

One of the major diagnostic dilemmas within this category is the differentiation of genuine delusions and hallucinations from malingering. Meyer and Deitsch (1996) identify characteristics of intentionally produced delusions and hallucinations (presented below in the Testing Tip).

   If your client's delusions or hallucinations meet the preceding criteria, you may want to administer tests with built-in validity scales such as the MMPI-2 or the Structured Interview of Reported Symptoms and consider the factors discussed in Chapter 2 on malingering.

   Some psychotic experiences, especially if they have religious or symbolic significance, may be culturally approved. At the onset consider the cultural context of the client's presentation and review Appendix I in the *DSM-IV* for culture-bound diagnoses. Tables 8.1 and 8.2 review the essential features of each of these disorders as described in this chapter and give corresponding test results.

   Rapid assessment of psychotic disorders may not require testing if diagnosis is solely required because the client's history and symptom profile will often be sufficient. The need for testing usually signals a more complex symptom picture and the need for you to create a clearer profile of the client.

Testing Tip
Characteristics of Fake Delusions and Hallucinations

Delusions	*Hallucinations*
Abrupt onset/finish.	Continuous versus sporadic.
Client calls attention to delusions.	Client obeys all commands.
Bizarre content, no hallucinations.	Vague, hard to hear, stilted language.
Behavior inconsistent with delusions.	Not associated with delusions.
Absolves client of responsibility.	No strategy to decrease voices.
	Exonerates client from blame.

TABLE 8.2
Key Test Findings for Psychotic Disorders

Disorder/ Syndrome	WAIS-III/WISC-III	MMPI-2/ MMPI-A	MCMI-III/ MAPI	Rorschach
Schizophrenia Undifferentiated Type (295.90)	VIQ > PIQ Increased Scatter Subtests: Higher scores on Block Design, Digit Symbol-Coding, Symbol Search Lower scores on Picture Arrangement, Arithmetic, Comprehension, Similarities, Matrix Reasoning Misses easy items, answers more difficult items	F > 65 Profiles: 2, 7, 8, 7-8, 8-7 Content: BIZ, FAM Elevations increase with chronicity	SS or S PP, 1, 2A	positive *SCZI* index X+% < .6 F+% < .6 Special scores > 4 High C, m-, FM-, CF-, PSV, Cn, Dd, F dominant Poor quality M Color Shock low P, W
Disorganized Type (295.10)	Use Schizophrenia signs Extreme scatter Subtests: Lower scores on Block Design, Digit Symbol-Coding, Symbol Search, Comprehension, Vocabulary	May be incomplete Profiles: silly 8-9, 9-8 flat 7, 2, low 9	Prominence C, S Elevated P, 1, 2A Moderate PP, SS	Low #R, F, high M-, Dd
Catatonic Type (295.20)	Use Schizophrenia signs or Depression signs or Bipolar Disorder signs	Profile 2-7, 7-8 2 dominant elevations: agitated: 8–9, 8–0 anger: 4 & 6, 6–8	SS, 1, 2A, C, S Stupor: CC Agitation: N	Schizophrenia signs
Paranoid Type (295.30)	Subtests: Higher scores on Similarities, Arithmetic, Picture Completion. Lower scores on Digit Symbol-Coding, Picture Arrangement, Comprehension, Matrix Reasoning, Symbol Search Errors of overinclusion	Profiles: 8-4, 8-6/6-8, 6-9/ 9-6, 1-6/6-1, 8-9/9-8 Elevations: None > 70 F, 2, 6 & 7, 3, 4 Content: BIZ	1, 2A, or C, PP prominence CC or SS presence	High Dd, F+%, M, W, HVI and Lambda and low C, edges
Residual Type (295.60)	Use Schizophrenia signs; not as severe	Elevations: 8, F Lower than acute Defensive: High L & K Low 9	CC, PP, SS, 1, A, C, & S Not as extreme as acute	Schizophrenia signs Not as severe

TABLE 8.2 (Continued)

Disorder/ Syndrome	WAIS-III/WISC-III	MMPI-2/ MMPI-A	MCMI-III/ MAPI	Rorschach
Schizophreno-form Disorder (295.40)	Use Schizophrenia signs. Lower scores on Digit Span, Arithmetic, and Digit Symbol-Coding	Higher F Profiles: 7-8-0 lower than acute	Schizophrenia pattern	Schizophrenia signs High CDI
Brief Psychotic Disorder (298.8)	Similar to 295.90 Not as impaired	As 295.90 High F significant turmoil	Schizophrenia pattern and high A, N, and 4	As 295.90, elevated CDI
Schizoaffective Disorder (295.70)	Combination depression and psychosis or mania and psychosis	Profiles: Spike 8, high 4, 7, F Depressed: high 2-7/2-8 Manic 8-9/9-8	Mood profile and S, SS, 2A	Mood and Schizophrenia signs
Delusional Disorder (297.1)	Subtests: High Arithmetic, Picture Completion, Similarities, Comprehension	Check Cannot Say? 6 may be normal Profiles: 6-8, 3-4	Prominence P, C, PP High 6A, 7 low	High HVI, F+%, Dd, rejections Low R, M & C
Shared Psychotic Disorder (297.3)	No consistent findings	Elevations 6, 2, 4 Moderate 7, 8 Males high 5	Dominant: 5, 6A Dependent: 3, 4	

Schizophrenia and Psychotic Disorders in *DSM-IV*

SCHIZOPHRENIA (295.xx)

Essential Features

The onset of Schizophrenia is typically in late adolescence or early adulthood. It is common for these clients to have multiple hospitalizations, but there is wide variation in the severity of Schizophrenia. Schizophrenia symptoms are commonly broken down into positive and negative symptoms.

Classically, Schizophrenia has an episodic course, characterized by an active phase and a residual phase. During the active phase, clients have "psychotic breaks" with florid symptoms. Symptoms then remit spontaneously or due to the use of medications, and the client enters the residual phase. For some, the residual phase can lead to high levels of functioning, but for most, psychotic symptoms usually remain. Schizophrenia impacts the ability to become socialized and to learn, making it hard for these clients to fit in.

For *DSM-IV*, these symptoms must be prominent and present for at least one month with some symptoms remaining for at least six months. If the

---

Testing Tip
Rapid Assessment of Psychosis-Based Disorders

For most of these clients, an efficient assessment might include:

Children   RATC or TAT, CBCL, Rorschach (possibly)

Adolescents   MMPI-A (preferred), CBCL, Rorschach, MACI

Adults   MMPI-2 (preferred) or MCMI-III, BDI-2, Rorschach

Elderly   MMPI-2 (preferred) or MCMI-III, Rorschach

To rule out cognitive complaints: Dementia Rating Scale, WMS-III

---

client's symptoms were successfully treated, the 1-month criteria may be shortened. The symptoms result in significant social and occupational impairment. In general, the more chronic or continuous the disorder, the greater impairment in functioning and the more pathological the test profile.

The causes of Schizophrenia are indeterminate. For many, there is a genetic association. Some clients with this disorder are more likely to have been exposed to problems during the second trimester of pregnancy (Mednick, Parnas, &

Testing Tip
Positive and Negative Symptoms of Schizophrenia

Positive Symptoms
- Delusions (mistaken beliefs, usually persecutory).
- Hallucinations (most common: critical, threatening, negativistic voices).
- Disorganized speech.
- Loose associations.
- Tangential speech.
- Derailment.
- Incoherence.
- Disorganized or catatonic behavior.

Negative Symptoms
- Restriction of range and intensity of emotion.
- Flat or blunted affect.
- Poverty of speech and thought.
- Anhedonia.
- Amotivation.
- Lack of goal-directed behavior.

Schulsinger, 1987). Finally, a minority of clients develop the disorder secondary to blood RH incompatibility.

Some individuals with chronic Schizophrenia self-medicate with alcohol or a range of street drugs, particularly if they are homeless and not actively involved in a treatment program. A full medical evaluation with drug screening may be required.

The current prognosis for Schizophrenia is not good. Clients hospitalized for the first time with Schizophrenia have a 50% chance of being readmitted within two years. The presence of affective symptoms in the acute stage is often a good prognostic sign.

Diagnosis

Frequently, persons with Schizophrenia do well on structured tasks that involve little interaction. Their test profile is often characterized by errors of overinclusion and unrelated associations. They may miss easy items while being able to answer more difficult ones (it is particularly useful to check these items for delusional content).

Within the Schizophrenia diagnosis are several types that determine the nature of the client's presentation:

- Undifferentiated (295.90)
- Disorganized type (295.10)
- Catatonic (295.20)
- Paranoid type (295.30)
- Residual (295.60)

The following discussions of these subtypes include a Testing Tip box for each type.

Undifferentiated Type. The Undifferentiated type does not meet criteria for any of the specific subtypes (see Testing Tip on page 162 for typical test results).

Paranoid Type. Paranoid Schizophrenia is characterized by a preoccupation with one or more prominent delusions or hallucinations. These clients may present with the belief they are being tormented, that the newspaper has coded messages, that alien thoughts are being inserted into their minds, or that they hear voices criticizing their behavior. Their delusions are often unshakable and impervious to logic. They may experience delusions of reference and grandiosity that are necessary to explain why the client has been singled out for such attention. These clients distrust others, expect to be exploited, and are hypersensitive to humiliation.

Testing Tip
Test Results Associated with Undifferentiated Schizophrenia

- On the WAIS-III, VIQ is often slightly greater than PIQ, with both in the low average range and with increased cognitive scatter. There may be higher scores on Block Design, Digit Symbol-Coding, and Symbol Search, concrete tasks that involve minimal interaction with the examiner (Block Design is more likely to be lower in clients with organic impairment). Picture Arrangement, Arithmetic, and Comprehension may be low due to impaired social judgment and difficulties with concentration. Matrix Reasoning may be lower due to thought disorder impairing executive function. Delusional content may result in low scores on Similarities.
- On the MMPI-2 or MMPI-A, an elevated Scale F (Infrequency) may occur, indicating emotional turmoil, distress, and the endorsement of unusual experiences. In early stages, a 2-7-8 profile may occur with Scale 8 being the highest score. Greater chronicity may create a 7-8 profile. Elevations on 6, 7, 8, and 9 is often referred to as the "psychotic tetrad." If Scale 1 is elevated, you may want to check for somatic delusions. A 9-8 profile may be associated with occupational problems. The content scale BIZ (Bizarre Mentation) may be elevated as may be FAM (Family Discord).
- On the MCMI-III, there may be elevations at the presence or prominence range for Thought Disorder (SS) or Delusional Disorder (PP). There may also be elevations on Schizotypal (S), Schizoid (1), Avoidant (2A), Depressive (2B), Dependent (3), Passive-Aggressive (8A), and Self-Defeating (8B). Finally, if there is a co-existing depression, Major Depression (CC) may be significant.
- On the Rorschach, the Schizophrenia Index should be significant (SCZI), and possibly the Suicide Constellation (S-CON). Impaired reality testing will be evidenced by lower X+%, and F+%, and an elevated X–%. Persons with Schizophrenia often respond with a high number of Level II special scores (>4), higher Lambda, and higher Sum Y shading responses. Responses tend to be of poor quality and form dominant. A high number of pure C, Cn, m–, and FM– responses indicates severe impairment in reality testing. High PSV is indicative of an inability to cognitively shift, and the prominence of delusions. Low W indicates difficulty in integrating information. In addition, there may be color shock and a low number of P responses, suggesting an idiosyncratic way of looking at the world. Content may be dominated by Abstract, Fire, Anatomical, Sex, and Blood responses.
- On apperception tests, stories may appear bizarre, confused, with loose associations and tangential thinking. The stories may also be incoherent or disorganized.

It may be extremely difficult to evaluate clients with this subtype as considerable time may be spent establishing rapport. Typically, this subtype has a later onset and clients present with less anxiety and impairment than others. They may appear meticulous, seeming very concerned about their performance, and commenting on it occasionally (see Testing Tip for typical test results).

Disorganized Type.   The essential features of this subtype include disorganized speech and behavior, with flat or inappropriate affect. These clients show

---

Testing Tip
Test Results Associated with Paranoid Schizophrenia

- On the WAIS-III, they present with a relatively higher IQ score. Similarities and Picture Completion may be elevated possibly due to intellectualization and hypersensitivity to their environment. Digit Symbol-Coding may be lowered due to perfectionism. Errors of over-inclusion may contribute to low scores on Comprehension and Picture Arrangement.
- On the MMPI-2 or MMPI-A there may be no scales with an elevation greater than 70. Several different profiles may occur: 8-4, 8-6, 6-9, 1-6, or 8-9. There may be elevations on Scale F (Infrequency), 2 (Depression), 7 (Psychasthenia), or 3 (Hysteria). Elevations on Scales 6 (Paranoia) and 4 (Psychopathic Deviate) suggest possible dangerousness. A low score on Scale 7 may suggest the presence of auditory hallucinations. Scales 2 and 4 may also be low. The content scale BIZ may be elevated. It may be useful to check the obvious versus subtle supplemental scales to assess insight or an attempt to hide symptoms from the examiner.
- On the MCMI-III, Schizoid (1), Avoidant (2A), Paranoid (P), or Antisocial (6) scales may be significant. Delusional Disorder (PP) may be at the prominence level while the Thought Disorder (SS) and Major Depression (CC) scales may be at the Presence level.
- On the Rorschach, there may be a high number of *Dd* and *F* responses, or an elevation on the *HVI* (Hypervigilance) index or Lambda. A high number of *M* and *W* responses suggests an overemphasis on intellectualization and overincorporation. There may be fewer C responses, suggesting emotional detachment. These clients may want to look at the backs of the cards and comment on the purpose of testing. Some may identify masks and eyes, and focus on the edges of the blots.
- On the apperception tests, the stories may be grandiose and pretentious; or if the client feels threatened, the stories will be short and concrete.

tangential speech, giggle for no reason, and appear disheveled. The prognosis is poor, particularly if the onset is slow and gradual. Responses to questions may include clang associations, tangential reasoning, and neologisms (see Testing Tip below for typical test results).

Catatonic Type.   The essential features include motor immobility, waxy flexibility, stupor, excessive purposeless activity, extreme motiveless negativism, peculiarities of voluntary movement, and echolia or echopraxia. These clients may rock back and forth for hours, or sit immobile for extended periods. When agitated, they may become dangerous (see Testing Tip at top of page 165 for typical test results).

Residual Type.   This subtype refers to clients who present with an absence of the main diagnostic symptoms of Schizophrenia (e.g., hallucinations, delusions). However, there usually remains evidence of negative symptoms. If there are positive symptoms, they appear in a milder form. For many of them, medication may mask the underlying psychotic processes. These clients can be easily misdiagnosed, making history taking very important in differential diagnosis (see Testing Tip at bottom of page 165 for typical test results).

Testing Tip
Test Results Associated with Schizophrenia,
Disorganized Type

- On the WAIS-III, significant subtest scatter is more likely due to the varying level of inappropriate affect and behavior. The completion of some items may be impossible. Block Design, Digit Symbol-Coding, Symbol Search, and Matrix Reasoning may be significantly lowered due to difficulty in focusing on the task at hand. Tests that rely on verbal responses will likely pick up disordered speech (e.g., Comprehension and Vocabulary).
- The MMPI-2 or MMPI-A may not be completed because of the level of disorganization. Silly or inappropriate clients with this disorder typically present with an 8-9 profile. If the presentation includes emotional flattening, a 7-2 profile may occur with a low Scale 9.
- On the MCMI-III, there may be a prominence on Schizotypal (S), Borderline (C), Paranoid (P), Schizoid (1), or Avoidant (2A) scales, and moderate elevations on Delusional Disorder (PP) and Thought Disorder (SS).
- The Rorschach will be characterized as a disorganized protocol with a low number of *F* responses and occasional M– responses.

Testing Tip
Test Results Associated with Schizophrenia, Catatonic Type

- On the WAIS-III, test profiles may have characteristics of both Schizophrenia and severe Mood Disorder due to extreme psychomotor retardation and agitation.
- On the MMPI-2 or MMPI-A, the client may show a 2-7-8 profile with Scale 2 dominating. With agitation, an 8-9 or 8-0 profile may occur. If there is anger, elevations on Scales 4 and 6 might occur.
- On the MCMI-III, there may be elevations on the Thought Disorder (SS), Schizoid (1), Avoidant (2A), Borderline (C), and Schizotypal (S) scales. If stupor is dominant, Major Depression (CC) may be at the prominence level. If the client is agitated, the Bipolar Manic (N) scale may be elevated.
- On the Rorschach, there will be a predominance of Schizophrenia signs (as described earlier) accompanied by indicators of severe depression or agitation.

Testing Tip
Test Results Associated with Schizophrenia, Residual Type

- On the WAIS-III, these clients can perform similarly, but less severely than in acute Undifferentiated Schizophrenia. However, higher functioning clients may not show characteristic test signs.
- On the MMPI-2 or MMPI-A, there may be elevations on Scales F and 8, though the elevations are lower than in the active phase of Schizophrenia. Scales K and L may be elevated, particularly if the client is defensive. Medication use may contribute to a low Scale 9.
- On the MCMI-III, the results will be similar but less extreme than the undifferentiated profile. The following scales may be significant: Thought Disorder (SS), Major Depression (CC), Delusional Disorder (PP), Schizoid (1), Avoidant (2A), Borderline (C), and Schizotypal (S).
- On the Rorschach, there will be signs similar to Undifferentiated Schizophrenia, but in a less severe form.

Older Adults

For the most part, there is little formal understanding of Schizophrenia in older adults. There is a reduced incidence of Schizophrenia in the elderly possibly due to the greater frequency of suicide in this diagnosis. However, there is evidence, too, for late-onset Schizophrenia, which is thought to have a more benign course. There is some research that suggests older adults with a chronic history of Schizophrenia show an exacerbation of symptoms with age (Koenig et al., 1996). Clients with Schizophrenia are at a lower risk for developing Alzheimer's disease.

Children/Adolescents

The diagnostic criteria for Schizophrenia are the same for children and adolescents as for adults. Paranoid and Undifferentiated are the most frequently occurring subtypes. While Schizophrenia's symptoms may appear to overlap with Autism, these are separate diagnoses. The differentiation of both are discussed at the end of this chapter.

Schizophrenia is exceptionally rare in very young children with the onset usually occurring after nine years of age, and the incidence increasing with age. Young children presenting with symptoms of these disorders warrant an extensive evaluation and a cautious diagnostic approach, especially considering developmentally appropriate behaviors (e.g., imaginary friends). Onset may be slow, characterized by unusual verbalizations, beliefs, and behaviors. Some clinicians find that the predominant presentation is severe anxiety associated with paranoia and thought disorder. They may present with delayed motor milestones, poor coordination, or bizarre mannerisms. They often report sensory sensitivities, unusual fears, suspiciousness, and strange preoccupations. These children often have difficulties with social adjustment, they can be clingy to attachment figures, and may be teased by peers who subsequently reject them. This can lead to social withdrawal.

When onset occurs in mid to late adolescence, the presentation is almost identical to the adult form. Drug experimentation has been identified as a risk factor for some adolescents' first psychotic break, though many stressors can be the impetus for a psychotic break. The *DSM-IV* diagnostic criteria for childhood Schizophrenia also specify that failure to achieve at the expected level must occur interpersonally and academically not just as deterioration in function.

A very small minority of children are at risk for developing a shared psychotic disorder from their parents. In this case, the symptoms are the same as the adult and, in general, diminish when the child is separated from the parent.

When interviewing children about hallucinations and delusions, be wary that symptoms are not produced to please the examiner or gain attention. Identify the feelings associated with these experiences and determine whether the child realizes the experiences are unusual and has compulsions to act in response to delusions or hallucinations. When interpreting test data, particularly projective data, it is important to consider other factors that may create a psychotic

> ## Testing Tip
> ## Test Results Associated with Schizophrenia in Childhood
>
> - On the WISC-III, there are inconsistent findings. These children may present with intense anxiety and misunderstand the instructions. Their FIQ, PIQ, and VIQ scores may be in the average or low average range. There may be a lack of a significant difference between VIQ and PIQ scores. There may be low scores on Similarities, Picture Arrangement, and Comprehension. The Freedom from Distractibility Index may also be low.
> - On the Rorschach, there may be a high number of F dominated responses. The protocol will be characterized by few responses in general, a low number of P responses, and a high number of C, C', or MOR responses. Interpret M–, low H, and high (H) cautiously as these may be due to imagination rather than reality testing. X+% should be < .6, while X–% should be > .3. These children may score > 5 on the special scores.
> - On the Child Behavior Check List, these clients may appear as hostile, withdrawn, passive, delinquent, hyperactive, and inattentive.
> - On apperception tests, stories may show evidence of thought disorder, with lack of sensibility, neologisms, and derailment. Content may also be bizarre.

profile such as anxiety, limited intellectual functioning, and misunderstanding instructions (see Testing Tip for typical test results).

Recommendations

If testing indicates a diagnosis of Schizophrenia, the following treatment recommendations may be appropriate.

- *Psychotherapy* (Behavioral, Cognitive-Behavioral) aimed at:

    Helping client accept that symptoms are due to mental illness.

    Increasing client's comprehension regarding the need for medication.

    Increasing medication compliance.

    Improving socialization and social awareness.

    Reducing depression associated with the disorder.

    Increasing self-esteem.

    Reducing social isolation.

    Reducing suicide risk.

- *Multidisciplinary* treatment approach (inpatient, partial, or outpatient).
- *Antipsychotic* or antidepressant medication.
- *Occupational therapy* aimed at:

    Identifying appropriate vocational and activity goals.

- *Milieu based or clubhouse program* stressing social skills, social support, and contact.
- *Family therapy or support groups* aimed at:

    Increasing the family's knowledge of the disorder.

    Creating reasonable expectations from family members.

    Reducing anxiety in family members.

    Reducing family stressors that affect the client (e.g., expressed emotion).

- *For older adults:* Monitor coexisting depression, social isolation, and suicide risk.
- *For children/adolescents:* Consider play therapy, behavior therapy, and strategic family intervention. Be alert for medication side effects.
- *Potential referrals:* Psychiatrist, neuropsychologist, vocational rehabilitation counselor, occupational and activity therapist, family support group, day treatment or residential program.

Recommendations for Subtypes

- *Residual.* Consider drug-free periods if client will return for treatment when symptoms return.
- *Disorganized.* Therapy may be impossible until symptoms abate. Initially, vocational, social skills, and behavioral therapy are very important followed by milieu therapy.
- *Catatonic.* If agitated or stuporous, medication may be necessary to control the symptoms or break through the stupor.
- *Paranoid.* At onset, address issues of trust, therapeutic intrusiveness, and medication compliance.

SCHIZOPHRENIFORM DISORDER (295.40)

Essential Features

This disorder is identical to Schizophrenia except that the duration of symptoms can be less than six months, and there is no requirement for a decline in function. Thus, these clients initially appear to have Schizophrenia, but don't have the same history or level of disturbance. As a result, these clients have a better prognosis and are more likely to recover to their premorbid level of function. This diagnosis is relatively rare, and poorly understood. Adolescents, Schizotypal, Histrionic, and Borderline Personality Disorders are more prone to receive this diagnosis.

Diagnosis

On intake, Schizophreniform Disorder clients may present as very upset or in acute emotional turmoil (see Testing Tip for typical test results).

Recommendations

If testing indicates a diagnosis of Schizophreniform Disorder, the treatment recommendations for Schizophrenia best apply, keeping in mind both that the client's premorbid history may not be as disturbed, and that treatment may not need to be as comprehensive. The priority for treatment is to ensure the client returns to the premorbid level of functioning as soon as possible with minimum disruption to occupational or interpersonal functioning. In particular, the client may need to be dissuaded from adopting the client or sick role.

BRIEF PSYCHOTIC DISORDER (298.8)

Essential Features

Clients with this disorder present with a sudden onset of psychotic symptoms. According to *DSM-IV*, the duration of the episode is longer than a day and less than a month. The episode is typically characterized by positive psychotic symptoms. The client's symptoms may be a response to extreme stress. In general, after the episode, the client returns to a normal level of functioning. Stressors may include rape, death of a loved one, or childbirth. A minority of clients are so disturbed by their experience they become suicidal.

Testing Tip
Test Results Associated with Schizophreniform Disorder

- On the WAIS-III, a profile similar to Schizophrenia may occur, except that increased emotional distress may lead to difficulties with attention and concentration (Digit Span, Arithmetic, and Digit Symbol-Coding). FIQ should be higher than in Schizophrenia.
- On the MMPI-2/MMPI-A, the F scale may be more elevated than for chronic Schizophrenia. However, the other scales will likely be in a lower range than in Schizophrenia, with lower elevations on 7-8-0.
- The MCMI-III profile will be similar to that for Schizophrenia.
- The Rorschach will be similar to that described for Schizophrenia. There may also be elevations on the Coping Deficit Index.

Diagnosis

The test profile may be similar to acute Schizophrenia. Cognitive skills may be more intact and there may be less evidence of an impairment of functioning (see Testing Tip for typical test results).

Recommendations

- *Psychotherapy* (Behavioral, Cognitive-Behavioral) aimed at:

    Preventing client from accepting the "patient role."

    Increasing client's comprehension regarding the need for medication.

    Reducing loss in socialization and preventing withdrawal.

    Reducing depression associated with the disorder.

    Increasing self-esteem and maintaining vocational involvement.

    Reducing suicide risk.

- *Multidisciplinary* treatment approach (crisis intervention, brief hospitalization, inpatient, partial, or outpatient therapy).
- *Antipsychotic* or antidepressant medication.
- *Crisis Intervention.*
- *Family therapy or support groups* aimed at:

    Increasing the family's knowledge of the disorder.

    Creating reasonable expectations from family members.

Testing Tip
Test Results Associated with Brief Psychotic Disorder

- Emotionally, these individuals may appear very confused and in significant emotional distress. Their test profile may even appear more severe than that of a person with acute Schizophrenia.
- On the MMPI-2 or MMPI-A, the overall profile will be suggestive of acute distress with elevations on 7 (Psychasthenia) and 8 (Schizophrenia). Given the good premorbid functioning, the 0 (Social Introversion) scale may be close to normal. It is unlikely for the 4 (Psychopathic Deviate) or 6 (Paranoia) scales to be elevated.
- On the MCMI-III, there will be a Schizophrenia profile with the following additional features: The Clinical Syndrome scales of Anxiety (A) and Bipolar: Manic (N) may be elevated indicating tension and emotional turmoil. There may also be an elevation of the Clinical Personality Pattern Scale 4 (Histrionic Personality).

Reducing anxiety in family members.

Reducing family stressors that affect the client.

- *Potential referrals:* Psychiatrist, family support group, vocational/occupational counselor.

SCHIZOAFFECTIVE DISORDER (295.70)

Essential Features

The primary features of this disorder are the presence of both significant psychotic and mood symptoms. Thus, this disorder is considered a "wastebasket" category because most clients are later diagnosed with either Schizophrenia or a Mood Disorder. Keep in mind that the presence of this disorder in *DSM-IV* suggests that part of your assessment clientele will include these patients. The mood symptoms can be depressive or bipolar, though the most common presentation is with depression. According to *DSM-IV*, there must be at least two weeks of psychotic symptoms in the absence of mood symptoms or at least one episode of Schizophrenia.

Diagnosis

The test profile for Schizoaffective Disorder consists of a combination of signs of Schizophrenia and Mood Disorder. The presentation in part will be determined by the nature of the Mood Disorder as well as the severity of the psychotic symptoms (see Testing Tip on page 172).

Recommendations

If testing indicates a diagnosis of Schizoaffective Disorder, treatment recommendations should follow a symptomatic approach, treating mood and psychotic symptoms as they occur (see treatment recommendations for mood (Chapter 6) and psychotic disorders as needed). Retesting after six months may help identify if the client's diagnosis has changed to Schizophrenia or a Mood Disorder.

DELUSIONAL DISORDER (297.1)

Essential Features

Due to their higher level of functioning, these clients are seldom seen for evaluation. The primary feature is the presence of a nonbizarre delusion (e.g., suspicion of a spouse having an affair), the most common being either a persecutory or paranoid nature. Delusional jealousy is also common. According to *DSM-IV*, the delusion must persist for at least one month, and not be due to or lead to

---

Testing Tip
Test Results Associated with Schizoaffective Disorder

- On the WAIS-III, in principle, scores should share features found in both Mood Disorders and Schizophrenia, resulting in numerous problems. Marked subtest scatter and disordered verbal content could occur due to psychosis, while depression might decrease PIQ scores with evidence of difficulty with attention and concentration (Digit Span, Arithmetic, Digit Symbol-Coding). In contrast, manic symptoms might lead to impulsivity with careless responding on Picture Arrangement, Matrix Reasoning, Symbol Search, or Block Design.
- On the MMPI-2 or MMPI-A, the characteristic profile is an elevation on Scale 8 (Schizophrenia) accompanied by Scales 2 (Depression), 7 (Psychasthenia), F, or an 8-2 profile, if the depressive mood predominates. Suicide risk increases as Scale 9 (Hypomania) increases. In contrast, if mania is the dominant feature, then an 8-9 profile may occur, with an elevated Scale 4 (Psychopathic Deviate).
- On the MCMI-III, there may be elevations characteristic of a mood disorder (see Chapter 6) with additional elevations on Schizotypal (S), Thought Disorder (SS), or Avoidant (2A) scales.
- The Rorschach may indicate schizophrenic signs associated with considerable affect, impaired coping, and poor stress tolerance. Check for elevations on the major indices SCZI, DEPI, S-CON, and CDI.

Schizophrenia. This is a rare disorder with a late onset, occurring typically in middle adulthood. However, the intensity of the delusion can lead to dangerousness, especially when it involves delusional jealousy. The presentation of the disorder varies depending on the delusional theme. The *DSM-IV* identifies six types including grandiose and somatic. During the evaluation, clients with Delusional Disorder may often be condescending and critical.

Diagnosis

The delusional theme usually impacts test results. Hostility and suspiciousness can lead to unanswered questions and test items (see Testing Tip for typical test results). This disorder may co-occur with Borderline Personality Disorder.

Older Adults

Delusions are more common in older adults. They may be a signal of the onset of dementia or a sign of overmedication. Chapter 11 describes cognitive and neuropsychological assessment in more detail.

Testing Tip
Test Results Associated with Delusional Disorder

- On the WAIS-III, there may be no impairment in cognitive functioning. Arithmetic and Picture Completion may be high, consistent with environmental alertness. A perfectionist and abstractionist style may result in high scores on Similarities or Comprehension.
- On the MMPI-2 or MMPI-A, elevations may occur on Scales 6 (Paranoia), 4 (Psychopathic Deviate), and 9 (Hypomania), but there is minimal evidence on whether this happens with any regularity. The K scale may also be high, consistent with a defensive attitude and lack of insight. An elevation on Scale 3 (Hysteria) suggests greater denial and projection. Greater paranoia may also lead to elevations on Scale 8 (Schizophrenia). Somatic delusions may lead to elevations on Scales 1 (Hypochondriasis) and 3. The content scales Over-Controlled Hostility (O-H), Cynicism (CYN), and Bizarre Mentation (BIZ) may all be elevated at onset.
- On the MCMI-III, there may be a prominence on the Paranoid (P), Delusional Disorder (PP), Borderline (C), Antisocial (6A), or Compulsive (7) scales.
- On the Rorschach, these clients mainly show evidence of resistance, which may include rejections and oppositional responses (high S, low R). There may be a high number of Dd responses that are form dominant, and Lambda and HVI may be high. The protocols may also be characterized by high F responses, and few M or C responses, with high $F+\%$.

Recommendations

- *Psychotherapy* (cognitive-behavioral) aimed at:

    Developing cognitive reframing.

    Establishing better boundaries.

    Improving anger control.

    Establishing therapeutic rapport and trust.

    Increasing self-efficacy, self-monitoring, and self-evaluation.

    Decreasing vigilance and suspiciousness.

- *Techniques* to interact with others in a nondefensive, nonangry manner.
- *Potential referral:* Family therapist.

SHARED PSYCHOTIC DISORDER (FOLIE A DEUX) (297.3)

Essential Features and Diagnosis

This is an uncommon disorder, and it is unlikely you will evaluate a client who has it. The essential features are the sharing of the delusional beliefs of a significant other with whom there is a dependent, intimate controlling relationship. The dominant and receiving party must present with identical symptoms. As expected, these clients are passive and dependent, and are psychologically susceptible to suggestion. Treatment usually involves separation from the primary client who has the Psychotic Disorder, psychotherapy, and assertiveness training.

MOOD DISORDER WITH PSYCHOTIC FEATURES (296.x4)

Essential Features

This category includes all Mood Disorders that can be coded with the modifier indicating the presence of psychotic symptoms (Major Depressive, Bipolar I or Bipolar II Disorders). It is a frequent diagnostic differential with the preceding disorders. Usually the psychotic symptoms are mood congruent. These clients often have a family history of Mood Disorders. The predominant and essential features of these disorders meet the criteria discussed in Chapter 6. Unlike Schizophrenia, psychotic symptoms dissipate with the remission of mood symptoms. In addition, it is rare to see severe thought disorder.

Diagnosis

Typical test results of Mood Disorder with Psychotic Features should be more consistent with test results for the primary mood disorder (see Chapter 6 for specific mood-related test results). However, on the WAIS-III, there may be increased scatter and the presence of psychotic content on test items. On the MMPI-2 or MMPI-A, the profile may show elevations on Scales 8 or 6. It is also useful to check the content scale Bizarre Mentation (BIZ). On the MCMI-III, elevations may occur on the Thought Disorder scale (SS). On the Rorschach, there may be lower F+% and X+% scores and elevated special scores.

Recommendations

See Chapter 6 for diagnostic specific recommendations.

Time as a Diagnostic Factor in *DSM-IV*

Key time-related features must be considered when assigning a diagnosis. The accompanying Testing Tip lists them by duration.

Testing Tip	
Important Durations to Consider for Psychotic Disorders	
Brief Psychotic Disorder	For at least 1 day, less than 30 days.
Schizophreniform Disorder	For at least 1 month, less than 6 months.
Schizoaffective Disorder	Delusions/hallucinations for at least 2 weeks.
	Major depression for at least 2 weeks.
	Manic for at least 1 week unless hospitalized; mixed for at least 1 week.
Delusional Disorder	Nonbizarre delusions for at least 1 month.
Schizophrenia	Continuous signs for at least 6 months.
	Significant symptoms for at least 1 month.

Differential Diagnosis

Psychotic symptoms may suggest a Psychotic Disorder, Mood Disorder, or Substance-Related Disorder (especially intoxication or withdrawal). Several of the most frequent or prominent differential diagnoses are discussed.

PSYCHOSIS VERSUS DRUG-INDUCED PSYCHOSIS (291.xx; 292.xx)

Clients with either disorder present with agitation, and poor reality testing characterized by hallucinations and paranoia. An accurate assessment of the onset of the episode will clarify the nature of the disorder. Drug-induced psychosis may include visual and olfactory hallucinations, which are rare in Schizophrenia. As the effects of the substance use diminish, psychotic symptoms typically abate. Loosening of associations, cognitive slippage, language impairment, social withdrawal, interpersonal difficulties, and a lower premorbid level of functioning are uncommon in drug-induced psychosis.

SCHIZOPHRENIA VERSUS SCHIZOAFFECTIVE DISORDER

Schizophrenia will not necessarily have an affective component. The primary characteristic of the disorder is the presence of psychosis. In contrast, Schizoaffective Disorder presents with concurrent affective and psychotic symptoms. The prognosis is better for Schizoaffective Disorder.

SCHIZOPHRENIA VERSUS BORDERLINE PERSONALITY DISORDER

Borderline Personality Disorder is characterized by impulsivity, difficulties with boundaries, chaotic interpersonal relationships, a poor self-concept, and lability of affect and behavior. These clients can present with intense anxiety, psychotic regression, and ego fragmentation that can appear, at times, delusional or disordered. In contrast, clients with Schizophrenia tend to be socially isolated and withdrawn. While they have a poor prognosis, their psychosis tends to be episodic. In contrast, Borderline symptoms are long-lasting.

SCHIZOPHRENIA VERSUS SCHIZOID OR SCHIZOTYPAL PERSONALITY DISORDER

Both Schizoid and Schizotypal Personality Disorders are characterized by withdrawn or odd interpersonal interactions. Schizoid clients are typically isolated with few relationships and have no psychotic symptoms. It is important to note, however, that this diagnosis and Schizophrenia frequently coexist. Schizotypal individuals may experience mild psychoticlike symptoms, such as magical thinking, and there is usually an absence of florid psychotic symptoms.

SCHIZOPHRENIA VERSUS POSTTRAUMATIC STRESS DISORDER

Posttraumatic Stress Disorder is characterized by flashbacks, and at times, olfactory hallucinations. These experiences are not psychotic as the person is aware of the impairment in reality and is disturbed by the experience. This disorder is a reaction to an extreme stressor. Impairment in interpersonal relationships and poor premorbid functioning that is characteristic of schizophrenics is usually absent.

PARANOID SCHIZOPHRENIA VERSUS DELUSIONAL DISORDER VERSUS PARANOID PERSONALITY DISORDER

Paranoid Schizophrenia presents with greater cognitive impairment, more bizarre delusions, and greater ego fragmentation than the other disorders. Delusional disorder has a later age of onset, usually a higher premorbid level of functioning, the delusions are relatively nonbizarre, and the impairment of functioning is usually restricted to the delusions. Paranoid Personality Disorder is a style of long-standing distrust, suspiciousness, and guarded interpersonal interactions, unrelated to a specific domain. Delusions are absent.

AUTISM VERSUS CHILDHOOD SCHIZOPHRENIA

Autistic clients typically lack psychotic symptoms (e.g., hallucinations). Rather, they show deviant language patterns and aberrant social relationships. Autism includes a pervasive lack of social responsiveness, early language deficits, echolalia, self-injurious behavior, or a resistance to change. Autistic preoccupations are not delusions. Autistic symptoms usually are visible before 3 years of age, and the majority have a diagnosis of Mental Retardation. In contrast, very few schizophrenic children are mentally retarded, with onset between 8 and 12 years of age and stereotypical psychotic symptoms. Childhood schizophrenics are more socially responsive, and echolalia is rare.

AUTISM VERSUS ASPERGER'S DISORDER

These disorders are similar in that these clients show severe impairment in social interaction and restrictive repetitive behaviors. Asperger's Disorder is less severe than Autism in that autistic clients show significant language delays and significant delays in cognitive development. Asperger's Disorder clients have greater intellectual function and more motor delays.

SCHIZOPHRENIA VERSUS MENTAL RETARDATION

Some clients with Schizophrenia may function in the low average or borderline range intellectually. Occasionally, a Schizophrenic client may score in the intellectually impaired range due to profound catatonia. While some mentally retarded individuals may experience psychosis, it is not a defining feature. Rather, impairment of cognitive functioning in the mentally retarded range and accompanying impairment in adaptive functioning are the diagnostic criteria. In addition, Mental Retardation must have an onset before age 18 years and is usually diagnosed at an earlier age than Schizophrenia. Don't mistake the concrete nature of Mental Retardation with thought disorder.

CHAPTER 9

Self-Control: Suicidality, Dangerousness, Substance-Related Disorders, Abuse, and Eating Disorders

Why These Problems Are Grouped Together

THESE PROBLEMS ARE RELATED to affect modulation and self-control, ranging from overcontrol (e.g., Eating Disorders) to the loss of control (e.g., Dangerousness) and its consequences. They are organized based on their likelihood of occurrence in your practice.

Practical Considerations

CONFIDENTIALITY AND MANDATED REPORTING

Although these clients have the same rights to confidentiality as others, there is a greater likelihood that you will have to break confidentiality or be involved in a nonconfidential relationship, especially for clients referred by the legal system. You will need to clarify your relationship, determine who accesses the report, and discuss what information is shared with others. Clients mandated for evaluation by the legal system still require the use of consent forms and releases.

Abuse

Your obligation to confidentiality may be superseded by legally mandated reporting of abuse, so you will need to be familiar with your local laws. Most counties have either a Child Abuse Registry, Child Protective Services, or Adult Protective Services. If in doubt about your responsibilities, consult these agencies or your colleagues.

Dangerousness

You also have obligations under the legal decision of *Tarasoff v. Board of Regents of the University of California* (1974, 1976). Specifically, if your client makes a direct threat to an identifiable victim, then it is your duty to notify both the police and the victim. Most states have variations on this law that consider danger to property, or variations on the details regarding what is a sufficient way of notifying the victim. Be familiar with the laws in the state where you practice.

Hospitalization

You may have to break confidentiality if clients pose a danger to themselves or others, and you decide that hospitalization is needed. You should learn the mechanisms for initiating hospitalization. Several factors help identify when and why a client should be hospitalized (see Testing Tip below).

ACCURACY OF CLIENT'S REPORT

Regardless of your level of rapport, the validity of the information provided by the client should be considered. Clients with a criminal record or a history of abuse may deny or exaggerate their actions. A discussion on malingering is included in Chapter 2.

Patients may also misrepresent themselves unintentionally. Clients with Eating Disorders or Substance-Related Disorders may lack insight, and minimize their symptoms. Suicidal clients may downplay their true intentions. Abused

---

Testing Tip
When to Hospitalize Clients with Self-Control Problems

- You remain concerned that your client will try a serious suicide attempt, regardless of outside support mechanisms.
- Your client shows a gross inability for self-care, resulting in ever-worsening health and safety (e.g., gross neglect; Anorexia Nervosa).
- Your client's living circumstances are sufficiently unsafe or chaotic that they present a danger (e.g., abuse).
- Your client has become dangerous to others or property and cannot be controlled even with outside support (e.g., Dangerousness).
- Your client is unable to comply with outpatient treatment and continues to worsen.

Testing Tip
When to Question the Validity of Your Client's Data

- Court-mandated referral.
- Past treatment compliance problems.
- Client shows marked concerns about confidentiality.
- Difficulty establishing rapport.
- Marked distancing by client.
- Lack of insight and minimization of issues on part of client.
- Presence of Alcohol or Substance-Related Disorder.
- Inappropriate reaction to your wanting to corroborate information.
- Marked hesitation about signing releases.

---

clients may repress recalling events, and the fear of further abuse may lead to unwillingness to talk.

DEALING WITH ISSUES OF SAFETY

You may need to address issues of safety, either for the client or potential victims. When safety becomes a primary issue, take a concrete, action-oriented intervention approach to de-escalate the situation. Assess the risk and potential lethality of your client, and if necessary, determine a plan to protect the client or others. Refer the client for a medical evaluation (e.g., self-injury, detox), as this essential procedure can be forgotten in a crisis. Plan to have a future reassessment because self-control difficulties wax and wane. At all times, pay attention to your own comfort level with the client.

If the client's behavior is inappropriate, set clear limits. A concrete contract can be implemented immediately to help maintain self-control. Have alternative interventions available, and be clear about the steps that you will take to ensure safety. Be prepared to involve the client's social support system if it is needed to provide structure and aid. These safety issues are addressed later for specific disorders; however, realize that you may have to deal with them at the start of your assessment.

RECIDIVISM

Several of these problems have high rates of recidivism. However, 70%–90% of abused children do not abuse others. Battering parents have a recidivism rate of 33%–50% (Melton, Petrila, Poythress, & Slobogin, 1987). For suicidality and dangerousness, a consistent predictor is a history of prior acts. Thus, have realistic expectations and recommendations. We suggest that you be skeptical of major and rapid changes, especially if the client has a problem-filled history.

Some clients who are mandated to treatment are so hostile that therapeutic rapport cannot be established. If this occurs, you may consider obtaining consultation, referring the case to a colleague, requesting a strategy session with the referring source, or discussing the issue with the client. Be very clear about your boundaries and follow through immediately if a contract is broken or if the client fails to appear for a mandated session.

PROBLEMS OF SELF-CONTROL

The detailed review provided here for each of these problems includes specific issues, test results, and treatment recommendations. A description of the behavioral presentation of these conditions and their associated test results is presented in Tables 9.1 and 9.2.

As mentioned before, you may find that testing is not appropriate or needed (e.g., performing an assessment to diagnose Anorexia in a grossly underweight teenager). Clarifying the needs of your referring source will help keep you on track.

Testing Tip
Rapid Assessment of Self-Control Problems

For most of these clients, an efficient assessment might include:

Children	CAT, TAT, Rorschach
Adolescents	MMPI-A, CAT, TAT, Rorschach
Adults	MMPI-2, Rorschach
Elderly	MMPI-2, Rorschach

Problem-Specific Scales

Eating Disorder	Eating Disorder Index
Suicide	Beck Hopelessness Scale, BDI-II
Abuse Victim	MMPI-A/MACI
Abuse Perpetrator	Child Abuse Potential Inventory

TABLE 9.1
Key Descriptive Features of Impulse Control Disorders

Disorder/Syndrome	Behavioral	Emotional	Interpersonal
Suicide	Self-destructive acts; risk-taking behaviors/ impulsivity; psychomotor retardation/agitation; weight and sleep changes; fatigue; diminished interest in activities; substance abuse; saying good-byes; putting affairs in order	Hopelessness; shame and guilt; depressed mood; worthlessness; poor concentration; suicidal thoughts	Social impairment; occupational impairment; social withdrawal; isolation
Dangerousness	Decreased sleep; talkative; self-destructive; impulsive; acting out; assaultive, threatening; low frustration tolerance; substance abuse	Expansive, irritable mood; inflated self-esteem; grandiosity; racing thoughts; selfish	Manipulative; disinterest in others' opinions; need for attention; demanding; exploitative
Alcohol and Substance Abuse	Risk taking, exhibitionism, extroversion	Difficulty concentrating; depressed/elated; chronic/flat affect	Solitary; superficial or codependent; substance using peers
Abuse Victim	Avoidance of stimuli associated with prior trauma; sleep disturbance; aggressiveness; accident proneness; extreme secrecy; excessive bathing; provocative or promiscuous sexual behavior	Shame/depression; hypervigilance; anger/rage; fear; inability to recall; low self-worth; anxious/insecure	Interpersonal problems; difficulty with intimacy; promiscuity; shrinking from physical contact; social withdrawal
Anorexia Nervosa	Dramatic weight loss; failure to gain weight; lack of menstruation; restrictive eating; excessive exercise	Overcontrolled; depression-masked; anxiety	Cheerful; family conflict
Bulimia Nervosa	Binging and purging; hiding of behavior	Depression; anxiety	Superficial; family conflict

In most cases, the MMPI-2/MMPI-A will be your best measure, although the Rorschach is recommended if you are skilled and have computerized scoring at hand. Despite its psychometric shortcomings, the MACI may be useful for adolescents because it specifically addresses suicidal tendency, impulsive propensity, delinquent predisposition, substance abuse proneness, and child abuse. We have also included several problem-specific measures for clinicians who work extensively with these clinical populations.

TABLE 9.2
Key Test Findings for Impulse Control Disorders

Disorder/ Syndrome	WAIS-III/WISC-III	MMPI-2/ MMPI-A	MCMI-III/ MACI	Rorschach
Suicide	VIQ > PIQ Subtests: Lower scores on Digit Span, Digit Symbol-Coding (Coding), Block Design, Symbol Search High scores on Comprehension	Profiles: 2-7, 2-4, 5-0 Elevations: 2, 4, 7, 6, 8, 0 Low Scale K	D, CC, A, C, B MACI: B, GG, DD	Positive *S-Con*, *DEPI* index Higher *V*, *MOR* Lower *R*
Dangerousness	PIQ > VIQ Subtests: Low scores on Picture Arrangement; school problems leading to lower Information, Arithmetic, Vocabulary High scores on Information, Comprehension	profiles: F-4-9, 4-3, 8-6-4, F-6-7 Elevations: 6, 8	6A, B, 5, 6B, T, P, PP	*CF + C > FC*, *CF > FC* Lower *M*, *R* Higher *C*, *Cn*, *S*, *L* Content *AG*, *Bl*, *Ex*, *MOR*, *An*
Alcohol and Substance Abuse	Long term: Organic signs and school problems Subtests: Low scores on Information, Arithmetic, Digit Symbol-Coding, Picture Arrangement	profiles: 2-4, 1-2, 4-7, 4-6, or 4-9 Elevations: 2, 4, 7, 8, or 9 Content: PRO, ACK Suppl: MAC-R	B, T, 2B, D, 2A, 3, 6A, 6B MACI: BB, DD, G, 6A, 8A	Higher *Dd*, *S*, *C* Lower *R F+%*
Abuse Victim	High overall IQ (possibly) Subtests: Low scores on Digit Span, Arithmetic, Digit Symbol-Coding (Coding), Block Design, Symbol Search	Profiles: F-2-8, 7-2, 8-2-7, 1-9 Elevations: 2, 7, 1, or 8 Content: PK	R, 2B, A, D MACI: B, G, H, FF	Extratensive style Low *Afr* High *L*
Anorexia Nervosa	May be similar to OCD with VIQ > PIQ Higher Vocabulary, Information, Arithmetic (in better educated clients)	Profiles: Conversion V, 2-4-8, 7-6-8, L-K	3, 7, 8A, 1, E, C	Higher *F+%*
Bulimia Nervosa	No specific findings	Profiles: Conversion V, 2-4-7-8 Elevations, 2, 4, 8	3, 7, 8A, 1, E, C	No specific findings

Suicide

SUICIDE RISK

Assessing suicidality is a normal part of a mental status exam, but many clinicians find it a stressful issue to cover. It is the second highest cause of death among males ages 15–19, and prevalence rates among the elderly are increasing. In general, men attempt suicide less often than women, but are more successful in their attempts. Bongar (1991) reported that there is a 15% chance that any attempt will be successful. Suicide coexists with many mental disorders. Nevertheless, clients commonly express suicidal thoughts and ideation on a frequent basis, usually with no behavioral consequences.

Many clinical signs can suggest a risk of potential suicide, though by themselves, they do not offer much predictive power. These include:

- Expressed statements of hopelessness or of being overwhelmed.
- Frequent crying.
- Drug use.
- Reckless driving.
- Fantasies of how others would react to their death.
- Death of a loved one.
- Recent end of a relationship.
- Recent release from psychiatric hospital (within 3 months).
- Feeling a lack of friendships.

If you identify one of these factors, follow up with an assessment of suicide potential, as discussed in the following section.

Testing Tip
Rapid Method to Assess Suicide Potential

1. Interview client and evaluate risk factors/trigger events.
2. Obtain collateral information, if needed.
3. Administer psychological tests if the client is defensive during the evaluation.
4. Assess lethality.
5. Develop a plan to protect.

INTERVIEW TO ASSESS RISK FACTORS/TRIGGER EVENTS

Your first step is to interview the client and identify factors that increase suicide risk. Ask direct questions, including the reasons for wanting to die, and the meaning of the present crisis. A client who states a wish to cease to exist is in a high risk category. If functioning has been decreasing recently, then risk can be assumed to be increasing. When functioning has been increasing after an episode of severe depression, then the risk can be assumed to be increasing, too. Because these clients give clues to peers or family members, you should interview significant others. The 10 most significant factors are discussed in this section. Keep in mind that the presence of a single risk factor does not in itself predict suicide.

- *Past history of suicide (individual and family).* Past attempts place clients at a higher suicide risk and the risk rises based on the level of lethality of the previous attempts. Having a parent or significant other (including a hero or idol) who has committed suicide increases the client's vulnerability, particularly around significant dates.
- *Intention, plan, means.* Clients are at greatest risk if they state clear intentions, describe a specific, organized, and detailed plan, and have the means available. It is your responsibility to ask for the details, the time frame, and any backup plans.
- *Diagnosis.* A history of mental illness puts a patient at higher risk for suicide, with greatest risk for the following disorders and symptoms: Major Depression, Schizophrenia, Borderline Personality, Anxiety Disorders (specifically Panic Attacks), paranoid symptoms, Substance Abuse, command hallucinations that are suicidal. Often the risk is greatest as the

---

Testing Tip
10 Suicide Risk Factors to Identify during an Assessment

1. Past history of suicide attempts or self-mutilation (client or family).
2. Clear intention, plan, means.
3. Diagnosis of Depression, Schizophrenia, Substance Abuse, chronic physical illness.
4. Hopelessness or dysphoria.
5. Behaviors suggesting the decision to die (e.g., selling possessions).
6. Communicating the desire to die to others.
7. Lack of social support.
8. Inability to see alternatives.
9. Stressful precipitating events, especially loss.
10. Assessment results consistent with suicide risk.

client begins to recover (e.g., immediately post-hospitalization). Chronic physical illness is also a risk factor which is more common in older adults.

- *Hopelessness or dysphoria.* Higher risk is associated with agitation, self-hatred, shame, dysphoria, panic, anxiety, or loss of pleasure. If the client presents with sudden cheerfulness after a depressive episode, this may suggest an increased risk, too. Clients who show a history of coping by escaping crises are at greater risk.

- *Behaviors suggesting the decision to die.* Certain behaviors may reflect a decision to die:

  Making a will.

  Giving away possessions.

  Severing relationships.

  Inappropriate and sudden calmness.

  Finishing up old business.

  Writing a suicide note.

  Fantasizing about how people would react to the death.

- *Communication of the decision to die.* Most suicide completers communicate their intention in advance, so you should ask clients directly if they have told anyone of the intention to commit suicide. Family members and peers can be interviewed.

- *Lack of social support.* Lack of social support is a risk factor. Specific events include lack of a therapeutic alliance, recent loss of key supports, and few friends. Lack of support may also be a misperception, and can be expressed as feeling rejection or betrayal by significant others. In particular, older urban males who are divorced or widowed and living alone are at higher risk.

- *Inability to see alternatives.* Clients are at risk when they see suicide as the only solution to their problems, or the only way to end chronic psychological pain. A client who appears rigid and unable to take another perspective probably has limited coping and self-control.

- *Precipitating events.* Acute stresses place an individual at higher risk. Important events include recent losses, a change in finances or employment, discharge from a psychiatric hospital in the past three months, or a diagnosis of a medical condition. If the loss is irrevocable and the person was unable to mourn the loss, the risk increases.

Assessment Results

A good clinical interview should be able to provide you with a clear basis for evaluating suicide risk, unless your client continues to take a defensive stance. In these cases, testing should be performed. In addition, some clients who deny

Testing Tip
Test Results Associated with Suicide Risk

- On the WAIS-III/WISC-III, depression and psychomotor retardation may lead to VIQ > PIQ with lower concentration, and the tendency to give up resulting in lower scores on Arithmetic, Digit Symbol-Coding (Coding), Block Design, and Symbol Search. Their sensitivity to the social environment may result in higher scores on Comprehension.
- On the MMPI-2/MMPI-A, elevations may include Scales 2 (Depression), 4 (Psychopathic Deviate), 7 (Psychasthenia), 0 (Social Introversion), and possibly Scales 6 (Paranoia) or 8 (Schizophrenia). Profiles may include 2-7, 2-4, or a 5-0 profile with low K in females. Increases in Scales 4, 8, and 9 suggest reduced self-control and poor judgment. Also check the client's responses to the suicide items: 150, 506, 520, and 524.
- On the MCMI-III, elevations may occur at the prominence level for Scales CC (Major Depression), and D (Dysthymia), sometimes accompanied by C (Borderline) and B (Alcohol Dependence). Elevated Scale N (Bipolar: Manic) combined with D suggests the client has the energy to commit suicide. Psychotic patients are also at higher risk so check Scales S (Schizotypal), P (Paranoid), SS (Thought Disorder), and PP (Delusional Disorder).
- On the Rorschach, clients may meet criteria for the *S-CON* (Suicide Constellation), *DEPI* (Depression), and *CDI* (Coping Deficit) indices. A significant *S-CON* identified suicide risk 83% of the time (Exner, 1993). The presence of color-shading blends suggests painful dysphoric affect that may accompany suicide. There are often few C (Color) and T (Texture) responses, suggesting unmet needs and a shutting down of emotions. Isolation is indicated by fewer H (human content) and more LS (landscape content) and V (Vista) responses. Any suicidal verbal content should automatically alert you to the client's risk.
- On the apperception tests, the stories may be short and lack an ending. There may be themes of hopelessness, guilt, and a preoccupation with death.
- On the Beck Hopelessness Scale (Psychological Corporation, 1993), suicidal clients will score above the suggested cutoffs.

suicidal ideation will reveal their intentions only through psychological testing (see Testing Tip on page 187 for typical test results).

Suicide Risk Scales

Many scales are available to assess suicide risk. A popular and useful one is the Beck Hopelessness Scale. This self-report questionnaire has 20 true-false items and has been found to be effective in predicting suicide. It measures three aspects of hopelessness: feelings about the future, loss of motivation, and expectations. It can be administered to an age range of 17–80 years and is available in English and Spanish. It takes between 5 and 10 minutes to administer.

Older Adults

Older adults are at risk because they are more likely to have lost significant others, to become isolated, or to experience chronic health problems.

Children/Adolescents

Suicide among young children, particularly adolescents, is more frequent than in the past. Suicide risk is indicated by acting out and risk taking, not only by depression or withdrawal. Risk also increases if a parent commits suicide. In addition, family crises or disruptions frequently precede the suicide of young children.

Adolescents, especially those who use alcohol and substances, represent a high risk population, and the same risk factors for adults apply to this group. Many adolescents who have completed suicides had threatened or attempted suicide within the previous 24 hours. Even in intact families, suicidal adolescents are sensitive to parental rejection, school disciplinary action, or the loss of an important relationship.

Test Results

In addition to the results mentioned previously, suicidal adolescents may present with elevations on the MACI Scales B (Self-Devaluing), GG (Suicidal Tendency), and DD (Impulsive Propensity).

Plan to Protect

The primary goal is to stabilize the crisis, determine the appropriate level of care, and implement a plan to protect. Identify the factors that precipitated the increase in suicidal thoughts and actions, develop a no-suicide contract, increase and strengthen the social support, and implement an ongoing risk-monitoring system. Keep thorough notes and consult with at least one colleague.

Recommendations

If the client's interview and test results suggest the presence of suicide potential, the following treatment recommendations may be appropriate.

- *Psychotherapy* (cognitive-behavioral, interpersonal, etc.) aimed at:

    De-escalating the crisis.

    Strengthening the therapeutic alliance.

    Decreasing negative affect.

    Increasing emotional control.

    Identifying positive things in life and reestablishing hope.

    Strengthening social supports.

    Developing more adaptive coping strategies.

    Involving client in self-esteem-enhancing activity.

- *Clarification* of your duty to protect.
- Choice of *outpatient versus inpatient* treatment.
- Agreement on a *no-suicide contract* and removal of the means.
- *Medication and medical evaluation.*
- *Family therapy* for children and adolescents.
- *Support group* for older adults to decrease social isolation.
- *Monitoring* of ongoing risk.
- *Potential referrals:* Psychiatrist, group therapy, peer support group, and activity group.

Dangerousness

Dangerousness, like suicide, can be hard to predict, and can appear episodically or chronically. Keep in mind, though, that most clients aren't dangerous, despite having violent thoughts or feelings. Because dangerousness intimidates many clinicians (and most people), it can be hard to determine a logical and rapid manner to assess it. If dangerousness is conceptualized as a loss of self-control, then your role is to:

- Recognize trigger situations.
- Conduct an appropriate assessment.
- Implement a plan to protect (if needed).

TRIGGER SITUATIONS

Trigger situations are events that raise your concern and alert you to conduct a more detailed evaluation. They are not verifiable predictors of violence, however, so don't "jump the gun" just because you encounter one of them. Another warning sign is your own level of comfort or sense of safety.

Testing Tip
Common Trigger Situations

- Client has a gun collection.
- Client has "lived for" a job and recently lost it.
- Diagnosis includes paranoid symptoms or substance abuse.
- Client is obsessed with a particular person.
- Verbal threats have been made by client.
- Client is "hot-tempered."
- There is a diagnosis of Antisocial Personality Disorder.
- There is a history of previous acts of violence.
- A third party informs you of a threat.
- Client has recently been released from inpatient psychiatric treatment.

ASSESSMENT OF DANGEROUSNESS

As with suicidality, dangerousness is usually considered during a typical mental status exam, and you will likely evaluate it in depth only when you identify trigger situations or risk factors.

Dangerousness assessments can occur as part of a regular evaluation or as part of an evaluation of a confined person (hospital, jail, etc.). Regardless of the context, resist the pressure to rush your evaluation due to discomfort.

When appropriate, gather as much collateral information as possible because the accuracy of your assessment increases as you collect multiple sources. Use the "Outline of Dangerousness Assessment Interview" provided in the Testing Tip on page 191 as a format for assessing dangerousness.

During the interview, one of your primary goals is to assess the client's lethality. The level of danger or threat to others that your client poses can be assessed in terms of risk factors. We have identified the most common risk factors associated with the potential of danger to others; these are by no means inclusive. The factors are not all equivalent, and each one has unique characteristics. The greater the number of factors the person has, the higher the risk to others:

- *History of previous violence.* The best predictor of future violence is a past history of violence. Identify the client's age at onset, type, frequency, and severity of incidents and the role of situational factors. Establish the consequences of these actions and the client's perception of the consequences. See if you can identify an underlying pattern. Patterns may be related to:

Specific emotions or stressors.

Impulsiveness versus premeditation.

Predatory versus opportunistic violence.

Social versus solitary violence.

Weapons versus physical force.

Stealth versus detection.

Testing Tip
Outline of Dangerousness Assessment Interview

Evaluate the threat
- Identify trigger events.
- Consider risk factors.
- Obtain history.
- Document critical data.

Assess the lethality
- Access to means.
- Determine level of self-control.
- Identify the victim.
- Consider duty to warn victim, police, others.

Discuss plan to protect
- Decide disposition.
- Strengthen outside supports; identify secondary monitor.
- Communicate limits and consequences.
- Create nonviolence contract.

Testing Tip
Clinical Risk Factors Associated with Dangerousness

- History of previous violence.
- Clear intention, plan, means, and target.
- Diagnosis of Substance Abuse or Antisocial Personality Disorder.
- Emotional lability/unemotional demeanor.
- Behavioral impulsivity.
- History of violence in family of origin.
- Precipitating events, suggesting rejection or betrayal.
- Assessment results consistent with violence.

- *Clear intention, plan, means, and target.* Directly ask the client about motivations, intention, any plans, available means, and potential targets. Clients with a fascination with weapons or access to weapons are at higher risk, so ask if they have a preference, knowledge, or experience with any specific weapons. Explore the relationship between the client and the potential target to identify other risk factors (e.g., stalking, rejection, precipitating events).

Testing Tip
Test Results Associated with Violence Risk

- On the WAIS-III/WISC-III, these clients appear impulsive, respond rapidly, and frequently do better on nonverbal tests (PIQ > VIQ). Awareness of their environment may lead to higher scores on Information and Comprehension. Performance on Picture Arrangement may indicate impulsivity if the client is seen hastily assembling the cards. A history of school-related problems will lead to lower scores on Information, Arithmetic, and Vocabulary.
- On the MMPI-2/MMPI-A, clients at risk for assaultive behavior may show an F-4-9 profile, with secondary elevations on Scale 6 (Paranoia) or 8 (Schizophrenia). These clients show lack of impulse control, social alienation, and resentment toward others. A 4-3 profile may also occur, with the amount of control increasing as Scale 3 increases. Females with a 4-3 profile may appear promiscuous. An increase in Scale 0 (Social Introversion) may indicate greater isolation, anger, and resentment. Paranoid clients with an 8-6-4 profile are at risk for hostile outbursts as are clients with an F-6-7 profile combined with low scores on Scales 1-2-3. The supplementary scale, Over-Controlled Hostility (O-H), may also predict violent outbursts, though African Americans and females tend to score higher on this scale.
- On the MCMI-III, Scale 6A (Antisocial) or B (Alcohol Dependence) may be at the prominence level. There may also be elevations on Scales 5 (Narcissistic) and 6B (Aggressive) if there is a narcissistic, exploitative vindictiveness to the individual's presentation. Elevations on the B, T (Drug Dependence), P (Paranoid), and PP (Delusional Disorder) scales alert you to potential aggressiveness.
- On the Rorschach, these individuals show difficulty modulating emotions (CF + C > FC, CF > FC) and containing their impulsivity (low M responses and the presence of Pure C and Cn responses). They may be defensive and guarded (low R, high S, and high L). Content may show AG (Aggressive content), Bl (Blood), Ex (Explosions), MOR (Morbid), and An (Anatomical) responses.

- *Diagnosis.* Clients with Antisocial Personality Disorder or Substance Abuse/Dependence are at a higher risk. Note that substance users are more likely to present a higher risk than alcohol users due to the stronger effects of the drugs and their withdrawal symptoms. Other disorders or primary symptoms include paranoia, delusions, mania, hallucinations (particularly command or demand hallucinations), obsession with people or weapons, and impulse control symptoms. The highest risk group are individuals with multiple diagnoses.
- *Emotional lability/unemotional demeanor.* Emotional lability is associated with a higher risk for violence. Clarify if it occurs exclusively with alcohol or substance use. In addition, emotionally detached clients are also more at risk for becoming dangerous.
- *Behavioral impulsivity.* Poor impulse control is associated with an increased risk of dangerousness, which may be evidenced by unstable school and occupational histories, multiple relationships, risk-taking behaviors, and noncompliance with prior treatments.
- *History of violence in family of origin.* Exposure to family violence is correlated with a higher risk of dangerousness, as evidenced by child abuse, or witnessing parental violence.
- *Precipitating events.* Any stressor can precipitate violence, including alcoholic binges, rejection by significant others, or unemployment. It is also useful to consider the trigger situations described earlier.
- *Assessment results.* A good clinical interview should be able to provide you with a clear basis for evaluating dangerousness, unless your client continues to take a defensive stance. In these cases, testing should be performed. In addition, some clients who deny dangerousness will reveal their intentions only on psychological testing (see Testing Tip on page 192 for typical test results).

Older Adults

The same trigger and risk factors for dangerousness apply to this population as discussed earlier.

Children/Adolescents

When considering child and adolescent dangerousness, be familiar with Oppositional Defiant Disorder and Conduct Disorder (Chapter 7). The earlier the onset of Conduct Disorder, the greater the likelihood of severe acting out. Many of the risk factors discussed earlier apply to children and adolescents. Closely examine the child's school history, attendance record, and any reports of disciplinary problems. The absence of adequate parental supervision is strongly related to adolescent aggressiveness, as is a coercive parenting style.

Plan to Protect

Should it be necessary, your primary goal will be to develop and implement a plan to protect anyone at risk. For the client, the goal is to help teach self-control and decrease the frequency of impulsive acts. Keep thorough notes and consult with at least one colleague.

Recommendations for Dangerous Clients

- *Psychotherapy* (cognitive-behavioral, interpersonal, etc.) is aimed at:

    Anger management and anger control techniques.

    Identifying and avoiding high risk situations and people.

    Increasing self-control and contingency management.

    Increasing self-observation and monitoring.

    Cognitive restructuring and relaxation training.

    Strengthening social supports.

    Developing more adaptive coping strategies.

    Enhancing self-esteem and communication skills.

- *Clarify* your duty to protect/warn.
- If there are identifiable victims and direct threats, *warn target(s) and police.*
- Decide whether *inpatient treatment* is needed.
- Make a *nonviolence contract* and remove the means to becoming violent.
- *Review medication and medical evaluation.*
- *Crisis management* to reduce the crises affecting client's self-control.
- *Examine family and parenting issues.* Be alert for abuse.
- *Monitor ongoing risk.*
- *Potential referrals:* Psychiatrist, group therapy, anger management, parenting group.

A VIOLENCE DISORDER: INTERMITTENT EXPLOSIVE DISORDER (312.34)

Essential Features

This is an impulse control disorder. Relatively rare, it is characterized by sudden eruptions of aggressive impulses and loss of control. These clients normally do not exhibit these impulses, and usually express regret and guilt after they occur. It is only diagnosed when other disorders that include violence are excluded (e.g., Conduct Disorder).

Test Results

On the WAIS-III/WISC-III, these clients may have low scores on Picture Arrangement, Comprehension, and Similarities, suggesting poor social judgment and difficulties with cause and effect reasoning. On the MMPI-2/MMPI-A, there may be a 4-6 or 4-3 profile accompanied by an elevation on Scale 7 (Psychasthenia), indicating guilty feelings, rumination, and brooding. They may also have a significant elevation on Over-Controlled Hostility (O-H). On the Rorschach, their protocol may appear constricted (low *R*, high *L*) and include passive movement responses and a higher number of blood *(Bl)* and explosion *(Ex)* content responses.

Substance-Related Disorders

The essential feature of these disorders is a maladaptive pattern of substance use that results in impairment and distress. The *DSM-IV* describes 11 substances including alcohol, cocaine, and amphetamines. It also makes two further subdivisions: Substance Use (including Substance Dependence and Substance Abuse) and Substance-Induced Disorders (e.g., Intoxication, Withdrawal, Dementia).

Some clients will present with their substance-use symptoms as the reason for treatment. More commonly, you will find the client resistant to discussing substance use openly.

ASSESSMENT

The typical method of assessing for Substance-Related Disorders is a clinical interview, with perhaps testing and interviews with significant others. Collateral sources are useful because of the denial commonly seen in these clients (see Testing Tip for typical test results).

Older Adults

The same issues for adults apply as previously discussed.

Children/Adolescents

Sudden changes in school performance or peer group, or increased conflict at home and curfew violations are all indicators of the potential presence of these disorders. In addition to the adult test data, you may find elevations on the MACI scales including BB (Substance Abuse Proneness), DD (Impulsive

Testing Tip
Test Results Associated with Substance-Related Disorders

- On the WAIS-III, results depend on the nature and length of the substance use. If the use was short-term, there may be no significant findings. After the client stops drinking alcohol, short-term deficits may include problems with attention (Digit Span), visual integration (Block Design), or abstract reasoning (Similarities, Comprehension). Chronic use may lead to problems with attention (Arithmetic, Digit Span), psychomotor speed (Digit Symbol-Coding), cause-and-effect reasoning (Picture Arrangement), executive function (Matrix Reasoning), and visuomotor skill (Block Design). If substance use contributed to school problems, lower scores may occur on Information and Arithmetic. Impulsivity and low frustration tolerance may result in lower scores on Symbol Search and Digit Symbol-Coding.

- On the MMPI-2/MMPI-A, the most likely elevations will be on Scales F (Infrequency), 2 (Depression), 4 (Psychopathic Deviate), 7 (Psychasthenia), 8 (Schizophrenia), and 9 (Mania). These elevations may be accompanied by low scores on L (Lie), K (Subtle Defensiveness), and 0 (Social Introversion) scales. Common profiles include 4-9 (impulsive and angry), 2-4 (acute use), 1-2 (episodic use), 4-7 (spree drinking), or 4-6 (chronic use). The supplementary scale MAC-R (MacAndrew), may be elevated. Ethnic minorities, especially African Americans, Hispanics, and Native Americans tend to score 1–2 points higher than others. Females tend to score 1–2 points lower than males.

- On the MCMI-III, elevations may occur on Scales B (Alcohol Dependence), T (Drug Dependence), 2B (Depressive), or D (Dysthymic) scales. Chronic alcoholics may have elevations on 2A (Avoidant), 3 (Dependent), 6A (Antisocial), 6B (Aggressive), S (Schizotypal), C (Borderline), or P (Paranoid) scales. During periods of intoxication, the profile may consist of elevations on Scales SS (Thought Disorder) and PP (Delusional Disorder). Substance users may also have elevations on Scales 3 and 5 (Narcissistic), with secondary elevations on 6A or 6B.

- On the Rorschach, these individuals present with a high number of Dd (uncommon detail), white Space (S), and pure color (C) responses, consistent with an impulsive, oppositional style. Defensiveness may lead to few responses (R). Psychotic symptoms will lower F+%.

Propensity), G (Family Discord), 6A (Unruly), and 8A (Oppositional). MMPI-A content scales that may be elevated include ACK (Alcohol Acknowledgment) or PRO (Alcohol Propensity).

Recommendations

A primary goal is the development of a substance-free lifestyle and support system. Your most difficult task is to break through denial, maintain motivation, and avoid manipulation and rationalization. Most clients require 9 to 15 months to adjust to a substance-free lifestyle, and 2 to 3 years to develop support systems and alternative coping and social skills. If testing indicates a diagnosis of substance-related disorder, the following treatment recommendations may be appropriate.

- *Psychotherapy* (cognitive-behavioral, interpersonal, etc.) aimed at:

  Achieving addiction-free life (providing education and support).

  Decreasing depression and anxiety.

  Improving self-monitoring and stimulus control.

  Addressing developmental delays.

  Increasing emotional regulation and anger management.

  Developing alternate coping and social skills.

  Enhancing self-esteem.

  Maintaining motivation and relapse prevention.
- *Medical detoxification* (if needed).
- *Decision for level of treatment* (outpatient, inpatient, or day treatment).
- *Medication and medical evaluation.*
- *Strengthen social supports.* Group therapy relapse prevention.
- *Family therapy* and family support group.
- *Monitor ongoing risk* for relapse.
- *Potential referrals:* Psychiatrist, neuropsychologist (to identify residual cognitive impairment), 12-step groups, bibliotherapy, family support group.

Abuse

Abuse is a frequent concomitant to a loss of self-control. *DSM-IV* clusters these diagnoses in Other Conditions That May Be a Focus of Clinical Attention. They include: Physical Abuse of Child, Sexual Abuse of Child, Neglect of Child, Physical Abuse of Adult, and Sexual Abuse of Adult. Perpetrators and victims are differentiated by separate diagnostic codes. We focus our review on identifying crucial issues in the assessment of perpetrators and victims of abuse.

ABUSE PERPETRATOR

Many of the factors discussed earlier on Dangerousness and Substance-Related Disorders are applicable here. You may also want to review Chapter 10 for the test profile of Antisocial Personality Disorder. When interviewing these clients, be aware of their characteristic high level of denial, defensiveness, and lack of insight. Collateral information, particularly police reports and interviews with significant others, are vital to conduct an accurate evaluation.

One of the first issues to determine is the client's level of dangerousness to others. The strategies described earlier in this chapter can provide assistance.

Assessment

If you have the option of administering assessment measures, consider the MMPI-2 because it has been widely used with this population (though there is no specific profile for a child abuser).

Testing Tip
Risk Factors Associated with Being a Perpetrator of Child Abuse

---

Individual Factors
- Emotional lability, inability to tolerate frustration and inhibit anger.
- Problems handling dependency needs of self and others.
- Low ability to express physical affection.
- Low self-esteem.
- High interpersonal and emotional isolation and a lack of support.
- Presence of alcohol or drug abuse or Mood Disorder.
- History as a child abuse victim or witness to abuse.
- Poor coping skills.
- Isolation.

Interactional Factors
- Anger associated with child interactions.
- Critical perceptions and evaluations of child behavior.
- Negative attributions regarding child behavior.
- Lack of parenting skills and knowledge of child development.
- Unrealistic expectations of child's performance.
- Use of corporal punishment as primary child-rearing technique.
- Problems in family functioning and communication.

The Child Abuse Potential Inventory (CAPI) has excellent psychometric properties and also is successful at identifying individuals who are at risk for being abusive. This scale was designed for use in child protective agencies (Milner & Wimberely, 1979/1980). It is a 160-item, true-false questionnaire that includes validity scales to measure random responding, inconsistency, and response biases. It can correctly classify 80% to 90% of physical abusers from a diverse population. It has good test-retest reliability, internal consistency, and predictive validity.

Recommendations

Treatment for these clients will be determined in part by their legal status. Treatment recommendations should follow those offered for dangerous clients. Be aware of the high recidivism rate for this population.

VICTIMS OF ABUSE

The consequences of abuse can appear in a range of disorders often within the Substance-Related, Mood, Anxiety, Dissociative, Eating, and Borderline Personality Disorders. The most frequent diagnosis assigned to abuse victims is Posttraumatic Stress Disorder. While many dangerous and abusive individuals grew up in abusive families, the majority do not go on to abuse.

Assessment

Assessment of abuse in children should only be done by experienced clinicians. Interviewing a victim of abuse requires that you avoid asking leading questions and contaminating testimony that may be later involved in legal proceedings. This is of greatest importance when the victim is a child. If you have any unfamiliarity with this area, get immediate consultation while avoiding abandoning your client.

You may notice physical signs of abuse, or the client or a significant other may allude to it. Behaviors may be seen, such as significant weight loss, regressive behaviors (e.g., bed-wetting, clinging) or inappropriate sexually provocative behavior in a young child (see Testing Tip on the following page for typical test results).

Recommendations

Once you have ensured the safety of your client from further abuse, the following treatment recommendations may be appropriate.

- *Psychotherapy* (cognitive-behavioral, interpersonal, etc.) aimed at:
    Building a trusting relationship with others.
    Relating story and letting go of self-blame.
    Addressing regressive behaviors and irrational fears.

Decreasing negative affect, rage, depression, and anxiety.

Resolving shame and grief.

Increasing capacity for intimacy.

Identifying positive aspects in life and reestablishing hope.

Encouraging self-esteem and assertiveness-enhancing activity.

- Clarification of your *duty to protect,* reporting responsibilities, and legal implications.
- *Medical evaluation.*
- *Family therapy* focusing on communication and support. Identify familial patterns and decrease secrecy.
- Strengthening of social supports though *peer or survivors groups.*
- *For children and adolescents,* school contact to address school problems.
    Decisions regarding safety of client, if abuse is at home.
    Treatment for perpetrator, if in the family.
- *Monitoring of ongoing risk* for revictimization.
- *Potential referrals:* Physician, bibliotherapy, survivor support group, assertiveness training.

Testing Tip
Test Results Associated with Victims of Abuse

- On the WAIS-III/WISC-III, these clients may show a relatively good FIQ. A hypervigilant style and sensitivity to the social environment may result in elevated scores on Picture Completion, Picture Arrangement, or Comprehension. Secondary to underlying anxiety, depression, and distractibility, these clients may have difficulty on subtests measuring attention and concentration (Digit Span, Arithmetic, Digit Symbol-Coding/Coding).
- On the MMPI-2/MMPI-A, most likely elevations include Scales 2 (Depression) and 7 (Psychasthenia). Scales 1 (Hypochondriasis) and 8 (Schizophrenia) may be elevated if there are somatic or physical complaints and feelings of alienation and family discord.
- On the MCMI-III, elevations may appear on Scales A (Anxiety), 2B (Depressive), R (Posttraumatic), and D (Dysthymia). On the MACI, there may be elevations on Scales B (Self Devaluation), G (Family Discord), H (Childhood Abuse), and FF (Depressive Affect).
- On the Rorschach, these clients will have a low number of responses (R) reflecting depressive withdrawal. Unmet needs for nurturance may be reflected by higher Vista (V) and Texture (T) responses. There may also be sexual content.

Eating Disorders

ANOREXIA NERVOSA (307.1)

Essential Features

This disorder typically occurs in females, either in puberty or early adulthood. The primary symptom is a fear of becoming fat, resulting in severe weight loss and failure to make expected weight gains. These clients can appear overcontrolled, stubborn, and overly sensitive. In *DSM-IV*, amenorrhea is required for postmenarcheal women. Anorexia can be lethal, so a primary goal is always to ensure the client's health. At its worst, the client can appear as thin as a labor camp victim, while still acting carefree and energized. Appetite is usually not diminished until the client is severely ill; thus, the disease has much to do with issues of self-control. Depression is common in these clients. Family conflicts often play a role in the disorder, as does child abuse. Although the stereotypical Anorexia client has been described as a well-educated female from a middle-class background, it can also appear in others, such as male athletes who overexercise. The *DSM-IV* distinguishes two subtypes: Restricting and Binge-Eating/Purging.

Many clinicians feel that suicide and Eating Disorders are linked, in that the underlying anger directed at self and others, expressed as starvation, is a more controlled form of self-destruction.

Diagnosis

Testing of these clients is seldom needed for diagnosis, but can provide essential information on the client's character and family dynamics (see Testing Tip on page 202 for typical test results). Also consider evaluating for a Mood Disorder.

Older Adults

There is little information on this disorder in the elderly.

Children/Adolescents

On the MACI, elevations may occur on Scales C (Body Disapproval), H (Childhood Abuse), G (Family Discord), and AA (Eating Dysfunction).

Recommendations

If testing indicates a diagnosis of Anorexia, the following treatment recommendations may be appropriate.

- *Psychotherapy* (cognitive-behavioral, family systems) aimed at:
    Increasing weight and normalizing eating habits.
    Addressing issues of control and self-esteem.

> ### Testing Tip
> ### Test Results Associated with Anorexia
>
> - As expected with the obsessive characteristics of the disorder, clients with Anorexia can show a similar WAIS-III profile to OCD, with VIQ > PIQ (see OCD in Chapter 6 for further discussion). Clients with better education may sometimes show better scores on Vocabulary, Information, and Arithmetic.
> - On the MMPI-2 or MMPI-A, elevations on Scales 1 (Hypochondriasis) and 3 (Hysteria) with a low scale score on Scale 2 (Depression) may occur. The L (Lie) and K scales may be elevated. Alternatively, a 2-4-8 or 7-6-8 profile may occur.
> - On the MCMI-III, elevations may occur on Scales 7 (Compulsive), 3 (Dependent), 8A (Passive-Aggressive), and 1 (Schizoid).
> - On the Rorschach, there may be lower R, M, or C responses, with higher Dd, $F+\%$, and food-related content. The lower scores may be a result of evasiveness, passivity, depression, and an avoidance of emotion, whereas the higher scores reflect an overdependence on appearance and attention to small physical details.
> - On the Eating Disorder-Inventory-2 (EDI-2; Garner, 1991), a self-report assessment of symptoms consistent with eating disorders, elevations are likely to occur on the Drive for Thinness scale, Body Dissatisfaction scale, and Perfectionism scale.

Confronting body distortion and maladaptive food-related thoughts.

Addressing underlying issues contributing to maladaptive behavior.

Reducing use of laxatives and exercises.

- Decisions to treat *inpatient versus outpatient.*
- *Referral for medical evaluation* and nutritionist consultation.
- *Family therapy* aimed at systemic issues, boundaries, and individuation.
- *Medication* during depressed periods.
- Participation in *support groups* for parents and client.
- *Potential referrals:* Nutritionist, medical evaluation, support group.

BULIMIA NERVOSA (307.51)

Essential Features

This disorder typically occurs in females, either in late puberty or early adulthood. The primary symptom is periods of binge eating, followed by methods to avoid gaining weight (e.g., use of laxatives, vomiting). Bingeing usually occurs as a result of stress or from experiencing dysphoria. These clients try to keep bingeing a secret, and have deep shame associated with it. Depression is common. Family conflicts often play a role in the disorder. Bulimia most often occurs in well-educated females, from middle-class backgrounds.

Diagnosis

Typical test results for Bulimic clients are provided in the Testing Tip on the following page. Also consider evaluating for a concurrent Mood Disorder.

Older Adults

There is little information on this disorder in the elderly.

Children/Adolescents

On the MACI, elevations may occur on Scales C (Body Disapproval), H (Childhood Abuse), G (Family Discord), and AA (Eating Dysfunction).

Recommendations

If testing indicates a diagnosis of Bulimia, the following treatment recommendations may be appropriate.

- *Psychotherapy* (cognitive-behavioral, family systems) aimed at:
    Stabilizing eating habits and decreasing purging activities.
    Addressing issues of control and self-esteem.
    Confronting body distortion and maladaptive food-related thoughts.
    Developing alternative coping strategies.
    Addressing underlying issues contributing to maladaptive behavior.
    Reducing use of laxatives and bingeing.
- Decisions to treat *inpatient versus outpatient.*
- *Referral for medical evaluation* and nutritionist consultation.
- *Family therapy* aimed at systemic issues, boundaries, and individuation.
- *Medication* during depressed periods.
- Participation in *support groups* for parents and client.

Differential Diagnosis

INTERMITTENT EXPLOSIVE DISORDER VERSUS ANTISOCIAL
PERSONALITY DISORDER

Intermittent Explosive Disorder is characterized by discrete, aggressive episodes. Unlike Antisocial Personality Disorder, these clients do not demonstrate a

---

Testing Tip
Test Results Associated with Bulimia

- On the WAIS-III, there aren't specific test findings for Bulimia.
- On the MMPI-2, elevations on Scales 1 (Hypochondriasis) and 3 (Hysteria) with a low score on Scale 2 (Depression) may occur. There may also be a profile with elevations on Scales 8 (Schizophrenia), 2, and 4 (Psychopathic Deviate), or sometimes a 2-4-7-8 profile.
- There is not a specific profile on the MCMI-III.

---

long history of disregard for the rights of others. In contrast, the explosive episode is frequently followed by regret. The outbursts are usually precipitated by psychosocial stressors and are not characteristic of the person's normal behavior.

CHAPTER 10

Personality Disorders

Practical Considerations

PERSONALITY DISORDERS are considered long-standing, chronic, and pervasive patterns of behavior and perception that affect functioning and cause distress. In *DSM-IV*, they are coded on Axis II. Table 10.1 summarizes the key descriptive features of each disorder. Table 10.2 summarizes the key test findings associated with each disorder.

DIAGNOSING PERSONALITY DISORDERS

Personality Disorders are not easy to diagnose. First, clinicians seldom can spend enough time with a client to get a sense of personality pathology. Second, informant information can be biased. Third, some personality questionnaires tend to overpathologize. Fourth, *DSM-IV* diagnostic criteria have considerable overlap. Thus, clinicians are often left wondering if there is Axis II pathology and what it is.

A CAVEAT

When a client meets criteria for both a Personality Disorder and an Axis I disorder, be sure to determine from historical information that the client's personality pathology was present before the Axis I disorder. Otherwise, you may incorrectly diagnose a Personality Disorder.

Personality Disorders are serious diagnoses. Claiming that someone is narcissistic or compulsive can create considerable distress or harm if that information is disclosed to the client and family, other medical providers, or employers.

TABLE 10.1
Key Descriptive Features of Personality Disorders

Disorder/Syndrome	Behavioral	Emotional	Interpersonal
Paranoid	Challenging, suspicious, mistrustful	Irritable, angry	Demanding, narcissistic, oppositional
Schizoid	Shy, poor social skills; desire for solitude	Withdrawn, detached	Uninterested; loner, solitary, friendless
Schizotypal	Odd, peculiar, eccentric	Magical thinking, superstitious; strange emotion	Socially anxious, socially immature, odd
Antisocial	Amoral, criminal behavior; impulsiveness	Superficial; repressed rage	Manipulative, narcissistic
Borderline	Impulsiveness; idealization; unstability; lability	Poor affect regulation, depression, anger	Idealization/devaluation, splitting
Histrionic	Theatrical, concerned with appearance	Overemotional	Attention seeking, insensitive to others
Narcissistic	Gradiosity; difficulty with criticism	Low empathy; low self-esteem	Superficial relationships, entitled
Avoidant	Poor social skills, withdrawn	Anxious, depressed, sad	Socially anxious, avoids social situations
Dependent	Clingy, fearful of solitude; fearful of independence; indecisive	Low self-esteem; passivity, anxiety, depression	Passive, complacent, lacks initiative
Obsessive-Compulsive	Rigid, slow; poor task management; perfectionistic	Indecisive; emotionally restricted	Rigid, litigious, controlling

In general, Personality Disorders are considered long-standing and untreatable. In reality, some of these disorders are amenable to psychotherapy, as will be discussed. Yet, many clinicians tend not to diagnose a Personality Disorder unless the circumstances are undeniable, or more harm would occur if the diagnosis wasn't recorded. Clinicians should weigh their options carefully whenever considering this diagnostic category.

IDENTIFYING PERSONALITY PATHOLOGY IS IMPORTANT

Identifying personality pathology can be useful when the client's behavior is not due to an Axis I disorder. For example, a client who is hospitalized for medical reasons and is "driving the staff berserk" may be treated more appropriately once personality symptoms are described under the framework of a diagnosis. A Personality Disorder may affect a client's ability to conform to treatment recommendations. In addition, being able to describe the personality style of a client can be remarkably helpful to the referral source.

TABLE 10.2
Key Test Findings for Personality Disorders

Disorder/ Syndrome	WAIS-III/WISC-III	MMPI-2/ MMPI-A	MCMI-III	Rorschach
Paranoid	Frustration with testing, overinclusion	Elevations: K, 1, 3, 6 (high or low)	6B, 6A, P	Higher *D*, Lambda, Animal, *P*
		Profiles: 4-8, 6-8, 1-3-8		Lower color, *HVI*
Schizoid	No specific findings	Elevations: 0	1	Higher animal content
		Profiles: 1-8, 4-8, 6-8		Fewer color, human content
Schizotypal	Peculiar responses may occur on Comprehension or Picture Arrangement	Profiles: 2-7-8, 7-8	2, S, 1, 8A, 8B	Higher animal content
				Fewer color, human content
				More special scores
Antisocial	VIQ < PIQ	Elevations: 4, 9, 2, 8	5, 6A, 6B	Higher Lambda, C, *P*
	Impulsive problem solving	Profiles: 4-8, 4-9	Sometimes: B, T, PP, P	Lower M
Borderline	May show signs of anxiety, frustration	Elevations: 2, 4, 8	C	Relative to other tests will show more pathology
	May show higher Picture Completion, Picture Arrangement, Comprehension due to social sensitivity	Profiles: 2-4-6-8	Sometimes: A, H, D, N, B, T, 8A, 8B, 2	*F+% > X+%*
		Check MAC-R		
Histrionic	May show a greater emotional response when making errors	Elevations: 2, 3, 4, 9	4, N, S	No specific findings
	May require structure to refrain from unnecessary talking	Profiles: 1-3, 3-4		
Narcissistic	May minimize significance of errors	Elevations: 4, 9	5	Poor form quality possible
	May maximize good performance	Profiles: 4-9, 3-6		Increased C, R, (2)
Avoidant	No specific findings, may see test anxiety	Elevations: 2, 7	2A	Increased *P*, inactive M, animal content
		Profiles: 6-7, 3-4	Sometimes: D, A, 8B, C	
Dependent	No specific findings, but may appear similar to depression	Elevations: 2, 3, 7, L, K	7, H, 3, P	Usually low R
		Profile: 7-8		Increased P, inactive M, animal content, *Dd*
		Low scores: 5, 4, 9		
Obsessive-Compulsive	VIQ > PIQ	Elevations: K, 3, 1, 9, 6, 7	7, H, 3, P	Increased R, D, Dd, F+%
	Subtests: Higher scores on Similarities, Vocabulary, Comprehension			Fewer W, color responses
	Lower scores on Digit Symbol-Coding, Block Design, Symbol Search			

> **Testing Tip**
> **Assessing Personality Pathology**
> _____
>
> 1. Observe the client's test-taking attitude.
> 2. Ask questions to elicit opinions about current events.
> 3. Challenge the client's opinions to see what type of reaction occurs.
> 4. Ask how others described the client in high school and college.
> 5. Ask client to describe relationships with others.
> 6. Administer MMPI-2, MCMI-III, or Rorschach.

ASSIGNING PERSONALITY DISORDERS TO CHILDREN AND ADOLESCENTS

Personality Disorders are considered long-standing characterological aspects of pathology. Thus, a diagnosis in children should not be done unless there is a long-term basis for the disorder, and there lacks a more appropriate Axis I disorder that could account for the symptoms.

Personality Disorder Summary

The *DSM-IV* organizes these disorders into three clusters (A, B, and C), based on similarities in symptoms. Clients with Cluster A disorders seem odd or eccentric. Cluster B clients appear dramatic or emotional. Cluster C patients present as worried or fearful.

Cluster A: Paranoid, Schizoid, Schizotypal

PARANOID (SUSPICIOUS/MISTRUSTFUL/MORALISTIC/SUPERIOR) 301.00

Essential Features

These clients are suspicious, mistrustful, and see others as inferior. Their mistrust is undeniable and is not accompanied by more pervasive symptoms such as psychosis. For example, they might read hidden meaning into benign remarks and avoid confiding in others. In some cases, the predominant symptoms are frustration and irritability from having to endure in a hostile and untrustworthy environment. Prevalence rates in clinic settings average around 18% (Livesley,

1995), but these clients seldom seek clinical help, unless their support system breaks down. Paranoid personality can overlap with other Personality Disorders, too, most likely Schizotypal Personality Disorder. Paranoid clients can appear somewhat narcissistic, but mistrust is the predominant feature.

Diagnosis

These clients tend to show obvious mistrust and irritation with assessment, sometimes at the point where a consent form is being signed. Rule out psychotic disorders and mania (see Testing Tip below for typical test results).

Older Adults

Paranoia is a common symptom in older adults, and should not be misdiagnosed as Paranoid Personality Disorder. A good psychiatric history should help to identify the nature of the symptoms. Consider the possibility of dementia.

SCHIZOID (SHY/WITHDRAWN/EMOTIONALLY UNATTACHED/ LONER) 301.20

Essential Features

These clients appear as shy and emotionally withdrawn. They tend to avoid social contacts and lack interpersonal skills. Their careers usually end up being ones that keep them away from others. Consequently, they can appear as unemotional

---

Testing Tip
Test Results Associated with Paranoid Personality Disorder

- On the WAIS-III, clients with Paranoid Personality Disorder may be distinguished by their frustration over not being told the answers to test questions, resulting in oppositional behavior. Errors of overinclusion may occur.
- On the MMPI-2, elevations can occur on Scales K, 1, 3, or 6, with 4-8, 6-8, or 1-3-8 profiles possible. Some clients with severe Paranoia will show significantly low scores on Scale 6, due to not wanting to admit suspiciousness of any kind.
- On the MCMI-III, significant elevations may appear on Scale 6B (Aggressive), 6A (Antisocial), or PP (Paranoid).
- On the Rorschach, these clients may appear resentful to the ambiguousness of the task. They are prone to give more D, Animal, and popular responses, have higher Lambda, and have few color responses. The *HVI* (Hypervigilance) Index may be positive.

> **Testing Tip**
> **Test Results Associated with Schizoid Personality Disorder**
>
> - On the WAIS-III, there aren't specific test findings that distinguish this disorder.
> - On the MMPI-2, elevations may occur on Scale 0 (Social Introversion), with 1-8, 4-8, or 6-8 profiles possible.
> - On the MCMI-III, elevations on Scale 1 (Schizoid) are most likely.
> - On the Rorschach, there are more likely to be fewer Color and human responses. Animal responses are more common.

as the mythical Vulcan. Prevalence rates in clinic settings average around 11% (Livesley, 1995), so they, too, are not seen very often. Unlike Avoidant Personality Disorder, they do not desire intimacy or fear social rejection. Rather, they tend to be impersonal, with almost no friends or sexual relationships. Unlike Schizotypal Personality Disorder, these clients do not have disturbances in their communication, or exhibit odd behavior. Yet, it is easy for a client with residual Schizophrenia or with Schizotypal Personality Disorder to appear to be a Schizoid Personality.

Diagnosis

Schizoid Personality clients appear cooperative, though reserved when being assessed. Rule out residual Schizophrenia (see Testing Tip above for typical test results).

SCHIZOTYPAL (ODD/SOCIALLY ANXIOUS/ECCENTRIC) 301.22

Essential Features

Schizotypal clients are considered an odder version of schizoid clients. In fact, Schizotypal Personality Disorder is genetically associated to Schizophrenia, and some researchers believe that it is a precursor to Schizophrenia (Mednick et al., 1987). Schizotypal Personality Disorder clients are more likely to have first-degree relatives with Schizophrenia.

These clients are behaviorally eccentric, socially awkward, and anxious; they may exhibit magical thinking or participate in strange organizations. They show more emotion than schizoid clients, but it can appear inappropriate and strange. Make sure to rule out an Axis I disorder prior to diagnosing Schizotypal Personality. They are not commonly seen for assessments.

Testing Tip
Test Results Associated with Schizotypal Personality Disorder

- On the WAIS-III, peculiar responses may occur on Comprehension or Picture Arrangement.
- On the MMPI-2, a 2-7-8 or 7-8 profile may occur.
- On the MCMI-III, elevations may occur on Scale 2 (Avoidant), S (Schizotypal), 1 (Schizoid), 8A (Passive-Aggressive), or 8B (Self-Defeating).
- On the Rorschach, there are more likely to be fewer Color and human responses. Animal content is more common, and there may be higher scores on the special scores items. The responses may appear more like that of Schizophrenia.

Diagnosis

Schizotypal clients can appear as initially cooperative, but odd. They may have a strange career history, and show peculiar affect. Rule out psychotic disorders (see Testing Tip above for typical test results).

Children/Adolescents

Precursors of Schizotypal Personality Disorder have been found in children (Olin et al., 1997).

Cluster B: Antisocial, Borderline, Histrionic, Narcissistic

ANTISOCIAL (AMORAL/IMPULSIVE BEHAVIOR/NARCISSISTIC) 301.9

Essential Features

Clients with Antisocial Personality Disorder, also called psychopaths or sociopaths, are disinhibited and lack a clear sense of conscience. In *DSM-IV*, a previous diagnosis of Conduct Disorder is required. These clients seek excitement and sensation, and do not care or feel remorse for their illegal, morally wrong, or hurtful behaviors. They can be irritable and aggressive interpersonally. They do not learn from experience when punished. The behavior pattern usually begins in childhood and is more frequent in males. In outpatient settings, these clients tend to appear as more manipulative, rather than like stereotypical criminals.

> ### Testing Tip
> ### Test Results Associated with Antisocial Personality Disorder
>
> - On the WAIS-III, clients with this disorder may show lower VIQ due to poor academic achievement. They have a tendency to solve problems impulsively with little reflection.
> - On the MMPI-2, significant elevations are most likely on Scales 4 (Psychopathic Deviate), 9 (Hypomania), 8 (Schizophrenia), and/or 2 (Depression), with a 4-8 or 4-9 profile possible.
> - On the MCMI-III, significant elevations may occur on Scales 5 (Narcissistic), 6A (Antisocial), and 6B (Aggressive), and possibly also B (Alcohol Dependence), T (Drug Dependence), PP (Delusional Disorder), or P (Paranoid).
> - On the Rorschach, there are more likely to be higher Lambda, C, P, and lower M responses.
> - The Psychopathy Check List-Revised (Hare, 1995), an interview rating scale, can assist in determining whether the client has Antisocial Personality Disorder.

Diagnosis

Typical test results of Antisocial clients on each of the major tests are provided in the Testing Tip above.

Children/Adolescents

This diagnosis cannot be made in clients under 18 years of age.

BORDERLINE (FEAR OF ABANDONMENT/IMPULSIVITY/
INSTABILITY) 301.83

These clients feel emotionally empty, have a very poor self-concept, and have difficulty regulating their emotions and behaviors. This is believed to be due to early chaotic or traumatic experiences, usually in the family. Their perception of the world is frequently distorted. Emotions can become wildly erratic and feel uncontrollable. Intense anger, anxiety, or depression can appear, but is usually transient. They are prone to form intense personal relationships, hoping others will fill their emptiness, but the desire for dependency conflicts with the need for independence. Because they have trouble seeing the complexity of life, these clients tend to use splitting as a defense mechanism (seeing things in black and white). They also have trouble knowing what limits are appropriate, and more than any other clients, are likely to ask personal questions or call you over trivial matters.

Higher functioning clients can appear emotionally healthy, having limited awareness that their perceptions and reactions are inappropriate. Thus, when seen for an evaluation, the primary symptoms may be anxiety or depression. Borderline Personalities are more likely than others to be suicidal. Clients with more severe forms of the disorder may be hospitalized multiple times, and have a high suicide completion rate.

Diagnosis

The Testing Tip below provides typical test results of Borderline clients on each of the major tests.

Children/Adolescents

There is some research suggesting that Borderline Personality may co-occur with Conduct Disorder in males. Diagnosis of this disorder in childhood is rare and does not predict its occurrence in adulthood. In addition, because this disorder is associated with trauma and abuse, making an assessment of abuse is important when Borderline Personality Disorder is being considered for an adolescent.

Testing Tip
Test Results Associated with Borderline Personality Disorder

- Answers on structured psychological measures (e.g., WAIS-III) may be normal, but in more severe clients, bizarre and sometimes psychotic responses may occur on unstructured tests such as the Rorschach.
- On the WAIS-III, Borderline Personality Disorder clients appear relatively normal, though anxiety over testing may occur. They may show frustration and a haphazard, trial-and-error response style to more difficult items, especially on performance subtests. Some clients may show added social sensitivity reflected in Picture Completion, Picture Arrangement, and Comprehension.
- On the MMPI-2, significant elevations on Scales 8 (Schizophrenia), 2 (Depression), 4 (Psychopathic Deviate), or sometimes a 2-4-6-8 profile. Also check the MAC-R Scale.
- On the MCMI-III, elevations on Scale C (Borderline), and possibly Scales A (Anxiety), H (Somatoform), R (PTSD), D (Dysthymia), N (Bipolar: Manic), 8A (Passive-Aggressive), 8B (Self-Defeating), and 2B (Depressive) may occur. Substance use may lead to elevated B or T.
- On the Rorschach, interpretation is based on finding relatively higher levels of pathology compared with other clinical scales. In particular, $F+\%$ may be greater than $X+\%$. Some clients show higher C, (2), and T responses.

HISTRIONIC (OVEREMOTIONAL/THEATRICAL/LOW INSIGHT) 301.50

Essential Features

Histrionic clients are seen more commonly in clinical settings, likely due to their attention-seeking and perceived environmental stressors. At their worst, they show little insight into their problems, are shallow and theatrical, and are entirely concerned with their appearance. Although they appear somewhat narcissistic, the predominant feature is theatricality. When they have empathy, it is very superficial. What is more commonly seen in clinic settings are clients with histrionic features who retain a certain degree of insight, but nevertheless seem to overreact to stress. They can burst into tears or anger, and enjoy having attention, but are not grandly hysterical. This disorder is found predominately in females.

Diagnosis

Histrionic clients overreact to failures on testing. Rule out psychotic disorders (see Testing Tip below for typical test results).

NARCISSISTIC (GRANDIOSITY/LACK OF EMPATHY/ENTITLED) 301.81

Essential Features

These clients show unrealistic self-importance, an inability to hear criticism, little empathy, are often exploitative, and feel bored. For example, these clients might ask to use your phone to make a long-distance call, and then act haughty when you set limits. In psychodynamic terms, these clients are thought to have low self-esteem, which results in a personality style that blocks

---

Testing Tip
Test Results Associated with Histrionic Personality Disorder

- On the WAIS-III, responses to negative performance are more common, and sometimes these clients need structure not to talk during the testing.
- On the MMPI-2, elevations may occur on Scales 2 (Depression), 3 (Hysteria), 4 (Psychopathic Deviate), or 9 (Hypomania), with 1-3, or 3-4 profiles possible.
- On the MCMI-III, significant elevation on Scales 4 (Histrionic), N (Bipolar: Manic), or S (Schizotypal) may occur.

Testing Tip
Test Results Associated with Narcissistic Personality Disorder

---

- On the WAIS-III, these clients are likely to comment on their strengths during the assessment. When they make errors, they will minimize them, perhaps suggesting that they were guessing. Some will want to know how they are performing.
- On the MMPI-2, elevations on Scales 4 (Psychopathic Deviate) and 9 (Hypomania), with 4-9 or 3-6 profiles are possible. Scale 0 (Social Introversion) is usually low.
- On the MCMI-III significant elevations on Scale 5 (Narcissistic) may occur.
- On the Rorschach, poor form quality may occur, with increased C responses, more responses (R), or more pairs ((2)).

---

feelings of inadequacy. Their relationships are usually very superficial. Clients with Narcissistic personalities should be distinguished from individuals with a healthy amount of narcissism (indicating a modicum of self-confidence).

Diagnosis

They are likely to comment on any mistakes made by the examiner. A good sign of narcissism is when the examiner is feeling his or her own shortcomings. Also look for more personalized responses, for example, providing unnecessary anecdotal details to WAIS-III information items (see Testing Tip above for typical test results).

Cluster C: Avoidant, Dependent, Obsessive-Compulsive

AVOIDANT (HYPERSENSITIVITY TO REJECTION/SOCIAL WITHDRAWAL/LOW SELF-ESTEEM) 301.82

Essential Features

These clients appear as shy and introverted, yet they wish for social support and affection. They avoid social situations because of fear of rejection, humiliation, or shame. When socially involved, it is with passive, uncritical people. They avoid taking risks in many circumstances, in addition to social or occupational settings. They blame themselves for their awkwardness. They may have specific social phobias.

Testing Tip
Test Results Associated with Avoidant Personality Disorder

- On the WAIS-III, there are not specific findings that coincide with this disorder, though anxiety may occur during testing.
- On the MMPI-2, significant elevations may occur on Scales 2 (Depression), 7 (Psychasthenia), 0 (Social Introversion) and 6-7 and 3-4 profiles are possible.
- On the MCMI-III, elevations may occur on Scale 2A (Avoidant), and possibly D (Dysthymia), A (Anxiety), 8B (Self-Defeating), or C (Borderline).
- On the Rorschach, Popular, Animal content, and passive M responses may occur.

Diagnosis

The Testing Tip above provides typical test results of Avoidant clients on each of the major tests.

DEPENDENT (CLINGY/FEAR OF SELF-CARE/ UNCOMFORTABLE ALONE) 301.6

Essential Features

Clients with Dependent Personality Disorder have total dependency. They strongly fear autonomy; they want others to make decisions. Clinginess occurs when threatened with separation, and their own desires are withheld if they fear that expressing them will hurt a relationship. Their low self-esteem leads to fearing that they won't be able to take care of themselves. They have poor motivation, and may appear overly "nice." Dependent Personality is more common in women. Anxiety or depression are common when the person is single.

Diagnosis

The Testing Tip at the top of page 217 provides typical test results of Dependent clients on each of the major tests.

OBSESSIVE-COMPULSIVE (RIGID/PERFECTIONISTIC/ MORALLY INFLEXIBLE) 301.4

Essential Features

Clients with Obsessive-Compulsive Personality Disorder are overly concerned with detail, organization, and control, to the point where it interferes with

---

Testing Tip
Test Results Associated with Dependent Personality Disorder

- On the WAIS-III, there are not specific findings for this disorder though clients with depression may show results consistent with those of Mood Disorder.
- On the MMPI-2, elevations may occur on Scales 2 (Depression), 7 (Psychasthenia), 3 (Hysteria), L, and K, with a 7-8 profile possible. Low scores on Scales 5 (Masculinity-Femininity), 4 (Psychopathic Deviate), and 9 (Hypomania) may occur, too.
- On the MCMI-III, elevations on Scale 3 (Dependent), A (Anxiety), H (Somatoform), D (Dysthymia), 2A (Avoidant), or 4 (Histrionic) may occur.
- On the Rorschach, responses are dependent on the client's comfort. A comfortable client may produce a large number of responses, but usually fewer than average responses will occur. Increased passive M, animal, Popular, and *Dd* responses can occur.

---

completing a task. They can be distant, insensitive, litigious, moralistic, perfectionistic, and hyperalert to criticism. They tend to hoard objects or money. They find these qualities ego-syntonic and rarely seek help (unlike clients with OCD). The disorder is more common in males.

Diagnosis

These clients present with fairly normal profiles on most personality tests; they do not freely self-disclose. They may express psychological disturbance through somatic symptoms. Unlike clients with OCD, they do not have a specific obsession or compulsive behavior (see Testing Tip on page 218 for typical test results).

Treatment Recommendations

GENERAL RECOMMENDATIONS

If testing indicates a diagnosis of Personality Disorder, the following treatment recommendations may be appropriate.

- *Individual psychotherapy* (cognitive/behavioral, insight oriented) aimed at:

    Building a trusting therapeutic relationship.

    Developing insight into maladaptive patterns of behavior.

Testing Tip
Test Results Associated with
Obsessive-Compulsive Personality Disorder

- On the WAIS-III, these clients tend to appear bright, with a detailed and overly precise response style that can lead to lower scores on speed-based subtests (see OCD for a discussion of findings), but more two-point scores on Verbal Subtests. VIQ is generally higher than PIQ.
- On the MMPI-2, elevations may occur on Scales K, 3 (Hysteria), 1 (Hypochondriasis), 9 (Hypomania), 6 (Paranoia), and 7 (Psychasthenia).
- On the MCMI-III, elevations may occur on Scales 7 (Compulsive), H (Somatoform), 3 (Histrionic), and P (Paranoid).
- On the Rorschach, protocols may include many D and Dd responses, with a high F+% and fewer W and Color responses. They may criticize the blots, describe their responses in great detail, and give a high number of responses.

Challenging underlying beliefs about self and relationships with others.

- *Couples or family therapy.*

SPECIFIC RECOMMENDATIONS

- *Paranoid.* Initially, accept the client's mistrust, and focus on less sensitive issues. Help clients test their beliefs and develop more effective ways of behaving.
- *Schizoid.* Help identify positive emotions. Build interpersonal skills to improve occupational functioning.
- *Schizotypal.* Address interpersonal isolation and potential psychotic signs. Help to develop more mature social behavior.
- *Histrionic.* Emphasize appropriate assertiveness. Avoid "rescuing" and treating as "special."
- *Narcissistic.* Clarify the limits and boundaries of therapy. Be alert for manipulations, underlying maladaptive patterns, and countertransference.
- *Antisocial.* Be alert for deception, resistance, and competitiveness. Reduce existing stimulus-seeking behavior.

- *Borderline.* Establish sense of identity, strengthen emotional and behavioral controls. Address crisis management and dichotomous thinking.
- *Avoidant.* Emphasize social skills building and assertiveness training.
- *Dependent.* Reinforce independence skills and assertiveness. Set limits on therapeutic relationship.
- *Obsessive-Compulsive.* Initially, provide consistent support. Covert conditioning and paradoxical intention may be useful.

Differential Diagnosis

Several of the most frequent or prominent differential diagnosis are discussed.

SCHIZOID VERSUS AVOIDANT

Both of these disorders involve people who are socially withdrawn. The key difference between these disorders is that the Schizoid client is unemotional and doesn't desire contact with others, whereas the Avoidant client wishes it.

PARANOID VERSUS NARCISSISTIC VERSUS OBSESSIVE-COMPULSIVE VERSUS HISTRIONIC

Paranoid, Narcissistic, Obsessive-Compulsive, and Histrionic clients all share narcissism, and an exaggerated sense of self-importance. However, clients who are Paranoid show mistrust as a primary feature, whereas Obsessive-Compulsive clients show a rigid and obsessive way of behaving. Histrionic clients, although narcissistic, are relatively more overemotional and dramatic.

PARANOID PERSONALITY DISORDER VERSUS SCHIZOPHRENIA

This is also discussed in Chapter 8. Briefly, clients with Schizophrenia show more marked symptoms, have a lower level of function, and are usually less irritable than clients with Paranoid Personality.

OCD VERSUS OBSESSIVE-COMPULSIVE PERSONALITY

This is discussed in the Differential Diagnosis section in Chapter 6.

CHAPTER 11

Cognitive Function from a Developmental Perspective: From Learning Disorders to Dementia Screenings

Why These Disorders Are Grouped Together

COGNITIVE FUNCTION is often determined as part of an assessment, but for some disorders, it takes primary focus. For children, cognitive function is important when there is a question of Mental Retardation or a Learning Disorder. For adults and older adults, cognitive function can be important when there is the question of a dementia or cognitive deficits associated with substance abuse. Taking a developmental approach, the disorders contained in this chapter include *DSM-IV* sections on Mental Retardation, Learning Disorders, and Dementia.

Consider the Underlying Factors Leading to the Disorder

Cognitive disorders are very descriptively defined. A client with Mathematics Disorder, for example, has difficulty with math. Cognitive testing is helpful because it can identify underlying problems that contribute to the disorder. Testing might identify whether the problem is due to math skills, visual-spatial processing, calculation abilities, attention, anxiety, depression, working memory, or motivation. Finding the underlying problem results in better and more specific treatment.

Advanced Cognitive Assessments: A Primer of Key Concepts

The ability to make sophisticated conclusions about a client's cognitive functioning requires knowledge of the numerous domains tapped by cognitive tests.

Many times, you need to be able to explain why Verbal IQ is greater than Performance IQ. Most cognitive tests and subtests measure multiple domains simultaneously, forcing you to deduce the most reasonable explanation that accounts for the client's pattern of performance. Some of the key dimensions tapped by cognitive tests are described in this section. Review these to help you identify possible explanations for your client's pattern of performance. Where appropriate, we also mention additional tests that you may want to consider administering. Their availability is described in Appendix A. Table 11.1 (on page 222) summarizes the relationship between cognitive function and specific tests.

LATERALITY

Many cognitive functions are localized to specific regions of the brain, which are the same for just about everyone except for a minority of left-handed persons. For the most part, the left hemisphere involves verbal abilities, whereas the right hemisphere involves nonverbal abilities. This distinction becomes relevant when a client's weaknesses seem to be localized.

For example, a client who shows poor performance in learning a list of words may have no trouble learning a list of symbols. Knowing that the client has a differential ability on two tests of memory suggests that the client's verbal performance could be due to left hemisphere neurocognitive deficits (as well as due to a lack of language skills, verbal attentional abilities, or poor hearing).

ATTENTION

Poor attention can reduce scores on almost every test in a cognitive assessment. Thus, you must rule out attentional problems before concluding that other deficits exist. Attention can be assessed using Digit Span, Spatial Span, Letter-Number Sequencing, and Arithmetic; they also capture processing (working memory) to some degree.

Global deficits in attention can be due to depression, dementia, medication interactions, anxiety, poor motivation, or sensory deficits. Yet, differences between attentional measures might be due to several factors, all of which have important treatment implications. First, problems with processing might lead to low digits backward or Arithmetic performance with intact function on the easier digits forward. Second, a problem in calculation ability or scholastic achievement might be seen with poor Arithmetic performance but good Letter-Number Sequencing or Digit Span. Third, differences between verbal and visual processing might lead to differences between Digit Span and Spatial Span. Fourth, shorter attention span might result in low scores on all the measures. Attention span increases throughout childhood and decreases slowly throughout adulthood.

TABLE 11.1
Specific Cognitive Areas and Tests That Measure Them

Cognitive Area	Tests
Attention	Digit Span, Spatial Span, Letter-Number Sequencing, Arithmetic
Attention to Detail	Picture Completion, Picture Arrangement, Matrix Reasoning, Rey Complex Figure Test
Executive Function	
Applied Social Judgment	Picture Arrangement
Initiation/Perseveration	Spatial Span, Matrix Reasoning, Wisconsin Card Sorting Test, Block Design
Planning and Sequencing	Picture Arrangement, Block Design, Matrix Reasoning, Color Trails 2
Shifting Set/Flexibility in Thinking	Block Design, Matrix Reasoning, Color Trails Test, Controlled Oral Word Association Test, Ruff Figural Fluency Test, Wisconsin Card Sorting Test, Color Trails 2
Fund of Knowledge	Information, Comprehension Vocabulary
Language Function	Boston Naming Test, Vocabulary, Information, Comprehension, Token Test for Children, Peabody Picture Vocabulary Test-III, Expressive One-Word Picture Vocabulary Test
Psychomotor Speed	Digit Symbol-Coding, Color Trails 1, Symbol Search
Praxis/Visual-Motor Ability	Digit Symbol-Coding, Visual Reproduction, Picture Arrangement, Block Design, Rey Complex Figure Test, Developmental Test of Visual-Motor Integration
Visuospatial Organization	Rey Complex Figure Test, Matrix Reasoning, Block Design, Picture Completion
Memory	Wechsler Memory Scale-III, Wide Range Assessment of Memory and Learning, Children's Memory Scale

Attention to Detail

Tests like Picture Completion, Matrix Reasoning, Picture Arrangement, and the Rey Complex Figure Test (Meyers & Meyers, 1995) all tap the client's ability to attend to visual details and discern relevant from irrelevant information.

EXECUTIVE FUNCTION

Executive function broadly embraces the domains of judgment, abstract think-ing, reasoning, planning, conceptualization, problem solving, and motivation. Deficits in these areas are common in Alzheimer's disease, Parkinson's disease, Vascular Dementia, chronic substance use, as well as in ADHD and Learning Disorders. Many tests that are sensitive to executive function tap other domains. The following areas are often considered aspects of executive function.

Applied Social Judgment

Sometimes impairment in one's judgment occurs despite having the necessary knowledge. Thus, you may see a low score on Picture Arrangement, but a high score on Comprehension. Yet, differences on these tests alone could be due to a lack of visual-spatial ability. Thus, it would be important to find corroborating evidence from outside the testing situation to substantiate this conclusion.

Behavioral Disinhibition

This is the tendency to be unable to contain one's actions or statements, or feel-ings. Some mildly brain-injured clients might demonstrate this when they are no longer able to curb spending habits. While some disinhibition in children is age appropriate, it is more commonly seen in ADHD (e.g., talking out of turn, an-swering questions prematurely). Disinhibition is usually noted from test behavior.

Initiation/Perseveration

Both of these domains reflect the client's flexibility in thinking. Initiation is the ability to commence a new task, and it can appear visually or verbally specific. Deficits in initiation might appear on WMS-III Spatial Span when the patient is unable to start copying your hand movements. Perseveration, on the other hand occurs when the client cannot stop doing the same thing, even when it is no longer correct. Perseveration can appear on the WAIS-III when the client keeps giving the same answer to multiple questions, or repeatedly using the wrong strat-egy to do Block Design or Matrix Reasoning items. The Wisconsin Card Sorting Test (Heaton, Chelune, Talley, Kay, & Curtiss, 1993) and Color Trails 2 (D'Elia, Satz, Uchiyama, & White, 1996) also measure perseveration.

Planning and Sequencing

Reasoning includes the ability to organize and apply information meaningfully, and deficits may be verbally or visually specific. Careful observation of the client's cognitive style can tell you a lot. For example, deficits on Picture Arrangement and Block Design might be due to poor planning. A client who incorrectly and hastily arranges the cards on Picture Arrangement has a different problem than a client who organizes them based on an irrelevant visual detail. Keep in mind, however, that visuospatial deficits might also decrease performance. You can rule this out by examining copy responses to Visual Reproduction on the WMS-III. Some Matrix Reasoning items tap sequencing as does the Color Trails Test.

Shifting Set/Flexibility in Thinking

Flexibility in thinking reflects executive functioning. This can be seen on Block Design, when the client is unable to master the concept of using multicolored sides to solve the latter items, or on Matrix Reasoning when the client incorrectly continues to use the same strategy to solve each item. Color Trails Test 2 is quite sensitive to the ability to shift sets.

These areas are also assessed with tests of verbal and visual fluency. Verbal fluency usually is assessed with the Controlled Oral Word Association Test (Benton & Hamsher, 1994), which asks the client to name as many words as possible starting with a specific letter of the alphabet. For visual fluency, the Ruff Figural Fluency Test (Ruff, 1996) is available.

FUND OF KNOWLEDGE

This is an assessment of the client's retention of learned information, and is usually captured by Information, and to a lesser degree Comprehension and Vocabulary. Impairment might be due to lack of schooling or to a loss of information associated with a dementia.

LANGUAGE FUNCTION

The centers in the brain that regulate speech are separate. One area focuses on the articulation of speech, while the other focuses on comprehension. *Expressive Aphasia* is difficulty in the expression of speech. *Circumlocution*, which is a component of expressive aphasia, is noted when the client uses general words instead of a specific one (e.g., "the thing you use to clean your teeth" instead of "toothbrush"). More pronounced aphasia leads to words missing from speech, or the misuse of words. Aphasia can be caused by stroke, dementia, or sedating medications. The Boston Naming Test (Kaplan, Goodglass, & Weintraub, 1983) is a good measure of naming ability. Expressive aphasia often lowers test scores that require verbal expression, particularly Vocabulary, Information, and Comprehension. To test for developmentally appropriate speech in children, consider using the Expressive One-Word Picture Vocabulary Test (Brownell, 1983; Gardner, 1990).

Receptive Aphasia is difficulty in comprehension of speech. A client with receptive aphasia may be able to read a newspaper aloud and have no idea what it means. This domain is assessed by giving the client a set of commands and seeing if they are performed correctly. A clue to receptive comprehension problems is noticing that you are slowing down your speech to be understood. Specific tests of receptive speech are the Peabody Picture Vocabulary Test-III (Dunn, Dunn, & Williams, 1997) and the Token Test for Children (Mecham, 1989).

PSYCHOMOTOR SPEED

Does the client do motor tasks more slowly? Slowed performance on Digit Symbol-Coding or Color Trails 1 is a good indicator. When the client does poorly on both Symbol Search and Digit Symbol, this may suggest a problem in intellectual processing speed, rather than with psychomotor speed. Block Design taps this ability, but to a smaller extent. Lower psychomotor speed may also be due to depression, medication side effects, or lack of motivation.

PRAXIS/VISUAL-MOTOR ABILITY

Praxis is a synonym for movement, and includes the ability to do sophisticated motor tasks. Praxis is assessed by Digit Symbol-Coding, as well as in part by Visual Reproduction, Picture Arrangement, Block Design, Color Trails, and the Rey Complex Figure Test. Children (3–18 years) can be given the Developmental Test of Visual-Motor Integration (Beery & Buktenica, 1997). Problems in praxis can have multiple causes, including fatigue, visuospatial difficulties, or depression.

VISUOSPATIAL ORGANIZATION

Visuospatial organization involves the skills that enable us to drive, and to organize information visually (e.g., our desktops). Often the tests involve visual puzzles. Matrix Reasoning, Block Design, and Picture Completion require being able to understand and deduce visuospatial concepts. The Complex Figure Test requires the client to be able to demonstrate visuo-organizational skill by being able to copy a complex image.

MEMORY

Memory involves the acquisition, retention, and retrieval of information. Acquisition is the ability to attend to and learn the information. Retention is the ability to store it over time. Retrieval is the ability to recall the information from memory when asked to do so. A client who cannot recall a list of words, but can recognize the words when they are read, shows a deficit in retrieval. A client who cannot recall or recognize information shows deficits in acquisition and also possibly in retention.

Verbal versus Visual Memory Performance

Memory can be assessed with both verbal and nonverbal methods, and many clients show differences between these areas. In addition, because memory usually involves other intellectual processes that aid in recall, some tests attempt to be more like everyday tasks. In principle, differences between verbal and visual memory performance are due to differential abilities in learning verbal information compared with visual information. However, there are many potential confounds to consider, including education and visual acuity that can account for the discrepancy. In addition, verbal subtests are more susceptible to cultural biases.

Differences between Memory Tests

For most clients, list learning is the hardest memory task because it requires accurate registration, retention, and recall of unrelated material. The advantage to list learning tests is that you can acquire a measure of the client's rate of learning over successive trials.

Paired associates is usually tested by exposing the client to sets of two items and then seeing if the client can recall the second item, after being reexposed to the first one. Problems in paired-associates learning might be seen as (a) clients who cannot learn any pairings (gross memory impairment) and (b) clients who learn all the items but mix them up incorrectly (inability to make any associations, but retention of verbal material).

Learning stories relies on the ability to comprehend and store text, and recall both the gist and details. Analogously, attempting to learn the details of a picture that shows a story of some kind requires being able to comprehend the image, store the information, and recall the gist and details. Thus, memory of pictoral situations is similar to story recall except that it relies less on language comprehension during the encoding process.

A client who does well on list learning is likely to do well on the other subtests unless there is a problem in either the ability to make meaningful associations or the ability to comprehend text (e.g., when English is a second language). When a client does well on learning stories, but poorly on list learning, it is likely due to story recall being an easier memory task.

Impaired Delayed Recall

When clients show impaired delayed recall, identify whether (a) this was consistent for all delayed measures, (b) the client's impaired score was due in part to a lack of material that was learned at the earlier trial, or (c) the client shows impairment in attention as assessed by Spatial Span, Letter-Number Sequencing, or WAIS-III Digit Span.

Recency and Primacy Effects

When learning, we have a tendency to remember the first few things we heard (primacy) and the last few things we heard (recency). These effects are easily seen on verbal learning tasks. Clients with dementia initially show both effects, but then later lose the primacy effect.

CONCLUSION

Understanding cognitive function requires having flexibility to consider test performance from a variety of angles. We now consider common disorders that involve cognitive function.

Cognitive Disorders of Childhood

PRACTICAL CONSIDERATIONS

Know What You're Doing

The diagnosis of a Learning Disorder or Mental Retardation has a tremendous impact on a client's life. It is your responsibility to ensure that the evaluation was done correctly, and that recommendations are appropriate. A poorly performed assessment can lead to malpractice suits, licensing board complaints, and poor treatment for the client.

For example, a clinician incorrectly diagnosed Mental Retardation in a patient with ADHD. The patient was placed in special education classes throughout elementary school, resulting in an inappropriate education. The moral of the story: Don't test children until you have received adequate supervision and training.

DSM-IV versus Reality

The diagnosis of cognitive disorders in children can be difficult. Most disorders are diagnosed based on discrepancies between different abilities or as across the board deficits. The *DSM-IV* suggests a discrepancy of 2 *SD* (standard deviation units) as clinically significant.

One benefit of testing children is to identify problems that will lead to special school interventions. States and school districts have their own criteria for what meets significance. Thus, you may diagnose a client with a Reading Disorder, but the level of impairment that was identified isn't significant enough to lead to special school intervention. When testing children for a cognitive disorder, know the local standards. If in doubt, seek consultation.

Identifying Significant Differences between Tests

Learning Disorders are diagnosed based on the discrepancy between achievement tests, or between achievement tests and intellectual tests. As discussed in Chapter 5, you can easily identify significant discrepancies between achievement and performance by comparing the WIAT to other Wechsler intelligence tests. This difference is sometimes defined in terms of standard deviation units (*SD*). For example, if the tests you are using both have a standard deviation of 15, a difference of 1 *SD* would require a discrepancy between tests of 15 points. In essence, when comparing achievement test scores with IQ test scores, you want to identify whether clients are performing at an expected level, based on their IQ score.

DYSLEXIA (DIAGNOSED IN *DSM-IV* AS READING DISORDER (315.2))

Essential Features

Dyslexia's primary symptoms are difficulty in learning to read and spell, with relatively better mathematical skills. There may be problems in articulation, naming, and memory. Some children show poor reading comprehension or math skills, and letter reversals. Yet, these children are often referred for evaluation because of secondary symptoms, such as anxiety or depression, school anxiety, or somatic symptoms.

The primary problem found most commonly is that the child cannot properly encode written text into speech (poor phonological encoding). Most children with dyslexia have little trouble comprehending the text itself when it is read to them. A significant minority of these patients also meet criteria for ADHD.

Some children work hard to hide their problems. For example, they may do well on weekly spelling tests by spending excessive time to memorize test words, while simple words that weren't on the list are misspelled. Keep in mind that for *DSM-IV*, the symptoms must interfere with academic achievement or relevant daily living skills.

Diagnosis

Dyslexia runs in families, so part of your evaluation should include an assessment of language-related problems in first- and second-degree relatives. Dyslexic symptoms are usually observed by the second grade. Early problems include difficulty in learning the alphabet or names of letters.

Pennington (1991) lists five primary reading errors:

1. *Dysfluency.* Slow and halting speech in oral reading. Less noticeable in older clients due to a large overlearned vocabulary.
2. *Function Word Errors.* Substitution of little words, usually misreading prepositions (e.g., "the" for "a").
3. *Visual Errors.* Substitution of content words that are visually similar (e.g., "crusted" for "crashed").
4. *Spelling Errors.* Errors that are not phonetically accurate, often with consonant errors (e.g., "hapness" for "happiness").
5. *Reversal Errors.* Considered less common, these errors are where visually similar letters are used (e.g., "bean" for "dean").

Testing Tip
Test Results Consistent with Dyslexia

- On the WISC-III, children with dyslexia tend to have lower scores on Arithmetic (taps inferential skills), Digit Span (attentional demands), and Information (everyday knowledge that aids reading). They also tend to have lower overall IQ scores.
- On the WIAT, lower scores on Basic Reading, Reading Comprehension, and Spelling should occur.
- On the WJ-R, lower scores on Word Attack and Dictation should occur.
- On the WRAT-3, lower scores on Reading and Spelling should occur.

We recommend using multiple tests of reading and spelling to ensure confidence in a test finding suggesting dyslexia (see Testing Tip for typical test results).

Recommendations

If testing indicates a diagnosis of dyslexia, the following treatment recommendations may be appropriate.

- *Psychotherapy* (cognitive-behavioral, interpersonal, etc.) aimed at:

  Educating family about dyslexia (e.g., to help develop appropriate expectations).

  Improving client's self-esteem.

  Reducing depression associated with dyslexia.

  Improving peer relationships.

  Removing emotional factors affecting learning.

- *Tutoring*, via an educational psychologist, aimed at:

  Improving reading skills with a phonics-based approach.

  For younger clients, segmental language skills.

  For older clients, reading comprehension and compensatory strategies and study skills.

- *Potential referral:* Neuropsychological assessment to refine clinical picture, support group for parents.

- *Advocacy* aimed at:

  Determining eligibility for special education programs.

DISORDER OF WRITTEN EXPRESSION (315.2)

Essential Features

The primary problem in this disorder is that the client's writing skills are (a) lower than should be expected, (b) interfere with academic performance, and (c) aren't solely due to sensory deficits. There are many facets to poor writing skills, so it is important to try to best characterize the problem. They include difficulties ranging from spelling errors to organizing pages of text together in a meaningful way. Writing skills can also be affected by a Reading Disorder when problems with encoding affect comprehension.

As with dyslexia, these children are often referred for an evaluation for a multitude of symptoms. It is only after careful evaluation that the specific cognitive deficit is identified.

Diagnosis

Like most cognitive disorders of childhood, diagnosis is based on identifying a discrepancy in writing skill compared to other abilities. Thus, an assessment should include measures of attention, memory, spatial processing, psychomotor speed, sequencing and planning, and intellectual function, as well as mood and personality (see Testing Tip for typical test results).

Testing Tip
Test Results Consistent with Disorder of Written Expression

- On the WISC-III, children with this disorder tend to have lower scores on tests that measure language skills, including Arithmetic, Digit Span, and Information. Because writing problems can be caused by many factors, your goal in testing will likely be to identify the factors leading to a writing problem, and not merely its diagnosis.
- On the WIAT, lower scores on Written Expression should occur. An examination of scores on the other subtests should help to elucidate other problems that contribute to poor writing (e.g., poor use of logic leading to lower scores on both Oral and Written Expression).
- On the WJ-R, lower scores should occur on subtests of written language (Dictation, Writing Samples, Proofing, or Writing Fluency). An examination of scores on the other subtests should also help elucidate other problems that contribute to poor writing.
- The WRAT-3 is not recommended because it does not have any tests of writing ability.

Recommendations

If testing indicates a Disorder of Written Expression, the following treatment recommendations may be appropriate.

- *Psychotherapy* (cognitive-behavioral, interpersonal, etc.) aimed at:
    Educating family about learning disorders.

    Improving client's self-esteem.

    Reducing depression associated with the disorder.

    Improving peer relationships.

    Removing emotional factors affecting learning.
- *Tutoring* aimed at:
    Improving writing skills with both a skills-based and holistic approach.
- *Potential referral:* Neuropsychological assessment to refine clinical picture, support group for parents.
- *Advocacy* aimed at:
    Determining eligibility for special education programs.

MATHEMATICS DISORDER (315.1)

Essential Features

The primary problem in this disorder is that the client's mathematical skills are lower than should be expected, interfere with academic performance, and aren't

---

Testing Tip
Test Results Consistent with Mathematics Disorder

- On the WISC-III, children with this disorder tend to have lower scores on Arithmetic, Digit Span, and Information. As with other Learning Disorders, testing is used more for identifying underlying problems than for diagnosis.
- On the WIAT, lower scores on Mathematics Reasoning and Numerical Operations should occur.
- On the WJ-R, lower scores on Calculation, Applied Problems, and Quantitative Concepts should occur.
- On the WRAT-III, lower scores on the Math subtest should occur.
- Administer tests of visuospatial function and executive function (Table 11.1).

solely due to sensory deficits. This disorder is usually due to either problems in spatial reasoning or executive function (and sometimes poor short-term memory). Because math skills rely on sequential instruction, it is important to identify the role of poor math teaching, and secondary factors such as absenteeism or missed lessons. An assessment should include measures of attention, memory, spatial processing, psychomotor speed, sequencing and planning, and intellectual function, as well as mood and personality.

Diagnosis

Like most cognitive disorders of childhood, diagnosis is based on identifying a discrepancy in mathematics skill compared to other abilities. When making your assessment, work to identify which factors lead to incorrect math responses. In addition, emotional factors can lead to incorrect responses, even when the skills are present (see Testing Tip on page 231 for typical test results).

Recommendations

If testing indicates a diagnosis of Mathematics Disorder, treatment should be geared to develop compensatory methods. There is no cure. The following treatment recommendations may be appropriate.

- *Psychotherapy* (cognitive-behavioral, interpersonal, etc.) aimed at:
    Educating family about the disorder.

    Improving client's self-esteem.

    Reducing depression associated with the disorder.

    Improving peer relationships.

    Removing emotional factors affecting learning.
- *Tutoring* (Pennington, 1991):
    If problems are due to difficulties with spatial reasoning:

    Have client use graph paper to ensure that numbers are properly lined up into columns.

    Have client use calculator to check answers.

    Have client learn to estimate solutions prior to starting the problem.

    If problems are due to difficulties in executive function:

    Teach client discrete steps in mathematical problem solving (e.g., "recipes," algorithms).

    Tutor should model problem-solving skills concretely so client can learn to use them.

- *Potential referral:* Neuropsychological assessment to refine clinical picture, support group for parents.
- *Advocacy* aimed at:
  Determining eligibility for special education programs.

MENTAL RETARDATION (317 TO 319)

Essential Features

Mental Retardation diagnosis is tightly bound to cognitive testing. In practice, these are clients whose intellectual function falls at around the second percentile or lower. A low IQ score isn't sufficient to make a diagnosis; patients must also show impairment in adaptive function (e.g., activities of daily living). Otherwise, you may be encountering someone whose low scores on intelligence tests are due to lack of schooling, motivation, or cultural factors. Most clients with Mental Retardation fall into the mild level. For adult clients with this disorder, that may translate to somewhere around the intellectual function of an 8- to 10-year-old. With greater severity comes fewer independent living skills. The *DSM-IV* requires onset prior to age 18.

Mental Retardation is due to many factors, though in half the cases, a specific cause cannot be identified. These clients are more likely to have other mental illnesses as well, including Mood and Anxiety Disorders.

Unlike some autistic clients, who may have IQ scores below 70, mentally retarded adults and children form social attachments, and are less likely to show echolalia, self-injurious behavior, or inappropriate affect.

Diagnosis

Mental Retardation is typically assessed using the WISC-III or WPPSI-R, and the Vineland Adaptive Behavior Scales. If a client meets criteria, the disorder is coded on Axis II (see Testing Tip on page 234 for typical test results).

Recommendations

If testing indicates a diagnosis of Mental Retardation, the following treatment recommendations may be appropriate (treatment is in part determined by level of impairment).

- *Psychotherapy* (behavioral) aimed at:
  Education for the family about the disorder.
  Psychosocial skill building.
  Setting of realistic, concrete goals.

Testing Tip
Test Results Consistent with Mental Retardation

- On the WISC-III, clients with Mental Retardation typically have a full scale IQ score of 70 or lower. Patients who score at the borderline range may have Mental Retardation, too, given the standard error of WISC-III scores. Typically, the subtest scatter is limited.
- On the WIAT, WJ-R, and WRAT-3, scores on all subtests should fall in the low borderline to impaired range.
- On the Vineland Adaptive Behavior Scales score should fall in the impaired range.

Increasing academic/vocational skills.

Focusing of treatment on a developmental framework.

Being alert for depression and risk for abuse.

Developing self-help skills using applied behavioral analysis.

- *Evaluation* for eligibility for special services.
- *Parent/family training and therapy.*
- *Potential referrals*: Physician, special services (e.g., regional center), vocational/academic services, national support organizations, family support groups.

Memory Assessments Used with Children

When children show cognitive difficulties in school or at home, it often is necessary to identify what contribution memory performance has on these problems. Alternatively, it may be needed to identify whether a Learning Disorder is affecting certain aspects of memory. The following two tests both provide comprehensive assessments of memory function.

WIDE RANGE ASSESSMENT OF MEMORY AND LEARNING (WRAML)

Description

The WRAML (Adams & Sheslow, 1990) is a popular assessment of memory function in children. It can be given to children ages 5 to 17 years. Most clinicians give the screening version; it includes four subtests and administration takes about

15 minutes, with an additional delay required to assess for delayed recall. Many clinicians find the screening a sufficiently rapid assessment of memory.

The complete test comprises nine subtests that are divided into three learning indices. The indices have a mean of 100 (*SD* = 15). The subtests and indices are:

1. *Visual Memory Index:*

   Picture Memory (recalling differences between two similar pictures; screener).

   Design Memory (ability to draw designs after a brief delay; screener).

   Finger Windows (nonverbal version of Wechsler Memory Scale Spatial Span).

2. *Verbal Memory Index:*

   Story Memory (recall of short stories; screener).

   Sentence Memory (recall of sentences).

   Number/Letter (similar to Wechsler Memory Scale Spatial Span).

3. *Learning Index:*

   Verbal Learning (4-trial list learning with optional delay; screener).

   Sound Symbol (4-trial paired-associates learning).

   Visual Learning (4-trial learning of visual designs).

The General Memory Index is a summary of all subtests.

Interpretation

In general, the WRAML is used to identify the client's learning strategies (e.g., the use of context as a learning aid) as well as to differentiate verbal versus visual memory skill.

CHILDREN'S MEMORY SCALE (CMS)

Description

The CMS (Cohen, 1997) is a broader assessment of memory than the WRAML, and is similar in concept to the Wechsler Memory Scale-III (described later in this chapter). It can be given to children between the ages of 5 and 16 years. It takes approximately 60 minutes to administer, although half of that time is taken up waiting to administer the delayed measures. We recommend administering it when you need a comprehensive memory assessment.

The CMS was standardized on a national sample of 1,000 children. It consists of six core and two supplemental subtests. Scores are standardized with a mean of 100 (*SD* = 15). The subtests comprise eight Index scores:

1. *Verbal Immediate Index:*

   Stories I (immediate recall of stories).

   Word Pairs I (learning of word paired-associates).

2. *Visual Immediate Index:*

   Dot Locations I (client learns location of colored symbols after a brief exposure).

   Faces I (facial recognition test).

3. *Verbal Delayed Index:*

   Stories II.

   Word Pairs II.

4. *Visual Delayed Index:*

   Dot Locations II.

   Faces II.

5. *Attention/Concentration Index:*

   Sequences (similar to WAIS-III Letter-Number Sequencing).

   Numbers (similar to Wechsler Digit Span).

6. *Delayed Recognition* (recognition measures of verbal and visual subtests).
7. *Learning* (rate of learning).
8. *General Memory Index* (overall measure of memory function).

Interpretation

Like the Wechsler scales, the General Memory Index can first be examined, followed by the indices and subtest scores. Marked heterogeneity between subtests can limit your confidence in summary scores.

Cognitive Disorders in the Elderly and Adults

PRACTICAL CONSIDERATIONS

Don't Diagnose a Cognitive Disorder without Sufficient Training

One of the most frequent forms of misdiagnosis in the elderly occurs when a patient with Major Depression is diagnosed with Dementia and vice versa. If you lack experience with this population, obtain consultation.

Aging Involves Cognitive Worsening

Part of aging involves the slow worsening of cognitive functions. With age, many abilities decline. Specific declines include:

- Shorter attention span.
- Smaller capacity to learn new information and retrieve it from memory.
- Slower processing speed.
- Reduced motor coordination.

Not Everything Ages

Although many cognitive abilities worsen with age, older adults tend to show good retention of information that was learned in the past. Thus, older adults are good historians and can recall many life experiences. Hence, when we think of wisdom in the elderly, it is usually due to their accumulated life experiences, rather than due to rapid memory or processing.

Age Is the Primary Risk Factor for Cognitive Disorders

Most studies show that with age comes an increased prevalence of cognitive disorders. By the time older adults reach their 80s, they are much more likely to become demented. Dementias are due to a variety of factors, which are not mutually exclusive. Thus, some clients show evidence of several dementing disorders.

Always Get Collateral Data

In the earliest stages of dementia, testing can often fail to reveal deficits, particularly in well-educated and intelligent individuals. Spouses, friends, co-workers, and loved ones often can report the specific symptoms that suggest forgetfulness or confusion. Always include them in your evaluation.

Significant Others Can Be Wrong

A spouse or loved one may complain about forgetfulness when it is in fact a sign of relationship issues. Make sure to identify current stressors that may lead to memory complaints, whether they come from the client or the partner.

PRIMARY COGNITIVE DISORDERS

Cognitive impairment is easy to identify when your client has gross impairment. Most common referral questions are either to make an initial diagnosis, or to measure current severity. Whenever cognitive impairment becomes salient, we recommend starting off coarsely with the Mini-Mental State Examination (MMSE; reprinted in Appendix B) or Dementia Rating Scale (described in this chapter). Follow-up testing with the Wechsler Memory Scale-III, WAIS-III, or other cognitive tests should be performed if a more detailed assessment of cognitive function is needed. If you find that you cannot adequately characterize the cognitive symptoms, based on the tests that you have given, immediately refer the client to a clinical neuropsychologist.

Alzheimer's Disease (290.xx)

Alzheimer's is the most frequent dementing disorder in the elderly. Initial clinical symptoms include short-term memory loss, problems in word finding, reduced visuomotor coordination, and sometimes delusions or depression. As the disease progresses, memory, language, and motor skills worsen, with increasing apathy and amotivation. Well-learned skills start to vanish. Thus, clients may forget how to make meals, then how to clean dishes, and then how to use the toilet. Many clients with Alzheimer's disease develop behavioral symptoms as the disease worsens, including agitation and combativeness. In the final stages, the client becomes unable to function without complete assistance, is bed-bound, and often dies from pneumonia. Alzheimer's is identified by microscopic examination of the brain. Deposits called plaques and tangles are found throughout. It is not well understood what leads to these deposits, though both genetics and environmental factors are known to play a role.

Vascular Dementia (290.xx)

The second most common dementia, Vascular Dementia is caused by damage to the capillaries that support the brain. The clinical symptoms are much like those of Alzheimer's disease, and usually the deficiencies are only obvious to a clinical neuropsychologist. Like Alzheimer's disease, clients with Vascular Dementia show memory impairment, impairment in language function, and in visuomotor skill. Yet, the stereotypical patient with Vascular Dementia shows milder cognitive deficits. They tend to show retained awareness of their problems, whereas there is apathy in Alzheimer's. They tend to show problems with reasoning earlier in the disease than in Alzheimer's. The course is more variable than in Alzheimer's.

Dementia Due to Parkinson's Disease (294.1)

Parkinson's is a movement disorder that causes symptoms such as rigidity and resting tremor. A substantial number of clients with Parkinson's develop a dementia later in the disease. The symptoms can include mild memory impairment, impaired executive function and reasoning, sometimes accompanied by delusions and visual hallucinations.

Dementia Due to Stroke (294.1)

Strokes occur when the supply of blood is cut off to a specific region of the brain, either by blockage or when a blood vessel ruptures. They can occur at any age. Strokes usually affect only the area where they occur. For example, damage to a blood vessel that runs to the left temporal lobe will affect language. At the moment when a stroke occurs, the client may become immobilized or unconscious, with function returning slowly thereafter. Strokes tend to occur in common areas, for example, at the junctions between the arteries at the base of the brain, or the arteries that feed the left parietal lobe. Because strokes are somewhat selective, cognitive deficits can appear in isolation.

Dementia Due to Head Trauma (294.1)

Head trauma can be caused by many factors, though a common one is automobile accidents. The trauma may be mild, resulting in a concussion that usually remits within days. More severe head trauma can create profound damage. When the head is struck by an object, the brain sustains injury at that site, which can lead to swelling, bruising, bleeding, and tissue loss. When trauma is sufficient to cause brain damage, it is usually isolated to the region of the brain where the trauma occurred. If the head is hit hard enough, the force will cause the brain to impact against the opposite side of the injured site, resulting in further (contra coup) damage. Keep in mind that problems with balance or vision can be due to trauma to the inner ear, rather than to the brain.

Cognitive Disorder NOS (94.9)

This category is for adults who show evidence of cognitive dysfunction due to a nonspecific cause, most typically substance abuse. However, if a substance-related cognitive disorder includes memory impairment, it would be coded as Substance-Induced Persisting Amnestic Disorder.

RECOMMENDATIONS

If testing indicates a diagnosis of a dementia, the following treatment recommendations may be appropriate. Not all dementia patients show global deficits. Many are able to return to work, despite measurable deficits.

- *Individual psychotherapy* for the client (cognitive/behavioral or behavioral, provided that the client can participate) aimed at:

    Increasing awareness of condition and confronting possible denial.

    Increasing ability to structure coping.

    Attaining optimal autonomy and self-sufficiency.

    Increasing activities and decreasing isolation.

    Monitoring anxiety and depression.

- *Individual psychotherapy* for the caregiver (cognitive/behavioral, insight oriented) aimed at:

    Increasing awareness of condition and confronting possible denial.

    Accepting changes in loved one.

    Helping caregiver make decisions regarding medical treatment, institutionalization, and estate planning (when relevant).

Testing Tip
Mini-Mental State Examination

When to Use It
- The client shows signs of confusion and forgetfulness.
- You are deciding whether neuropsychological assessment is needed.
- You are considering dementia.

Advantages
- Fast screen of dementia symptomatology.

Disadvantages
- Can misidentify schizophrenic and depressed clients as having dementia.
- Can miss the presence of cognitive impairment in nonglobal dementias (e.g., stroke).
- Overpathologizes dementia in clients with low education.

    Increasing coping ability.

    Increasing activities and decreasing isolation.

    Monitoring anxiety and depression.

- *Medical and medication evaluation.*
- *Family therapy* aimed at:

    Fostering communication and support.

    Alerting/educating about potential for physical abuse.

- Regular follow-up testing (every 6–12 months).
- *Potential referrals:* Neurologist, psychiatrist, neuropsychologist, support group, clinical trials group, occupational therapist, physical therapist, disease-related support organization (e.g., Alzheimer's Association, senior care facilities).

Assessment Instruments Used in Adult Cognitive Assessment

MINI-MENTAL STATE EXAMINATION (MMSE)

Description

Folstein, Folstein, and McHugh (1975) designed the MMSE as a brief and thorough assessment of cognitive mental status. It is typically used as a screening for

---

Testing Tip
Dementia Rating Scale

When to Use It
- You need a more thorough screen of cognitive function than the MMSE.
- You have more time to spend.
- You want to make greater distinctions between cognitive areas, but do not have the training or time to perform a full neuropsychological workup.

Advantages
- Provides more comprehensive information than the MMSE.
- Established reliability and validity.

Disadvantages
- Not suited for nondemented population.
- Criticized for potential insensitivity to mild dementia.

---

dementia, but can also be used in inpatient settings where level of delirium is being assessed. It has excellent test-retest and interrater reliability, takes about five minutes to administer, has a total score of 30 points, and can be rapidly scored and understood. It is available in numerous languages. This instrument briefly assesses orientation to time and place, attention, verbal memory, praxis, and language function. Lower scores indicate lower function. A cutoff of 23/24 is indicative of dementia. It is reprinted in Appendix B.

Testing Tip
WMS-III

When to Use It
- You need an index of the client's overall memory function.
- You are concerned about memory performance.

Advantages
- A comprehensive assessment of memory.
- Standardized with the same sample as the WAIS-III, allowing cross-comparisons.

Disadvantages
- Time consuming to administer the whole battery.

Items assess: (a) orientation, (b) registration and recall, (c) attention, (d) confrontational naming, (e) constructional praxis, (f) gross sentence writing ability, (g) gross reading ability, and (h) simple ideational praxis.

Scoring and Interpretation

Any client scoring below 24 points should have further evaluation to rule out why the performance is low. Clients who are unable to recall more than one word, and are not clinically depressed, should be further evaluated. Well educated and intelligent clients, who score between 24 and 26 points, may also be showing cognitive symptoms and should be given further assessment.

DEMENTIA RATING SCALE (DRS)

Description

The DRS (Mattis, 1988) consists of 36 items constituting five subscales: Attention, Initiation/Perseveration, Construction, Conceptualization, and Memory. Items are hierarchically weighted in many cases, so that if a client does one difficult item, easier items are skipped. This saves time in higher functioning clients. Higher scores suggest intact functioning. Published norms of both healthy and demented older adults are provided. Norms range from 65 to 81 years of age.

Relative to the MMSE, the DRS is a lengthy dementia screening, though it takes about 15 minutes to perform.

Interpretation

Patients who score near or below the cutoff for the total score should be referred for further neuropsychological assessment. Patients who score above the cutoff on the total score, but below the cutoff on half of the subtests, should also be given further evaluation. In particular, examine the types of errors made by the client.

WECHSLER MEMORY SCALE-III (WMS-III)

Description

The WMS-III is the latest revision (1997) of this popular test. It can be given to clients between the ages of 16 and 89. This version comprises 12 primary subtests of which 4 are delayed measures and 6 are supplemental subtests (2 are delayed measures). The test has solid psychometric properties.

WMS-III Subtests

Table 11.2 describes the WMS-III subtests and their typical interpretations.

TABLE 11.2
WMS-III Subtest Summary

Subtest	Delayed Recall Trial	Recognition Trial	Clinical Issues and Interpretation
ORIENTATION			
Information and Orientation.* Client is asked questions assessing orientation and overlearned information.	No	No	Standard interpretation: orientation to self, time, and location; familiarity with grossly overlearned information
AUDITORY/VERBAL MEMORY DOMAIN			
Logical Memory I and II. Client is asked to learn two short stories.	Yes	Yes	Standard interpretation: verbal memory of story recall. • Easier verbal memory test. • Depressed clients score on average at 16th percentile. • Elderly usually anticipate longer stories. • Warn clients not to interrupt during the reading with negative reactions (e.g., "I'll never remember this"). • Identify if clients remember the stories from previous administrations of the test.
Verbal-Paired Associates I and II. Client learns eight word pairs.	Yes	Yes	Standard interpretation: ability to generate and recall word associations. • Some clients learn all the words but not the pairings, suggesting problems in making associations. • Note when clients have learned all or none of the pairs.
Word List I and II.* Client learns a 12-item word list over four learning trials.	Yes	Yes	Standard interpretation: ability to learn unrelated verbal material. • Hardest memory test. • Test can frustrate clients. • Examine learning trials. Some clients learn many words at Trial 1, but learn no more over subsequent trials, suggesting good attention, but poor acquisition. Some clients show a good learning curve, but don't learn many of the words.
VISUAL/NONVERBAL MEMORY DOMAIN			
Family Pictures I and II. Client is shown pictures of people in stereotypical middle-class settings and is then asked to recall details.	Yes	No	Standard interpretation: nonverbal learning ability, ability to consolidate and describe visual information. • Low scores may be due to cultural differences. • Low scores may be due to executive funcitons affecting interpretation of social information. • Test requires client to have sufficient incidental learning skills.

(Continued)

TABLE 11.2 (Continued)

Subtest	Delayed Recall Trial	Recognition Trial	Clinical Issues and Interpretation
Faces I and II. A recognition test. Client is shown 24 pictures of faces and is asked to discriminate them from a set of distractor ones.	Yes	N/A	Standard interpretation: ability to recognize faces. • Low scores are usually localized to right hemisphere impairment. • Low scores may correlate with impairment in executive abilities (e.g., reasoning, planning, judgment).
Visual Reproduction.* Client is shown four figures and copies each from memory.	Yes	Yes	Standard interpretation: visual-memory, visual-constructive ability. • Low scores on immediate reconstruction may be due to visual-constructive ability. To rule this out, do a copy trial.
WORKING MEMORY DOMAIN			
Letter-Number Sequencing. Same as in WAIS-III.	No	No	Standard interpretation (see page 42)
Spatial Span. Client views board with raised blocks and is asked to observe blocks tapped in a sequence. Client then copies the sequence, which increase in length. Backward trials are included.	No	No	Standard interpretation: Visual version of WAIS-III digit span, measures attention, visual-motor ability, nonverbal attention • Backward trials are more demanding, requiring added working memory. • Identify if errors are due to (a) problems in sequencing, (b) rote memory (e.g., omitting an item), (c) inattention, (d) anxiety. • Better backward performance may suggest variation in effort. • Be wary of conditions that reduce performance (noise, hearing problems). • Susceptible to anxiety.
Digit Span.* Same as in WAIS-III.	No	No	Standard interpretation (see page 41)
Mental Control.* Client is asked to do simple tasks of attention; recite the alphabet, etc.	No	No	Standard interpretation: gross measure of attention, overlearned abilities. • Inability to recite alphabet or count backward from 20 to 1 suggests profound inattention, very low education, loss of overlearned abilities, malingering.

*Supplemental Subtests

Eight Primary Indices are derived from a combination of WMS-III subtest scores. They are:

1. *Auditory Immediate Index:*

   Logical Memory I, Verbal Paired Associates I.

2. *Visual Immediate Index:*

   Faces I, Family Pictures I.

3. *Immediate Memory Index:*

   Composite of Auditory, Immediate, and Visual Immediate subtests.

4. *Auditory Delayed Index:*

   Logical Memory II, Verbal Paired Associates II.

5. *Visual Delayed Index:*

   Faces II, Family Pictures II.

6. *Auditory Recognition Delayed:*

   Logical Memory II Recognition, Verbal Paired Associates II Recognition.

7. *General Memory:*

   Composite of Auditory Delayed, Visual Delayed, Auditory Recognition Delayed.

8. *Working Memory:*

   Letter-Number Sequencing.

   Spatial Span.

Interpretation

Like the WAIS-III, one of the keys to interpreting the WMS-III is to examine the scatter between subtests to ensure homogeneity in the Primary Index scores. Scatter is defined as the difference between the highest and lowest scores in the subtests that comprise a Primary Index.

First, identify if there was significant scatter for each of the Primary Indices using Table F.4 in the WMS-III manual. If there was significant scatter for a particular Index, don't use it, and consider why the scatter occurred. Next, calculate each of the Index scores and note if there were significant differences between

---

Testing Tip
Choosing a Dementia Screening

You want a very rapid screen:

   Use the MMSE.

You want a rapid screen, but require more detailed information:

   Use the DRS.

You need a detailed assessment of memory function:

   Administer the WMS-III.

them (using Tables F.1 and F.2 in the WMS-III manual). These values are recorded on the Discrepancy Analysis page. Listed below are the primary questions asked by these difference scores:

- *Auditory Immediate–Visual Immediate:* Are there differences in immediate memory based on the type of stimulus?
- *Auditory Immediate–Auditory Delayed:* Does the client have problems in long-term storage of auditory information?
- *Visual Immediate–Visual Delayed:* Does the client have problems in long-term storage of visual information?
- *Auditory Delayed–Auditory Recognition Delayed:* Does the client have retained auditory recognition memory, relative to long-term storage?
- *Auditory Delayed–Visual Delayed:* Are there differences in delayed recall based on the type of stimulus?
- *Immediate Memory–General Memory:* Does the client have problems in long-term storage?
- *General Memory–Working Memory:* Is the client's working memory playing a part in long-term storage of information?

Auditory Process Composites

The WMS-III Auditory Process Composites are supplemental scales that are still considered experimental, pending further validation studies. However, they offer valuable data and we recommend their use. These scales are derived from portions of Logical Memory I and II and Verbal Paired Associates I and II, and are scored as percentiles. The four scales are:

- *Single-Trial Learning.* This scale reflects the client's ability to learn based on one exposure to stimulus material. Low scores suggest inattention and anxiety.
- *Learning Slope.* This scale reflects the rate of learning from the first trial to the last. Higher scores suggest good learning, whereas lower scores suggest that learning does not increase over successive trials. Low scores may be due to a dementia, as well as gross inattention.
- *Retention.* This scale provides an assessment of the degree of forgetting. Retention compares delayed recall to performance on the final learning trial. Thus, you can identify if delayed recall performance was due to poor retention (first learning 12 words and later remembering only 6) versus acquisition (first learning 6 words and later remembering them all). Poor retention is often associated with retrieval.
- *Retrieval.* This scale is a comparison of recognition memory with delayed recall. It measures whether the client is having trouble with retrieval (defined by much better recognition memory compared with delayed recall). Higher scores suggest a greater problem (as with Alzheimer's).

Testing Tip
Alzheimer's Disease versus Depression

Historical and Behavioral Variables

Factor	Alzheimer's	Depression
Psychiatric History	Less common	More common
Patient Complaints	Varies	Vocal
Emotional Distress	Varies	Yes
Mood Congruent Delusions	No	Yes

Qualitative Variables

Measure	Alzheimer's	Depression
Impaired Recognition Memory	Yes	No
Intrusion Errors	Greater	Fewer
Performance on "Automatic" Tasks	Impaired	Intact
Effort–Motivation	Good	Reduced
Performance Consistency	Yes	No
Awareness of Impairment	Limited	Intact

Adapted from Kaszniak and Ditraglia-Christenson (1995).

Comparing WAIS-III to WMS-III Scores

The WMS-III Discrepancy Analysis page allows you to compare WAIS-III to WMS-III scores. There are two methods of calculating differences: Simple and Predicted-Actual. As mentioned before, we prefer the Predicted-Actual method because it is a statistically better technique to compare scores.

In the Simple method, you calculate the difference score between a WAIS-III IQ score and a WMS-III Primary Index, record it in the Simple column, and then identify if the value was statistically significant (using Tables C.1–C.3 in the WAIS-III-WMS-III manual), and infrequent in the standardization sample (using Tables C.4–C.6 in the WAIS-III-WMS-III manual).

In the Predicted-Actual method, you first use the actual IQ score to calculate a predicted WMS-III index score (using Tables B.1–B.3 in the WAIS-III-WMS-III manual), and record it in the Memory Index Score, Predicted column. Next, you calculate the difference score between each WMS-III Primary Index, and the predicted WAIS-III score. Then, identify if the difference was statistically significant (using Tables B.4–B.6 in the WAIS-III-WMS-III manual), and infrequent in the standardization sample (using Tables B.7–B.9 in the WAIS-III-WMS-III manual).

Ethnic and Cultural Diversity

The WMS-III used approximately half of the same standardization sample as the WAIS-III ($N = 1,250$). The WMS-III is designed for use in older adults, and is standardized for adults up to age 89.

Differential Diagnosis

ALZHEIMER'S DISEASE VERSUS DEPRESSION

Misdiagnosis of depression with dementia is very common in the elderly. The Testing Tip "Alzheimer's Disease versus Depression," based on an excellent review by Kaszniak and Ditraglia-Christenson (1995), presents key features that can help you distinguish between them.

DEMENTIA VERSUS MALINGERING

For the most part, clients who are malingering complain and perform markedly worse on tests of cognitive function than actual dementia clients. You might see clients who cannot recall any elements of a story, are unable to remember the most simple word pairing, cannot recall any elements of a figure after seeing it for 10 seconds, and so on. Malingering is also discussed in Chapter 2. Because malingering and neuropsychological impairment are associated most often with forensic psychology, we recommend that only clinicians who could qualify as experts in a legal setting perform forensic evaluations.

Marked inconsistencies are often seen. For example, a malingering client may call you to confirm the time and location of an appointment, and then be unable to recall any of 10 words after 20 minutes. In addition, patterns of performance make little sense. A client may show marked memory impairment without any other cognitive signs. A client may be unable to copy a simple figure, but then have no difficulty in filling out complicated registration forms, or drawing a picture of the scene of an accident. A client claiming cognitive impairment due to an injury may claim to be unable to remember the actual accident (like an actual head trauma), but then go on to claim an inability to remember job responsibilities or coworkers' names.

Clients with actual dementia or head trauma typically show a sophisticated pattern of deficits. It is rare to find someone who has lost only one measurable ability, or someone who shows losses in every ability.

SECTION III

COMPLETING THE EVALUATION

CHAPTER 12

Integration: Methods and Models of Test Interpretation

R EPORT WRITING is the end point in the assessment process, and we now provide a clear method for going through what some clinicians consider the hardest part of the assessment.

Raw Data Organization

There are four elements in organizing raw data:

1. Recall the referral question.
2. Gather all pertinent information.
3. Review initial hypotheses.
4. Identify and prioritize pertinent results.

RECALL THE REFERRAL QUESTION

Before you begin, reconsider the referral question. This provides a framework, reminds you of the evaluation's purpose, and directs you to pertinent issues. By doing so, you may find that information is lacking from your assessment.

GATHER ALL PERTINENT INFORMATION

Organizing test data is a process of filtration that involves sifting through all the test responses and identifying the clinically significant data. Do this with all the information you have gathered (e.g., relevant history, past evaluations, behavioral observations, notes, and all test results). In some cases, the tests themselves provide organizational strategies based on summary and composite scores (see Chapters 4 and 5 for a review). At this point, it is better to keep data rather than toss too much out.

REVIEW INITIAL HYPOTHESES

During and after the evaluation it is likely that you have been generating working hypotheses. These hypotheses may be based on test data as well as your own knowledge about assessment. Have them in mind before you identify significant results.

IDENTIFY AND PRIORITIZE PERTINENT RESULTS

Start laying out all the pertinent results. A pertinent result is not a poor result or a strength, but any finding that might have a significant bearing on the referral question, your working hypotheses, diagnosis, or treatment recommendations. At this stage, it is usually helpful to organize the results test by test. Some clinicians also create summary forms for the test they commonly use.

Next, prioritize the data in terms of clinical strength, organizing the information so that the most significant finding is highest on the list, regardless of how consistent the list looks. In general, composite scores carry more weight than single findings, and supplemental scales are usually not as psychometrically sound as primary ones. (Chapter 2 can help identify the factors needed to evaluate the tests' psychometric properties.)

Data Integration and Interpretation

There are three elements in integration and interpretation:

1. Consider the results based on four models:
   a. Your working hypotheses.
   b. Your theoretical orientation.
   c. Overarching commonalities (e.g., diagnosis, treatment).
   d. Strengths and weaknesses.
2. Develop an individual profile.
3. Render a diagnosis.

FOUR MODELS OF INTERPRETING TEST DATA

Once you have organized your test data, you will need to draw conclusions, based on what the results mean. We have identified four key models to consider test data. Note that these models are all interrelated, so we do not suggest that all test data needs to be considered exhaustively using each strategy. Rather, each model allows you to consider a critical component that may be of use to you. With more assessment experience, you will likely find yourself taking a less structured approach.

Consider the Test Data Based on Your Working Hypotheses

By now, you should be considering different ways for explaining the data, based on hypotheses that you have generated. Taking the test data, make note of hypotheses that have significant strength and can be cross-validated and those that are more tentative. You may want to organize the test findings based on these hypotheses. Often, this review is used in the report to justify your impressions, diagnosis, and recommendations. In addition, you may find yourself modifying your hypotheses based on the data.

Do not ignore inconsistent data; instead, find the source of the divergence. You may see a need to gather additional information, but more commonly, you will generate alternative hypotheses that are then evaluated with the test data. To understand the divergence, examine the inconsistent findings and compare those results with consistent findings. Alternatively, you will find data that do not make sense, or data that you had not previously considered. Discrepancies may be due to environmental variability, normal variability, differences, between measures, or motivation. For children and adolescents, situational demands can often cause discrepancies.

Consider the Test Data Based on Your Theoretical Orientation

All clinicians consider their own theoretical orientation when integrating test findings, though this becomes most noticeable with emotional test data. You may have already used your theoretical approach to generate working hypotheses. In either case, consider whether the data fit your theoretical models. For example, you may find it easiest to sort the test data into sections that fit common behavioral or psychodynamic elements. One danger to this process is the tendency to force the data to fit a theory, when there is evidence to support the contrary.

For cognitive test data, consider the categories and models specified in Chapters 4, 5, or 11 (including Table 11.1) to help organize the data.

Consider the Test Data Based on Overarching Commonalities

You may want to consider the data in terms of how it applies to larger scale themes, such as diagnosis, overall emotional and cognitive function, and treatment recommendations. These general categories are often used as the structure for a report.

Consider the Test Data Based on Strengths and Weaknesses

Examining the test data in terms of strengths and weaknesses helps you generate further hypotheses and create explanations. In addition, most referring sources, as well as your clients and their families, will find this information useful. Strengths and weaknesses can be defined in both basic terms (e.g., computational skill) as well as more global ones (e.g., coping skills). Make sure to identify the relationship between cognitive and emotional data to see which elements lead to strengths and weaknesses. For example, anxiety may be leading to lower scores on tests measuring attention. In addition, make sure to consider the psychometric strengths of the data.

Of greater importance, do not overinterpret isolated weaknesses or deficits, particularly when one or two findings fall into the impaired range. Given the number of scores created in the average test battery, probability theory alone would predict an isolated deficit. Weaknesses are most justifiable when they are found on several measures and supported by other nontest data.

DEVELOP AN INDIVIDUAL PROFILE

This step is the end point in the interpretive process. Having evaluated the clinical data as suggested, you now should be able to create an individual profile. This profile is simply a composite of the data that you have been analyzing (e.g., significant findings, strengths and weaknesses, diagnostically relevant data, emotional and cognitive function, treatment recommendations). Using the template for report writing described in this chapter, you will be able to report these results in an efficient and clear way.

RENDER A DIAGNOSIS

Psychological assessments are not always required to have a diagnosis in them, and we do not believe it is needed in every one that you do. Diagnosis is important when it is part of the referral question, when you identify a disorder that was previously unknown, when it is critical to providing services to the client (e.g., Regional Center services), or when you are required for insurance purposes to make one.

You can use this book, along with *DSM-IV*, to make a diagnosis. Keep in mind that many clinicians are aware of the *DSM-IV*'s limitations. They may find it more useful to know the client's features that are within the range of a disorder's criteria than to have a perfunctory listing of diagnoses. For assistance in making a *DSM-IV* diagnosis, review the primer in Chapter 1, as well as the relevant chapters in Section II.

Diagnostic Confidence

Sometimes you will not be sure of a final diagnosis, and have several plausible possibilities. We recommend listing the potential disorders in order of confidence, with each written as a "Rule Out" (e.g., "Rule Out Schizophrenia"). Make sure to mention in the report why you could not make a final diagnosis, and do not become overly dependent on this term.

Another common occurrence is assessment of a client who meets criteria for a "Not Otherwise Specified" disorder. There is nothing to fear with this category. Again, clarify why the client didn't meet criteria for a more specific disorder.

Personality Disorder Diagnoses

A common mistake made by clinicians is to give clients several Personality Disorder diagnoses because the client seems to meet multiple criteria (or shows multiple significant elevations on the MCMI-III). This tendency reflects both the shortcomings of the *DSM-IV* Personality Disorder diagnostic criteria as well as the MCMI-III. In addition, recall that these disorders have the tendency to negatively label the client. When you find yourself wanting to give multiple Axis II diagnoses, reconsider your data and the diagnostic criteria.

Writing the Psychological Report

The primary purpose of a psychological report is to communicate your findings in a way that helps the referring source understand and treat the client. If you have followed the preceding steps, you will find the bulk of your work has already been accomplished.

SORT RESULTS BY SECTION

For this step, organize the test results into clusters that mirror the sections of the report (e.g., cognitive functioning, emotional functioning). This will allow you to check hypotheses and generate alternatives. Don't worry if you place findings into multiple sections. Table 12.1 on pages 256–257 presents an annotated psychological report format.

CLUSTER SECTION DATA INTO ISSUES

Within each report section, organize the test findings based on the relevant issues being discussed. For example, you may find that the client did poorly on all

TABLE 12.1
Annotated Psychological Assessment Report

Psychological Assessment Report
Confidential Material

Name   Date of Birth
Dates of evaluation   Referral source
Date of report

Identifying Information:

[Write a sentence that lists the client's name, age, ethnic group, marital status, level of education, and occupation.]

Referral Question:

[Summarize the referral question in a sentence or two. If the client was referred to identify potential ADHD, that's all you have to say. The referral source or setting should also be clearly identified. You may also want this section to be where you describe the primary symptoms that led to the referral. Otherwise, add this information to the history.]

Relevant History:

Family History, Academic History, Social and Family History, Medical History, Psychiatric History, History Relevant to the Complaint.

[This section reviews the client's pertinent history and includes the interview information you collected (Chapter 2). Subheadings can be used to report this information. While there is usually a considerable amount of data, the key here is to only include relevant material. This section can be three to four paragraphs in length. Some referring sources are comfortable with extremely brief history sections because of their familiarity with the client. Clarify when you obtain information from earlier reports or other sources.]

Tests Administered:

[List each test, with its complete title, edition, and abbreviation. Many reports have this information arranged in columns, with a column listing the test result as a percentile; a verbal descriptor is included (e.g., Average). When the report includes a comparison of earlier test data, a column is usually added to place the results side by side.]

Mental Status Examination and Behavioral Observation:

Appearance, Handedness, Mood, Affect, Behavior, Intellectual Function, Language, Orientation, Memory, Attention, Insight, Judgment, Thought Process, Dangerousness.

[Summarize the exam, as listed in Chapter 2. The focus is on behavioral descriptions of the client's presentation. Direct quotes from the client can be used. Also report that consent was discussed and obtained from the client, commenting on any exceptions or special circumstances in relation to confidentiality.]

[Document the client's ability to establish and maintain rapport. Discuss the client's approach to testing, motivation to complete test items, examples of resistance, and odd behavior. Conclude with a statement commenting on the overall validity of the assessment, and its potential limitations.]

Cognitive Function:

[Use your notes from integrating test findings to organize these results. You may want to consider the section on advanced cognitive assessment in Chapter 11, as well as

TABLE 12.1 (Continued)

Chapters 4 and 5 as a guide. A common format for this selection is a statement on overall function, the assessment's validity, verbal versus nonverbal performance, index scores, individual strengths and weaknesses, and any clinical or diagnostically significant patterns of subtests. Report cognitive test findings as verbal descriptors and/or as percentiles (e.g., "Mr. Jones's Full Scale IQ score was in the average range at the 50th percentile."). Exact scores are frowned on because of their inherent standard of error and because they can be easily misinterpreted. Add comments indicating surprises. Report any variations in test procedure, clinical behavior that affected test responses, and specific limitations of the test items. Comment on the interrelationship between cognitive and emotional test data. Some clinicians also add comments regarding how the data fits with the referral question, though you can also save these remarks for the Impressions sections. For clients where cognitive function is of secondary importance, we recommend a simple summary of FIQ, PIQ, and VIQ and their respective ranges (e.g., high average).]

Personality and Emotional Function:
[When this section is the focus of the referral question, it may include several tests. The actual organization of this section will vary with your working hypotheses and theoretical orientation. One outline for considering the data would be to consider: (a) the client's view of self; (b) issues related to the individual's cognitions and emotions; (c) current stressors, defenses, and coping mechanisms; (d) impulse control and self-destructive behavior; and (e) the client's relationship with others and social supports. If you have given only one instrument, you may also find yourself describing personality based on its structure (e.g., MMPI-2).]

Diagnostic Impressions:
[This section should lay out your rationale for the diagnosis. Start with your diagnostic impression and then provide the justification. Explain overlapping diagnoses and how you discarded them. If you assign a diagnosis, rather than describe a diagnostic impression, it is important to verify that the individual meets all the diagnostic criteria, particularly the exclusionary ones. Try to use all five *DSM-IV* axes, unless this is unimportant to your referring source. If there is more than one diagnostic consideration, identify the primary and secondary diagnoses and their relationship with each other. Alternative diagnoses that require further evaluation should be discussed.]

Summary:
[Begin with a general orientation statement, followed by a summary of the relevant findings. One or two sentences on each section and on the major finding are usually sufficient. Restate the diagnostic impressions, setting the stage for your recommendations.]

Recommendations:
[Discuss recommendations, crisis issues, and client factors that may impact the implementation of the recommendations. Issues that need immediate attention (e.g., dangerousness, hospitalization) should be addressed first. Recommendations should be made that are possible to implement and that consider the client's resources. Be as specific as possible. Anticipate the difficulties the client may encounter with your recommendations and develop prevention plans or strategies to avoid these. Check Section II for common recommendations made for specific disorders.]

Name, Signature, Date, Telephone

Testing Tip
Practical Tips for Good Report Writing

- Keep the report referral focused.
- Your impressions, summary and recommendations are most important.
- Base it on the data, not intuition.
- Be user friendly.
- Be relevant, not redundant.
- Address inconsistencies.
- Discuss alternative diagnoses.
- Provide resource-appropriate referrals.
- Proofread and check your data.

---

timed tasks, so it would make sense to cluster those tests together. You may find it useful to organize some sections so that global issues are first mentioned followed by specific ones, or by considering strengths and weaknesses. Do not make inferences based on single findings, but rather cross-validate with multiple data points. You must also consider the strength of the data. Treatment issues should consider risk factors, crises, impulse control, and abuse (Chapter 9).

RAPID REPORT WRITING

In the ideal world, a psychological assessment report could be very short and simple. You would merely answer the referral question, summarize the client's diagnosis, cognitive and emotional function, and provide treatment recommendations. However, the following circumstances conspire to slow you down, and some of them are avoidable.

Ethics

If laypeople are going to read a report, it must be understandable and written in a way that prevents harm. This usually requires you to write more descriptive information, so that nonclinicians can make sense of it. However, you can usually provide a summary report for laypeople when it is requested, saving you time.

In addition, you may write a short report that assumes sophisticated knowledge in your referring source. However, it is possible that your report will be sent by the referring clinician to the client. Although this report may not be understandable to the client, because you were not the one to send it out, your conduct is not unethical. A simple remedy is to meet with the client or write a summary report.

Obsessiveness

Assessments create a huge amount of data, and most poorly written reports describe and treat it all equally. Some items are more important than others. For example, you may have gathered a detailed history, looking for early developmental clues. If nothing significant was uncovered, it's fine to make a simple summary statement, rather than wasting both your time and the reader's, too. Some clinicians also have difficulty omitting information from lengthy computer-generated interpretive narrative test reports.

Redundancy

Redundancies occur most frequently when the clinician makes clinical comments on test findings that are also discussed later in the Diagnosis or Impressions section of the report. Keep in mind that most referral sources focus first on the concluding sections of the report, and may not have the time or interest to read the findings on individual tests.

TIPS FOR REPORT WRITING

Referral Focus

Your report should be focused on the referral question. Although additional data will come to light that alter the report's focus, don't overlook the original reason for referral. If the summarized test data does not answer the referral question, address these limitations. For example, the client may not have cooperated sufficiently.

Format and Style

Write your report with the referring source in mind. When your assessment involves a new site or colleague, discuss their needs in advance. Use headings to divide the report into its component parts. Use lists to summarize the tests that were administered and to lay out treatment recommendations. Using the client's name can help personalize the report.

Choose Your Words Carefully

We urge caution when using inflammatory or emotional terms such as "brain damaged," "dysfunctional," or "impaired" without proper justification. Be careful not to use emotionally laden or evocative terms.

Avoid Jargon and Formulas

In general, avoid the sole use of technical terms and formulas, unless this is what is desired by your referring source. It is better to use percentiles rather than raw or standardized scores, unless the report is being provided to a school psychologist or a clinician skilled in testing. If you desire to report MMPI-2 or MCMI-III profile codes, keep in mind that only experienced clinicians can comprehend them. Behavioral descriptors (e.g., Chapter 4, Appendixes D and E) are far more informative.

Report Length

There are no rules for determining report length, though this is usually heavily determined by your referral source. It can be anywhere from 2 to 12 pages, though we hope that most adult assessment reports fall within 4 to 6 pages. Child assessment reports tend to be lengthy due to the need to provide a developmental history. Whenever a report is requested by the client or a family member, you will need to write in more understandable terms, resulting in a longer report.

Use of Raw Data

Make efforts not to release raw test data in your reports because it can be easily misinterpreted and cause harm to the client. It is also potentially unethical. Most assessments express scores in terms of percentiles and/or verbal descriptors. These terms are usually sufficient. Similarly, refrain from quoting the client, unless such statements could increase the reader's understanding and would not be taken negatively.

Releasing raw test data to the client should be done in a manner that avoids the client's harm, minimizes any invasion of privacy, and maintains test security. A good feedback session usually will provide enough feedback to the client so that raw data will not be requested. Often a summary report is sufficient for the client's needs.

Prediction and Prognosis

After you release a report, you have no control over it. Your evaluation is limited in its ability to predict the future. Thus, base your interpretations on specific findings that can be supported by the data. Don't extend the data and interpretations beyond their scope, no matter how good it sounds.

Report Variations and Feedback Formats

While the report is the primary means of providing feedback, you are often required to provide verbal summaries with the client, parents, or significant others. The American Psychological Association encourages you to initially discuss how feedback will be provided, by clarifying the nature of the results, the format of the feedback, and with whom the information will be shared. Here are a range of settings in which one may be required to provide verbal feedback.

Testing Tip
Report Writing Do's and Don'ts

- *Do* gear your report to the referral source.
- *Do* document informed consent and relevant confidentiality issues.
- *Don't* provide irrelevant history, no matter how interesting.
- *Don't* use raw data, particularly IQ scores, unless the report is going to a professional who needs this data (such as a school psychologist).
- *Don't* use jargon.
- *Do* focus on strengths.
- *Don't* use words like "impaired" or "poorly" unless there is supporting test data.
- *Do* provide a clear diagnostic impression.
- *Do* provide recommendations that are useful and feasible.

CLIENT OR FAMILY REPORT

Clients and families should not receive a report without first having a feedback session. The major role of the report is to provide information that will increase the client's or parents' understanding of the presenting problems. You may use a similar outline as discussed in this chapter. Use lay terms that are easily understood. Do not report clinical labels or specific cognitive test scores unless you believe the information will be beneficial to the patient and has already been discussed in advance. Avoid the use of emotionally charged terms or negative predictions because they can become self-fulfilling, especially when the client has limited insight. Similarly, consider that parents who are dealing with a challenging child or adolescent may have lost sight of individual strengths. Overall, you are trying to convey to the client and the family an empathic understanding of the client.

CLIENT FEEDBACK

There are several ways of starting the session. You may want to ask the client to restate the reason for referral and any prior concerns. For more anxious clients, you will likely take the lead. Because the amount of information can be overwhelming, it is helpful, prior to the session to identify three to four major points that will be addressed. Present results in simple language. Asking clients to rephrase what they have heard ensures that you got your point across. It is important that throughout the session the client feels validated and heard, that you address any concerns, and that you avoid negative terms or labels. You may need to help the client reframe deficits.

Some clinicians provide test data in terms of confidence intervals rather than as percentiles or verbal descriptors. In this case, if the client had a test score that fell in the average range, but with a standard error that placed the true score somewhere between average and high average, you may want to tell the client that performance fell within the average to high average range. Always be willing to clarify the psychometric limits of tests.

PARENT FEEDBACK OR FAMILY CONFERENCES

The issues for a parent feedback session are very similar to those previously described. You may or may not have the child included in the feedback session. At the onset, ask the parents for their perception of the problems. Give the parents adequate time to talk about their parenting experiences and time for adequate closure. You may want to invite the treating or referring therapist to attend, though this should not occur if it will lead to greater parental anxiety. Some parents are not ready to accept your findings so be alert for guilt, denial, and over-identification. Parents who have struggled with similar problems may be reluctant to become involved and appear as hostile, rejecting, or defensive. The feedback session should not be problem dominated. Provide adequate time to discuss recommendations and develop a follow-up plan. Parents should also be encouraged to call you after the evaluation if any questions or issues arise on reflection.

INPATIENT REPORT

Inpatient reports can be identical to outpatient ones, except that you may be called on to place more attention to risk issues, crisis intervention, and therapeutic management. If you have dictation privileges, this service will provide a rapid method for doing your work. Because the report will typically be placed in the patient's chart, language and style need to be appropriate for a wide audience.

CLINICAL ROUNDS OR REFERRAL FEEDBACK

You may be requested to present the assessment results at clinical medical rounds. In general, you need to present the report highlights in bulletin format, usually not exceeding 5 to 10 minutes. Similarly, the referring therapist may call to inquire about your immediate impressions and concerns. In these cases, the format of the answer is determined by the request (see Testing Tip for an outline for rapid feedback).

Testing Tip
Rapid Feedback for an Assessment

- Reiteration of the referral question.
- Validity of the assessment, rapport, and motivation.
- Risk issues or immediate concerns.
- Diagnosis or diagnostic impressions.
- Treatment recommendations (short- and long-term).

Give feedback in a format that the recipient will relate to and understand. Given the time constraints on many professionals, it is important to allow adequate time to discuss the recommendations and any factors that may affect prognosis. We strongly recommend not waiting for the referring therapist to call you, but rather keeping the therapist informed of progress throughout the evaluation.

SCHOOL REPORT

You will likely need to work with the school system to implement your assessment's recommendations. Besides having releases, keep parents informed of your contact with the school and review in advance the information that will be shared. During the evaluation, teachers usually offer valuable insights and you may need them to complete rating scales. School reports should include only pertinent family and emotional issues that affect the child's academic functioning. In contrast, raw test data and scaled scores are frequently included. When making recommendations, consider what is available in the child's school and suggest alternatives if necessary. When the assessment is completed, organize a meeting with the parents and teachers to discuss your recommendations. Many school districts provide individualized educational plans (IEP).

SCHOOL FEEDBACK

You may find that the hardest part of providing feedback to school personnel is in dealing with scheduling. One aspect of providing feedback is to help the school personnel form a similar understanding of the client as your own. Allow the teaching staff to share their impressions and concerns, and do it in a way that is respectful. Create a specific plan to put your recommendations in place that has concrete goals and a time frame to reassess their effectiveness. Make sure that there is a communications mechanism between the parents and the school.

FORENSIC REPORTS

Forensic evaluations initially appeal to many clinicians because they are relatively lucrative. However, unless you have specific training or supervision in forensic psychology, we strongly discourage you from getting involved in any assessments that place you in the position of being an expert witness.

COURT TESTIMONY

It is possible that you may be called into court to render an opinion on a client that you tested in the past. If you have never had a deposition taken or given testimony, you must get consultation immediately from a forensic psychologist or an attorney. Do not rely on support from the attorneys who request your services. Their primary responsibility is to their client and to do whatever it takes to assist their client.

Child custody evaluations often create the most difficulty for clinicians, leading to an increased risk of lawsuits and licensing board complaints. Again, consultation will be needed. Be aware of the APA guidelines on custody evaluation.

MANAGED CARE REPORT

When you are requested to write a report specifically for a managed care organization, you should clarify the length desired and type of information preferred. Clarify confidentiality with all relevant parties (releases), and identify who will have access to the report and where it will be filed. Review with the client the information that will be shared with the insurance company prior to its release. Many managed care companies are satisfied with a brief summary that includes tests administered, time spent on administration, diagnostic impressions, and recommendations.

TESTING A CLIENT WHO HAS MANAGED CARE INSURANCE

Frequently, managed care companies only reimburse for certain tests and have upper limits to the number of hours they will reimburse. You may need to petition for more time or for the use of more tests. Keep in mind that you are responsible for the most appropriate assessment, not the managed care company.

Test Availability and Test Publishers

Sources	Scoring Software Available	Interpretive Software Available
The Anser System		
Educators Publishing Service, Inc.	No	No
Beck Depression Inventory (BDI-II)		
The Psychological Corporation	Yes	Yes
Brown Attention-Deficit Disorder Scales		
The Psychological Corporation	No	No
Psychological Assessment Resources, Inc.	No	No
Child Behavior Checklist (CBCL/4-18, CBCL/2-3, TRF, YSR)		
Thomas M. Achenbach, Ph.D.	No	No
Children's Apperception Test (CAT)		
Psychological Assessment Resources, Inc.	No	No
The Psychological Corporation	No	No
Children's Depression Inventory (CDI)		
MHS	Yes	Yes
NCS Assessments	No	No
Pro-Ed	No	No
The Psychological Corporation	No	No
Children's Memory Scale (CMS)		
The Psychological Corporation	Yes	No
Psychological Assessment Resources, Inc.	No	No
Color Trails Test		
Psychological Assessment Resources, Inc.	No	No
Confrontational Naming Subtest (Boston Naming Test)		
The Psychological Corporation	No	No
Psychological Assessment Resources, Inc.	No	No
Riverside Publishing	No	No
Conners' Rating Scales—Revised (CRS-R; includes CPRS, CTRS)		
NCS Assessments	No	No
MHS	Yes	Yes
Pro-Ed	No	No
Psychological Assessment Resources, Inc.*	Yes	No
The Psychological Corporation	Yes	Yes

(Continued)

Sources	Scoring Software Available	Interpretive Software Available
Developmental Test of Visual-Motor Integration (VMI)		
Psychological Assessment Resources, Inc.	No	No
Pro-Ed	No	No
Western Psychological Services	No	No
Draw a Person: Screening Procedure for Emotional Disturbance (DAP:SPED)		
Pro-Ed	No	No
Riverside Publishing	No	No
The Psychological Corporation	No	No
Eating Disorder Inventory-2 (EDI-2)		
Psychological Assessment Resources, Inc.**	Yes	Yes
Expressive One-Word Picture Vocabulary Test		
Pro-Ed	No	No
Psychological Assessment Resources, Inc.	No	No
Riverside Publishing	No	No
Western Psychological Services	No	No
Hare Psychopathy Check List		
The Psychological Corporation	No	No
Psychological Assessment Resources, Inc.	No	No
House-Tree-Person Technique		
Western Psychological Services	No	No
Psychological Assessment Resources, Inc.	No	No
Kinetic Family Drawing		
Western Psychological Services	No	No
Millon Adolescent Clinical Inventory (MACI)		
NCS Assessments**	Yes	Yes[†]
Millon Clinical Multiaxial Inventory-III (MCMI-III)		
NCS Assessments**	Yes	Yes[†]
Psychological Assessment Resources, Inc.	No	Yes
Minnesota Multiphasic Personality Inventory-Adolescent (MMPI-A)		
NCS Assessments**	Yes	Yes[†]
MHS	No	Yes
Psychological Assessment Resources, Inc.	No	Yes
Minnesota Multiphasic Personality Inventory-II (MMPI-II)		
NCS Assessments**	Yes	Yes[†]
MHS	No	Yes
Psychological Assessment Resources, Inc.	No	Yes
National Adult Reading Test (NART, 2nd Ed.)		
American Guidance Service	No	No

Sources	Scoring Software Available	Interpretive Software Available
Peabody Picture Vocabulary Test-III (PPVT-III)		
American Guidance Service	No	No
Rey Complex Figure Test and Recognition Trial		
Psychological Assessment Resources, Inc.	No	No
The Psychological Corporation	No	No
Roberts Apperception Test for Children		
Western Psychological Services	No	No
Rorschach Inkblot Test		
NCS Assessments	No	No
MHS	Yes	Yes
Psychological Assessment Resources, Inc.	Yes	Yes
The Psychological Corporation	Yes	Yes
Ruff Figural Fluency Test		
Psychological Assessment Resources, Inc.	No	No
Structured Interview of Reported Symptoms (SIRS)		
Psychological Assessment Resources, Inc.	No	No
Test of Memory Malingering (TOMM)		
MHS	Yes	Yes
Thematic Apperception Test (TAT)		
NCS Assessments	No	No
Psychological Assessment Resources, Inc.	No	No
Riverside Publishing	No	No
The Psychological Corporation	No	No
MHS	No	No
The Token Test for Children		
Pro-Ed	No	No
Riverside Publishing	No	No
Psychological Assessment Resources, Inc.	No	No
Traumatic Symptom Inventory (TSI)		
Psychological Assessment Resources, Inc.	Yes	No
The Psychological Corporation	No	No
Traumatic Symptom Checklist for Children		
Psychological Assessment Resources, Inc.	Yes	No
The Psychological Corporation	No	No
Vineland Adaptive Rating Scales (VARS)		
American Guidance Service	Yes	No
Wechsler Adult Intelligence Scale-III (WAIS-III)		
The Psychological Corporation	Yes	No
Wechsler Individual Achievement Test (WIAT)		
The Psychological Corporation	Yes	Yes

(Continued)

Sources	Scoring Software Available	Interpretive Software Available
Wechsler Intelligence Scale for Children-3rd ed. (WISC-III)		
The Psychological Corporation	Yes	Yes
MHS	No	Yes
Wechsler Memory Scale-III (WMS-III)		
The Psychological Corporation	Yes	No
Wechsler Preschool and Primary Scale of Intelligence (WPPSI)		
Psychological Assessment Resources, Inc.	No	Yes
The Psychological Corporation	Yes	Yes
Wide Range Achievement Test-Revised (WRAT-III)		
Riverside Publishing	No	No
Psychological Assessment Resources, Inc.	Yes	No
Pro-Ed	No	No
MHS	No	No
Wide Range Assessment of Memory and Learning (WRAML)		
The Psychological Corporation	No	No
Psychological Assessment Resources, Inc.	No	No
Pro-Ed	No	No
Riverside Publishing	No	No
Wisconsin Card Sorting Test		
The Psychological Corporation	No	No
Psychological Assessment Resources, Inc.	Yes	No
Pro-Ed	No	No
MHS	Yes	No
Woodcock-Johnson-Revised (WJ-R)		
Riverside Publishing	Yes	Yes

*Paper-and-pencil and computer administration formats available.

**Paper-and-pencil, audiocassette, and computer administration formats available in English. Paper-and-pencil and audiocassette versions available in Spanish.

[†] Scoring service available by modem or mail-in.

Note: Psychological Assessment Resources, Inc., carries MCMI-III interpretive software but not the test itself. MHS and Psychological Assessment Resources, Inc., carry DOS and Windows interpretive software for the MMPI-A but not the test itself. MHS, Pro-Ed, and Psychological Assessment Resources, Inc., carry DOS and/or Windows interpretive software but not the test itself.

Test Publishers and Suppliers

Thomas M. Achenbach, Ph.D.
Phone: 802-656-8313
Fax: 802-656-2602
Web site: www.uvm.edu/~cbcl

American Guidance Service (AGS)
Phone: 800-328-2560
Fax: 612-786-9077
Web site: www.agsnet.com

Educators Publishing Service, Inc.
Phone: 800-225-5750
Fax: 617-547-0412
Web site: www.epsbooks.com

MHS
Phone: 800-456-3003
Fax: 416-424-1736
Web site: www.mhs.com

NCS Assessments
Phone: 800-627-7271
Fax: 612-939-5199
Web site: www.ncs.com/ncscorp/top
/prodserv/assessmt.htm

Pro-Ed
Phone: 800-897-3202; 512-451-3246
Fax: 800-397-7633
Web site: www.proedinc.com

**Psychological Assessment
Resources, Inc. (PAR)**
Phone: 800-331-8378
Fax: 800-727-9329
Web site: www.parinc.com

Riverside Publishing
A Houghton Mifflin Company
Phone: 800-323-9540
Fax: 630-467-7192
Web site: www.riverpub.com

The Psychological Corporation
Harcourt Brace & Company
Phone: 800-211-8378
Fax: 800-232-1223
TDD: 800-723-1318
Web site: www.psychcorp.com

Western Psychological Services
Phone: 800-648-8857
Fax: 310-478-7838
TDD: None available
Web site: None

APPENDIX B

Mini-Mental State Examination

Orientation
- Year, month, day, date, season.   _____/5
- State, county, town, place (hospital, street address),
  floor of the building.   _____/5

Registration
- Say to the client: "I'm going to name three objects. After
  I say them, I want you to repeat them. Remember
  them because I'm going to ask you to say them again in
  a few minutes." Name three objects (ball, flag, tree), and
  repeat all three for up to five trials until the client is able
  to say all three. Score one point for each word correctly
  repeated at the first trial.   _____/3

Attention
- Ask client to subtract 7s from 100, repeat each result
  aloud, until told to stop. Stop the client after 5: 100, 93,
  86, 79, 72, 65 (do not correct if errors are made).
  Subtract one point each time the client incorrectly
  subtracts seven from the previous number, regardless of
  whether the previous calculation was correct.
  Alternatively, if unable to do serial 7s: have client
  spell "world" forwards, and then ask client to spell
  "world" backwards: DLROW. Score 1 point for every
  letter in the correct sequence. Score client's best
  performance on either task.   _____/5

Recall
- Ask the client to recall the three words learned earlier.   _____/3

Language
- Hold up a pencil and ask the client to name it; repeat with a watch. Score 1 point for each item correctly named. _____/2
- Ask the client to repeat the spoken phrase: "No ifs, ands, or buts." The client must pronounce the whole phrase correctly. _____/1
- Give the client the following three stage command: Take this piece of paper in your right hand, fold it in half, and put it on the floor. Score 1 point for each stage correctly performed. _____/3
- Ask client to read and obey the following command written on a piece of paper: Close your eyes. _____/1
- Ask the client to write a sentence. Score if it is sensible, and has a subject and a verb. Spelling mistakes are acceptable. _____/1

Copying
- Ask the client to copy two intersecting pentagons. All angles must be present and two must intersect. _____/1

Total Score: _____/30

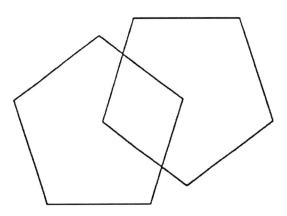

APPENDIX C

Statistical Translations

Percentile Ranks	Standard Scores	T-Scores	Scaled Scores	Z-Scores
>99	145	80	—	3.0
>99	137	75	—	2.5
99	133	72	17	—
98	130	70	16	2.0
97	127	69	—	1.82–1.95
96	126	67	—	1.70–1.81
95	124	66	15	1.60–1.69
94	123	—	—	1.52–1.59
93	122	65	—	1.5
92	121	64	—	1.38–1.43
91	120	—	14	1.32–1.37
90	119	63	—	1.26–1.31
89	118	—	—	1.21–1.25
88	—	62	—	1.16–1.20
87	117	—	—	1.11–1.15
86	116	61	—	1.06–1.10
85	—	—	—	1.02–1.05
84	115	60	13	1.0
83	114	—	—	.94–.97
82	—	59	—	.90–.93
81	113	—	—	.86–.89
80	—	—	—	.83–.85
79	112	58	—	.79–.82
78	—	—	—	.76–.78
77	111	—	—	.73–.75
76	—	57	—	.70–.73
75	110	—	12	.66–.69
74	—	—	—	.63–.65
73	109	56	—	.60–.62
72	—	—	—	.57–.59
71	—	—	—	.54–.56

Percentile Ranks	Standard Scores	T-Scores	Scaled Scores	Z-Scores
70	108	—	—	.51–.53
69	—	55	—	0.5
68	107	—	—	.46–.48
67	—	—	—	.43–.45
66	106	54	—	.40–.42
65	—	—	—	.38–.39
64	—	—	—	.35–.37
63	105	—	11	.32–.34
62	—	53	—	−.30–.31
61	104	—	—	.27–.29
60	—	—	—	.25–.26
59	—	—	—	.22–.24
58	103	52	—	.19–.21
57	—	—	—	.17–.18
56	—	—	—	.14–.16
55	102	—	—	.12–.13
54	—	51	—	.09–.11
53	101	—	—	.07–.08
52	—	—	—	.04–.06
51	—	—	—	.02–.03
51	—	—	—	—
50	100	50	10	0.0
49	—	—	—	−.03
48	—	—	—	−.06
47	99	—	—	−.08
46	—	49	—	−.11
45	98	—	—	−.13
44	—	—	—	−.16
43	—	—	—	−.18
42	97	48	—	−.21
41	—	—	—	−.24
40	—	—	—	−.26
39	96	—	—	−.29
38	—	47	—	−.31
37	95	—	9	−.34
36	—	—	—	−.37
35	—	—	—	−.39
34	94	46	—	−.42
33	—	—	—	−.45
32	93	—	—	−.48
31	—	45	—	− 0.5
30	92	—	—	−.53
29	—	—	—	−.56
28	—	—	—	−.59
27	91	44	—	−.62
26	—	—	—	−.65

(Continued)

Percentile Ranks	Standard Scores	T-Scores	Scaled Scores	Z-Scores
25	90	—	8	−.69
24	—	43	—	−.72
23	89	—	—	−.75
22	—	—	—	−.78
21	88	42	—	−.82
20	—	—	—	−.85
19	87	—	—	−.89
18	86	41	—	−.93
17	—	—	—	−.97
16	85	40	7	− 1.0
15	—	—	—	− 1.05
14	84	39	—	− 1.10
13	83	—	—	− 1.15
12	82	38	—	− 1.20
11	—	—	—	− 1.25
10	81	37	—	− 1.31
9	80	—	6	− 1.37
8	79	36	—	− 1.43
7	78	35	—	− 1.51
6	77	—	—	− 1.59
5	75	34	5	− 1.69
4	74	33	—	− 1.81
3	72	31	—	− 1.95
2	70	30	4	− 2.0
1	67	28	3	− 2.16
< 1	63	25	—	− 2.5
< 1	55	20	—	− 3.0

APPENDIX D

Interpretations of MMPI-2 and MMPI-A Code Types

Two-Point Code Types

12/21

These clients may have somatic discomfort, without a real organic basis. They react to stress with physical symptoms and are overly concerned with their health. They often report feeling anxious; they frequently report dysphoria and self-consciousness/shyness. They may seem attention-seeking or dependent. They are most often diagnosed with Anxiety, Depressive, or Somatoform Disorders, and less frequently, Schizophrenia. Adolescents may report weakness or fatigue.

13/31

These clients usually present with somatic complaints and try to appear as normal, optimistic people; they may have conversion symptoms (especially if combined with lower Scale 2). People with the 13/31 code type can use defense mechanisms extensively, are not grossly incapacitated, and lack psychological insight. These individuals are often immature, egocentric, insecure, attention-seeking, passive-aggressive, and have social difficulties. They are usually diagnosed with Somatoform Disorders. They may be difficult to motivate in psychotherapy; adolescents, on the other hand, may show a greater willingness to participate in psychotherapy.

Note: Adapted from Archer (1997), Graham (1993), Greene (1991), and Groth-Marnat (1997).

14/41

These clients may report extreme somatic symptoms, act anxious or uncertain, or have substance abuse problems. Having a negative outlook, they lack well-defined goals. They are demanding in interpersonal relationships and often disliked by peers. Hypochondriasis or personality disorders are common diagnoses. They may be resistant to psychotherapy. Adolescents with this code type may appear more defiant, pushy, and proactive than adults with this code type.

15/51

This code type is uncommon in adults. Adolescent clients often complain of physical illness, appear passive, and are prone to conflicts with parents. They may have a prior history of serious medical problems. They may not be open in therapy, and have difficulty forming tight attachments to others. They may seem effeminate.

16/61

This profile is not common in adults, and is described as a combination of hostility and hypochondriacal complaints. Adolescent clients appear evasive, and avoid close emotional connections with others. Suicidal attempts may be more common. They may come from homes where the father is absent or rejecting.

17/71

These clients report many physical symptoms that reflect tension, anxiety, or pain. Along with the somatic complaints, anxiety, insecurity, obsessive thoughts, social fears, and depressive symptoms are likely. This code type is not mentioned in adolescent literature.

18/81

These clients have strong feelings of anger, but are unable to express them appropriately. They feel socially inadequate, suspicious of others, and may feel isolated. Flat affect, dysphoria, somatic concerns, confused thinking, and distractibility may be present. Poor work history and social relationships are common. Common diagnoses are Schizophrenia, Anxiety Disorders, or Schizoid Personality Disorder.

Adolescents with this profile may show thought disorder, poor academic skills, and trouble forming peer relationships.

19/91

Although verbal, extroverted, agitated, and belligerent, these clients are covering underlying passive-dependency. They tend to experience significant distress, with anxiety, restlessness, and somatic complaints. They are reluctant to accept psychological interpretations of their symptoms. They have high aspirations but lack clear goals, and are frustrated by falling short. Diagnoses may include Hypochondriasis or Bipolar Disorder. This code type is not mentioned in adolescent literature.

23/32

These clients are characterized by reports of significant depression coupled with anxiety symptoms. They are often passive or insecure, and do not subject themselves to situations of potential failure. They overcontrol their feelings and deny unacceptable impulses, and sexual maladjustment is common. 23/32 is more common in women, and the most frequent diagnosis is Depressive Disorder. Adolescents with this profile may have poor social relationships, resulting in loneliness and isolation.

24/42

There are two types of clients who may show this profile. Those of the first type appear to have significant sociopathic features. Their depression is temporary and insincere, and future episodes of acting out are likely. When Scales 2 and 4 are very elevated, suicidal ideation and attempts are possible. Those clients of the second type show chronic depression, and have anger associated with dissatisfying aspects of their lives. They may appear as dependent or immature. Personality Disorder diagnoses are most common, as is alcohol abuse. Adolescents with this profile may have parents who are inconsistent or unavailable, or may feel there is no one whom they can turn to for support.

25/52

These clients may appear as anxious and socially isolated, and report somatic symptoms. Adolescents with this code type also may appear as anxious and uncertain, depressed, and were not described as masculine (e.g., poor athletes). They may do well in school while being teased by others.

26/62

These clients are angry, depressed, sensitive to real or imagined threat, misinterpret neutral statements as rejecting, and ruminate over any criticism. They are seen as hostile or resentful, and they have interpersonal difficulties. They reject others, first as a protective mechanism, but have little insight about how this causes others to avoid them. Moderate elevations suggest a paranoid style, and higher elevations (in addition to higher 7, 8, and 9) suggest Schizophrenia (paranoid type). Another possible diagnosis is Dysthymic Disorder. This code type is not mentioned in adolescent literature.

27/72

These clients are noticeably anxious and depressed; they worry excessively. Somatic and depressive symptoms are frequent. When they don't achieve personal goals, they experience feelings of inferiority. They are indecisive, insecure, and blame themselves for their problems. They tend to be perfectionistic, rigid thinkers, but are excellent candidates for psychotherapy. If Scale 3 is also elevated, they can be docile or passive-dependent in interpersonal relationships and get clingy when under stress. Always assess for suicidality in these clients. Anxiety Disorders (e.g., OCD) and Depressive Disorders are common diagnoses. Adolescents with this code type appear similar to adults.

28/82

These clients typically report significant depressive and anxiety symptoms (e.g., somatic or sleep complaints and/or cognitive slowing). They can appear dependent or unassertive. They may have difficulty in forming close relationships, which increases feelings of worthlessness. They appear clinically depressed. Suicidal ideation is common in adults and adolescents and should be carefully assessed. Common diagnoses include Bipolar Disorder and Schizoaffective Disorder. Adolescents with this profile appear similar to adults.

29/92

These clients are narcissistic, in a manner consistent with hypomania. They may have worries about being successful, while at the same time sabotaging their own efforts. Tension, agitation, and somatic symptoms may occur. History may include periods of serious depression, and alcohol or drugs may be used. Bipolar Disorder is common. This profile is not found in adolescent literature.

20/02

These clients exhibit mild dysthymia along with social isolation. They feel inadequate and lack social skills. They are passive, conventional, and may show an increased suicide risk. They show less motivation to change, having accepted their unhappy lifestyle. However, active or cognitive-behavioral treatment methods might lead to some benefit in improving social skills. Similar to adults, adolescents with this profile appear as meek, isolated loners.

31/13

These clients develop somatic symptoms when under stress that disappear when the stress has been eliminated. There are usually secondary gains associated with the symptoms, which are often pain-based. These clients also tend to be anxious, nervous, and are prone to brief outbursts or crying. If L or K are elevated, they try to act normal, resulting in a defensive stance that prevents them from admitting to psychological problems. There is no adolescent literature related to this profile.

34/43

These clients have difficulty dealing with their anger. Higher Scale 3 indicates indirect expression of anger, while higher Scale 4 indicates overcontrol, followed by violent or emotional outbursts. They lack insight about their behavior. They frequently blame others for their problems, which may be due to anger from earlier family conflicts or trauma. They feel easily criticized. Suicidality is common, especially after losing control and alcohol or drug abuse. They may have somatic complaints (e.g., tiredness, headache). The most frequent diagnosis is a Personality Disorder. Adolescents with this profile do not show the levels of hostility seen in adults. Rather, they appear as depressed, and are likely to have parental conflicts.

35/53

This profile is relatively uncommon and most literature pertains to adolescents. Adolescents with this profile tend to come from moralistic and religious homes.

They may appear depressed, withdrawn and inhibited, attention-seeking and insecure. Some may show weight problems (e.g., obesity, anorexia).

36/63

These clients tend to be angry, defiant, hostile, and resentful but will not admit any of these feelings. They may report anxiety or somatic complaints. The hostility may be due to unconscious family issues. They may be difficult to engage in psychotherapy. Adolescents with this profile are more likely to show suicidal behavior than adults.

38/83

These peculiar clients are often anxious and under significant distress which results in the development of somatic symptoms. Depression and hopelessness are common. They can seem apathetic and pessimistic. They can show histrionic signs, such as immaturity, dependency, and a need for affection. They may complain of cognitive deficits, but instead have a thought disorder. A diagnosis of Schizophrenia is most likely, followed by Somatoform Disorder. A supportive therapeutic relationship can be beneficial, insight-oriented therapy may be too intense due to thought disorder. This profile is not found in adolescent literature.

39/93

These clients are dramatic, outgoing people who like attention. They often have somatic complaints that remit with medical attention, but appear again in the future. They are hostile, grouchy, and unwilling to consider psychological explanations for their problems. There is no adolescent literature pertaining to this code type.

45/54

Clients with this profile are most often male. They are defensive, satisfied with their behavior, report little distress, and think rationally. They may be somewhat unconventional, rebelling against social rules. Dominance and dependence may be central themes. Male college students may be having problems with peers, or adjustment problems related to heterosexuality. Adolescents with this profile appear differently than adults. They have greater ego strength and may appear better adjusted. Yet they are more prone to antisocial behavior (e.g., truancy, suspension, low grades, drug use).

46/64

These clients are immature, angry, narcissistic, resentful, self-indulgent, passive-dependent, and suspicious of others. They have interpersonal and job problems and avoid interpersonal closeness. They repress their chronic anger and mistrust authority. They blame others for their problems, and are thus poor candidates for psychotherapy. Anxiety, depression, and somatic symptoms are frequently reported. Women with this profile may tend to identify with traditional female stereotypes and are dependent on men. A Personality Disorder or Schizophrenia (paranoid type) are common diagnoses. Adolescents with this profile tend to be provocative, in conflict with parental figures, and prone to impulsive acting out.

47/74

These clients vacillate between insensitivity and excessive concern for the social consequences of their behavior. Acting out (including substance abuse) may be followed by short-lived feelings of remorse. However, the pattern invariably repeats. They may complain of vague somatic symptoms, tension, or fatigue. They are insecure and guilt-ridden people who require reassurance of self-worth, but despite this, psychotherapy often has little success in breaking their cyclical behavior. Antisocial Personality and Anxiety Disorders are common diagnoses. Adolescents with this code type appear similar to adults.

48/84

These clients fit poorly into society; they seem moody, resentful like social misfits. Their erratic behavior and poor impulse control is reflected in their antisocial behavior. When they commit crimes, they tend to be vicious, assaultive, and poorly planned and executed. Substance abuse, prostitution, and promiscuity may occur. Their history may indicate poor adjustment. These people are essentially insecure. They have few social skills, are socially isolated, and have poor self-concepts. They do not trust others and see the world as threatening or rejecting. They blame others for their problems. They may have periods of suicidal ideation which require careful assessment. Antisocial, Schizoid, and Paranoid Personality Disorders and Schizophrenia (paranoid type) are the most frequent diagnoses. This code type is more frequent among child molesters, rapists, and sex offenders. Adolescents with this profile may have poor grades, and are more likely to have been sexually abused.

49/94

These clients lack appreciation for social mores, appearing antisocial. They often are in trouble with the authorities due to their excessive need for excitement. Thus, behavioral history may include substance abuse, fighting, relationship difficulties, and sexual acting out. They are narcissistic, selfish, irresponsible, impulsive, and hostile. They have poor judgment, don't take responsibility for their behavior, and fail to learn from experience. They blame others for their problems. They make an initially good first impression, yet interpersonal relationships are superficial. Antisocial Personality Disorder is the most common diagnosis, although some patients receive the diagnosis of Bipolar Disorder. Adolescents with this profile appear similar to adults, though they are more likely to show the potential for change (due to their age).

40/04

This code type is not typically seen in adults. Adolescents with this code type appear mistrustful, grandiose, resentful, and may feel socially awkward. They may seem shy, and socially uninvolved, having few friends and tending to overreact to minor events.

56/65

This code type is not typically seen in adults. Adolescents with this code type tend to admit to their problems, but avoid forming close relationships with others. They can be resentful and insecure, resulting in frequent acting out (e.g., drug use, violent behavior). Some adolescents may show preoccupation with themes of death, murder, and brutality.

59/95

This code type is not typically seen in adults. Adolescents with this code type tend to have fewer psychological problems relative to other code types. A common conflict is between dependency and assertiveness. They seldom have school problems, though parents may describe them as difficult to handle, with family conflicts common.

50/05

This code type is not typically seen in adults. Adolescents with this code type tend to appear as cautious and withdrawn, fearing close relationships. They may seem anxious due to conflicts centered around sexuality or assertiveness. They tend to be obsessive thinkers, preferring isolation over help-seeking behavior. Some may be in special education courses.

67/76

These clients are anxious, hypersensitive, suspicious, rigid, and stubborn. They express their hostility indirectly, resulting in intense and unstable relationships, and poor social skills. They are resistant to change. There is no adolescent literature pertaining to this profile.

68/86

These clients often manifest psychotic symptoms including thought disorder, cognitive deficits, delusions, hallucinations, blunted affect, or bizarre/incoherent speech. They feel insecure, inferior, and guilt over personal failures. They are withdrawn, poorly socialized, and are suspicious of others. They may cope with stress is by daydreaming, and it can be hard for them to separate fantasy from reality. Others see them as hostile, suspicious, or strange. Some are diagnosed with Paranoid or Schizoid Personality Disorders, while those with more severe profiles tend to be diagnosed with Schizophrenia (paranoid type). Consultation for psychotropic medication should be considered, and the risk of suicide requires careful assessment. They may be difficult to engage in psychotherapy because of their level of mistrust. Adolescents with this profile have been found to have been physically punished as children. They are disliked by their peers, and may have a bad temper.

69/96

Clients with this code type may appear as dependent, worried, and tearful. Others are described as angry, irritable, and grandiose. They overreact to stress and may respond by withdrawing into fantasy. Emotional expression may alternate between overcontrol and direct outbursts of emotion. Psychotic symptoms may be present, including thought disorder, cognitive difficulties, disorientation, poor judgment, obsessional thought, irrelevant/incoherent speech, delusions, and/or hallucinations. Schizophrenia (paranoid type) is a common diagnosis. They are often seen in inpatient settings. This profile is not found in adolescent literature.

78/87

These clients are in a high level of distress. They may feel chronically anxious and depressed; they are introspective, ruminative, and overideational. They may appear confused (due to thought disorder), show poor judgment, and fail to profit from experience. These persons lack social skills, feel inferior, withdraw from social involvement, and show poor judgment. To compensate for poor interpersonal relationships and sexual performance, they may develop involved sexual fantasies. Common diagnoses include Schizophrenia, Depressive Disorders, Obsessive-Compulsive Disorder, and Personality Disorders (especially schizoid). Psychotic disorders are more likely as Scale 8 becomes greater relative to Scale 7. Adolescents with this profile appear similar to adults.

79/97

These clients are anxious, agitated, and energetic. They obsessively ruminate, and may talk excessively about loosely connected ideas. They have trouble relaxing, form awkward, superficial relationships, and sometimes become manic or hypomanic. Behavior may include impulsive acting out followed by remorse. Adolescents with this code type tend to show fewer manic signs than adults.

70/07

This code type is not typically seen in adults. Adolescents with this code type tend to be extremely shy and sensitive. They tend to work well in therapy, show few academic problems, and are achievement oriented. They may react to stress by becoming emotionally overcontrolled. Their primary conflict may center around dependency versus assertiveness.

89/98

This code suggests serious psychopathology, especially if the scales are very elevated. Severe thought disorder, psychotic symptoms, and bizarre speech patterns may be present. These clients are self-centered and immature, becoming hostile if their needs are unmet. Due to fear of emotional involvement, they are socially isolated. Poor sexual adjustment is common. Others see them as egocentric or fickle, and they may appear hyperactive, labile, or excited. They are vague about their problems and may deny needing help. While they desire achievement, performance tends to be mediocre, and low self-esteem limits participation in competitive situations. Schizophrenia is the most common diagnosis, followed by mania due to Bipolar Disorder.

Three-Point Code Types

Note: Three-point code types are not reported in adolescent literature.

123/213/231

These clients are usually diagnosed with Somatoform Disorder, Anxiety Disorder, or Depressive Disorder, and somatic complaints typically have a secondary gain. They are often in conflict about dependency versus assertiveness. While marital and job adjustment are usually good, they take few chances.

132/312

This V-shaped configuration is known as the "conversion valley," or "conversion V"; classical conversion symptoms are likely, with diagnoses of Conversion Disorder or Somatoform Pain Disorder. These clients convert stress into physical symptoms, relying on denial and repression, resulting in a lack of insight and resistance to psychological interpretations of their symptoms. They are often passive-dependent and socially conforming. They may terminate treatment if pressed to deal with the psychological issues causing their somatic symptoms.

138

These clients are likely to have bizarre or delusional somatic symptoms, depression, suicidal ideation, and thought disorder. They are easily irritated and excitable. They are usually diagnosed with Schizophrenia (paranoid type) or Paranoid Personality Disorder.

139

These clients are often diagnosed with Somatoform Disorder or Organic Brain Syndrome.

247/274/472

Symptoms of anxiety and depression are common, as are substance abuse and family/marital problems. They are often hostile and immature, with unmet emotional needs. The most common diagnosis is a Personality Disorder. They respond best to directive, action-oriented treatment.

278/728

Clients with this code type report symptoms of anxiety and depression, have trouble concentrating, and often ruminate about suicide. Affect is blunted or inappropriate, appearing schizoidal. They lack social skills and are shy, withdrawn, socially isolated, and passive in relationships. They may cope by using drugs or alcohol. Women with this code type may have Eating Disorder symptoms. Anxiety or Psychotic Disorders are possible.

687/867

This V-shaped configuration is called the "psychotic valley"; it suggests serious psychopathology. Schizophrenia (paranoid type) is the most common diagnosis. Hallucinations, delusions, and thought disorder are common. These clients tend to be socially withdrawn.

MMPI-2 and MMPI-A Content and Supplementary Scales

MMPI-2 Content Interpretation

ANXIETY (ANX)

Reflects symptoms of anxiety, worries, nervousness, insomnia, somatic arousal, indecision, or feeling overwhelmed.

FEARS (FRS)

Reflects the presence of multiple specific fears.

OBSESSIVENESS (OBS)

Reflects rumination, indecision, rigidity of thought, worries, compulsive or repetitive behaviors, and possible dysphoria, anhedonia, and lack of self-confidence.

DEPRESSION (DEP)

Reflects symptoms of depression including (but not limited to) fatigue, anhedonia, dysphoria, pessimism, hopelessness, crying easily, feelings of guilt or emptiness, loneliness, or suicidal ideation.

Note: Adapted from Archer (1997), Graham (1993), Greene (1991), and Groth-Marnat (1997).

HEALTH CONCERNS (HEA)

Reflects a preoccupation with bodily functioning, subjective poor physical health, specific somatic complaints, tension, and fatigue. Somatic complaints frequently involve gastrointestinal, neurological, skin, sensory, cardiovascular, and/or respiratory systems.

BIZARRE MENTATION (BIZ)

Reflects positive symptoms of schizophrenia or psychotic thought processes, including hallucinations, paranoid beliefs, delusions, or feelings of unreality.

ANGER (ANG)

Reflects difficulty controlling anger. Person is often irritable, hotheaded, stubborn, annoyed, or hostile, and may swear, have temper tantrums, throw or smash objects, or act physically abusive.

CYNICISM (CYN)

People who score high on CYN are hostile, unfriendly, and overbearing, mistrust others, are guarded and wary in interpersonal relationships for fear of being used, and believe that people are dishonest, selfish, and only interested in personal gain.

ANTISOCIAL PRACTICES (ASP)

Reflects past legal or academic problem behaviors, interest in, or participation in criminal behavior, disdain for authority or law, and cynical attitudes about others. They are often seen as dishonest, unhelpful, hostile, and mistrusting of others.

TYPE A (TPA)

Reflects a tendency to be hard-working, driven, and time-pressured. They are seen as tense, hostile, and/or irritable; they are easily annoyed and critical in relationships. They dislike waiting or being interrupted, and they hold grudges.

LOW SELF-ESTEEM (LSE)

Reflects poor self-concept, sensitivity to criticism and rejection, passivity, indecision, fears and worries, difficulty accepting compliments, and general or context-specific feelings of insignificance and inadequacy.

SOCIAL DISCOMFORT (SOD)

Reflects shy and introverted people who prefer to be alone than to be in social situations.

FAMILY PROBLEMS (FAM)

Reflects discord (and possible abuse) in the family of origin, feelings of dissatisfaction, resentment, or anger toward current family or family of origin, and descriptions of marriage or current family as lacking in love, warmth, or support.

WORK INTERFERENCE (WRK)

Reflects behaviors or problems that interfere with work performance, career indecision or dissatisfaction, problems with coworkers, problems with concentration and making decisions, lack of energy or ambition, poor self-concept, worries, or a lack of support from others regarding career.

NEGATIVE TREATMENT INDICATORS (TRT)

Reflects the beliefs that no one can understand or help them, they cannot or do not want to change, and that they have problems they cannot share with anyone. These people have negative attitudes toward health professionals and give up easily when faced with a crisis.

Harris-Lingoes and Scale 0 Subscales

These subscales are useful when considering a recommendation of individual psychotherapy.

SCALE 2 (DEPRESSION)

Subjective Depression (D1)	Dysphoria, anhedonia, low self-confidence, social unease.
Psychomotor Retardation (D2)	Low energy, listless, socially withdrawn, immobilized.
Physical Malfunctioning (D3)	Somatic symptoms, preoccupation with poor health.
Mental Dullness (D4)	Problems with concentration, memory, alertness, attention; anhedonia, low energy, apathy, pessimism.
Brooding (D5)	Rumination, crying, feels as though losing control over thoughts, feels inferior and sensitive.

SCALE 3 (HYSTERIA)

Denial of Social Anxiety (Hy1)	Socially comfortable, extroverted, does not feel bound by social standards.
Need for Affection (Hy2)	Does not have negative feelings for others, trusts others, needs affection and attention but fears these needs will not be met. Leads to avoidance.
Lassitude-Malaise (Hy3)	Dysphoria, poor concentration, fatigue, subjective poor health, discomfort.
Somatic Complaints (Hy4)	Reports physical symptoms, denies hostility.
Inhibition of Aggression (Hy5)	Interpersonally sensitive, denies hostility.

SCALE 4 (PSYCHOPATHIC DEVIATE)

Familial Discord (Pd1)	Family was critical, unsupportive, and did not foster independence. Lacking love.
Authority Problems (Pd2)	Problem behaviors, disdain, and disregard for societal norms or rules.
Social Imperturbability (Pd3)	Outspoken, socially confident, opinionated.
Social Alienation (Pd4)	Socially isolated, feels misunderstood.
Self-Alienation (Pd5)	Feels guilt or regret for own behavior, unhappy with self, may use alcohol.

SCALE 6 (PARANOIA)

Persecutory Ideas (Pa1)	Feels misunderstood, sees world as dangerous, distrusts others.
Poignancy (Pa2)	Hypersensitive, feel lonely or tense, seek excitement.
Naivete (Pa3)	Optimistic, high moral standards, deny hostility.

SCALE 8 (SCHIZOPHRENIA)

Social Alienation (Sc1)	Feels mistreated, unloved, persecuted; has no close interpersonal relationships.
Emotional Alienation (Sc2)	Feels depressed, afraid, possibly suicidal. May be sadistic/masochistic.
Lack of Ego Mastery, Cognitive (Sc3)	Bizarre thoughts, poor concentration/memory, loss of control over thoughts, sense of unreality.
Lack of Ego Mastery, Conative (Sc4)	Depressed, worried, withdraws into fantasy, life seems too difficult, possible suicidality.
Lack of Ego Mastery, Defective Inhibition (Sc5)	Labile, sense of loss of control over thoughts, feelings, or impulses; cannot control or recall behaviors.
Bizarre Sensory Experiences (Sc6)	Hallucinations, delusions, strange thoughts or sensory/motor experiences.

SCALE 9 (HYPOMANIA)

Amorality (Ma1)	Selfish, manipulative, poorly developed conscience; believes others are also this way.
Psychomotor Acceleration (Ma2)	Hyperactive, restless, quick, excitement-seeking.
Imperturbability (Ma3)	Insensitive to others' feelings and opinions, are not socially anxious.
Ego Inflation (Ma4)	Unrealistically positive perceptions of personal qualities or abilities; resents demands made by others.

SCALE 0 (SOCIAL INTROVERSION) (FROM BEN-PORATH,
HOSTETLER, BUTCHER, & GRAHAM, 1989)

Shyness (Si1)	Socially uncomfortable, easily embarrassed, avoids initiating relationships.
Social Avoidance (Si2)	Dislikes and avoids group social situations or activities.
Self/Other Alienation (Si3)	Low self-esteem and confidence, self-critical, feels ineffectual, external locus of control.

MMPI-2 Supplementary Scales

ANXIETY (A)

High scores reflect general unhappiness and maladjustment; these clients are anxious, shy, insecure, overcontrolled, inhibited, upset, stressed, conforming, indecisive, defensive, apathetic, pessimistic, and fussy. They are usually motivated in therapy.

REPRESSION (R)

Elevated scores characterize internalizing, cautious clients who are submissive, unexcitable, conventional, logical, methodical, and slow. They avoid unpleasant interpersonal situations and use denial and rationalization.

EGO STRENGTH (Es)

Elevations indicate good prognosis for psychotherapy in anxious or depressed clients; they are reliable, self-confident, intelligent, tolerant, alert, persistent, have good coping repertoires and social skills, can tolerate confrontations in therapy, and know how to seek help in a crisis.

MACANDREW ALCOHOLISM SCALE-REVISED (MAC-R)

High scores suggest the *possibility* of an alcohol or other substance abuse problem. High scores reflect extroversion, exhibitionism, self-confidence, competitiveness, risk taking, possible blackouts, problems at school or with the law, and trouble concentrating. Some minorities and individuals in recovery who are not currently using alcohol may present with elevations on this scale.

ADDICTION ACKNOWLEDGMENT SCALE (AAS OR ACK)

Clients with high scores openly acknowledge substance abuse problems. Low scores indicate either a lack of substance abuse problems or an active attempt to hide substance abuse problems.

ADDICTION POTENTIAL SCALE (APS) [ALSO KNOWN AS ALCOHOL DRUG PRONENESS SCALE (PRO)]

Like the MacAndrew Alcoholism Scale, high scores are indicative of a lifestyle or personality style conducive to developing an alcohol or substance abuse problem. If persons with low scores do have a substance use problem, it is probably for self-medication of psychological distress rather than due to substance abuse.

MARITAL DISTRESS SCALE (MDS)

High scores reflect marital distress or difficulties; the scale should only be interpreted in those who are married, separated, or divorced (Scale 4 or FAM is applicable to nonmarital relationships).

OVERCONTROLLED HOSTILITY SCALE (O-H)

High scorers hold anger inside rather than freely expressing it, but occasionally may explode and become aggressive. The scale reflects past behavior more than predicting current or future danger of aggression. These people are usually emotionally constricted and highly socialized.

DOMINANCE (Do)

High scorers are socially skilled, confident, poised, realistic, task oriented, persistent, dutiful, and opinionated. This scale is often used in personnel selection.

SOCIAL RESPONSIBILITY (Re)

High scores reflect a strong sense of fairness, honesty, justice, standards, adherence to values, dependability, self-confidence, and trustworthiness. Frequently used in personnel selection.

COLLEGE MALADJUSTMENT (Mt)

Among college students, high scores reflect maladjustment, symptoms of anxiety and somatization, procrastination, and a pessimistic outlook that life is generally stressful.

FEMININE GENDER ROLE (GF)

High scores on this scale suggest stereotypically feminine attributes, and a tendency toward religiosity and substance abuse. Males may be critical, religious, bossy, and have a temper.

MASCULINE GENDER ROLE (GM)

High scores on this scale reflect confidence, persistence, and lack of anxiety. Females with high scores are open and honest. Concurrent high GF suggests androgyny, concurrent low GF suggest stereotypically masculine interests and orientation; low GM combined with high GF suggests stereotypically female interests and attributes, while low GM and GF suggests an undifferentiated gender orientation.

POSTTRAUMATIC STRESS DISORDER SCALE (PK)

High scores reflect symptoms consistent with PTSD, but do not determine whether trauma has occurred.

POSTTRAUMATIC STRESS DISORDER SCALE (PS)

A second, experimental trauma-related scale used to diagnose veterans.

MMPI-A Specific Content and Supplementary Scales

ANXIETY (A-anx)

Reflects symptoms of anxiety that are perceived and reported (e.g., worries, insomnia, somatic arousal, poor concentration, indecision, or feeling overwhelmed). They may have suicidal ideation.

OBSESSIVENESS (A-obs)

Reflects rumination, indecision, worries, and possible dysphoria, anhedonia, and lack of self-confidence. Associated with general maladjustment, dependence and anxiety in clinical boys and suicidality in clinical girls.

DEPRESSION (A-dep)

Reflects symptoms of depression including (but not limited to) fatigue, anhedonia, dysphoria, pessimism, hopelessness, loneliness, low self-esteem, crying spells, feelings of guilt or emptiness, and/or suicidal ideation.

HEALTH CONCERNS (A-hea)

Reflects a preoccupation with bodily functioning, subjective poor physical health, specific somatic complaints, tension, and fatigue. Somatic complaints frequently involve gastrointestinal, neurological, skin, sensory, cardiovascular, and/or respiratory systems. Health concerns interfere with school activities and attendance.

BIZARRE MENTATION (A-biz)

Reflects psychotic thought processes including hallucinations, paranoid beliefs, delusions, or feelings of unreality. May have problems with impulse control.

ANGER (A-ang)

Reflects difficulty controlling anger. Client is often irritable, stubborn, annoyed, or hostile, and may swear, have temper tantrums, throw or smash objects, or be physically abusive.

CYNICISM (A-cyn)

Adolescents who score high on A-cyn have misanthropic attitudes. They mistrust others, are guarded and wary in interpersonal relationships for fear of being used, and believe that people are dishonest, selfish, jealous, and only interested in personal gain.

ALIENATION (A-aln)

Adolescents scoring high on A-aln feel emotionally distant from others, and think no one (including parents) cares for them or likes them. They are socially uncomfortable, reserved, and unappreciative of others' opinions or sympathy.

CONDUCT PROBLEMS (A-con)

Reflects problem behaviors and poor impulse control (e.g., stealing, lying, swearing, destroying property), interest in or participation in criminal behavior, disdain for authority or law, and cynical attitudes about others. They are often seen as dishonest, unhelpful, bullying, and mistrusting of others.

LOW SELF-ESTEEM (A-lse)

Reflects poor self-concept, sensitivity to criticism and rejection, passivity, indecision, fears and worries, difficulty accepting compliments, and general or context-specific feelings of insignificance and inadequacy.

LOW ASPIRATIONS (A-las)

Reflects disinterest in school, serious topics, or being successful, and expectations of failure. They let others solve problems for them and avoid challenges, preferring to be careless. They report difficulty starting or finishing tasks, are seen as lazy, and blame others for blocking their progress.

SOCIAL DISCOMFORT (A-sod)

Reflects shy and introverted people who prefer to be alone than to be in social situations.

FAMILY PROBLEMS (A-fam)

Reflects discord (and possible abuse), poor communication, or a lack of love, warmth, and understanding in the family. Feelings of anger, resentment, or jealousy with parents or siblings is common. They feel unable to count on their family, think their parents' punishments are unfair, and desire to leave home.

SCHOOL PROBLEMS (A-sch)

Reflects behaviors or problems that interfere with school performance, low grades, truancy, negative attitudes about school, and poor participation in school activities. These adolescents are often perceived as lazy; they think school is a waste of time (other than seeing friends), and report frequent boredom and sleepiness in class. Consider Learning Disorder diagnosis.

NEGATIVE TREATMENT INDICATORS (A-trt)

Reflects the beliefs that no one can understand or help them, they cannot or do not want to change, and that they have problems they cannot share with anyone. These clients have negative attitudes toward health professionals and give up easily when faced with a crisis.

ANXIETY (A)

Reflects general unhappiness and maladjustment; these adolescents are anxious, fearful, guilt-prone, and self-critical.

REPRESSION (R)

High scores characterize internalizing, inhibited, overcontrolled adolescents who are submissive, unexcitable, conventional, and rarely spontaneous.

MACANDREW ALCOHOLISM SCALE-REVISED (MAC-R)

High scores suggest the *possibility* of an alcohol or other substance abuse problem. High scores reflect extroversion, exhibitionism, self-confidence, competitiveness, risk-taking, possible blackouts, problems at school or with the law, and trouble concentrating.

ADDICTION ACKNOWLEDGMENT SCALE (ACK)

Adolescents with high scores openly acknowledge substance abuse problems. Low scores indicate either a lack of substance abuse problems or an active attempt to hide substance abuse problems.

ALCOHOL/DRUG PROBLEM PRONENESS SCALE (PRO)

Like the MacAndrew Alcoholism Scale (but possibly better than the MAC-R), high scores are indicative of a lifestyle or personality style conducive to developing an alcohol or substance abuse problem. If persons with low scores have a substance use problem, it is probably for self-medication of psychological distress instead of following a typical addictive pattern.

IMMATURITY SCALE (IMM)

Adolescents scoring high on IMM have a higher incidence of academic difficulties, disobedience, and antisocial behaviors. They may appear impatient and easily frustrated. Scores naturally decrease with age.

References

Achenbach, T. M. (1991a). *Manual for the child behavior checklist/4-18 and 1991 profile*. Burlington: University of Vermont Department of Psychiatry.

Achenbach, T. M. (1991b). *Manual for the teacher's report form and 1991 profile*. Burlington: University of Vermont Department of Psychiatry.

Achenbach, T. M. (1991c). *Manual for the youth self-report and 1991 profile*. Burlington: University of Vermont Department of Psychiatry.

Achenbach, T. M. (1992). *Manual for the child behavior checklist/2-3 and 1992 profile*. Burlington: University of Vermont Department of Psychiatry.

Achenbach, T. M. (1997). *Manual for the young adult self-report and young adult behavior checklist*. Burlington: University of Vermont Department of Psychiatry.

Adams, W., & Sheslow, D. (1990). *Manual for the wide range assessment of memory and learning*. Wilmington, DE: Jastak Association.

American Psychiatric Association. (1994). *Diagnostic and statistical manual of mental disorders* (4th ed.). Washington, DC: Author.

Archer, R. P. (1992). *MMPI-A: Assessing adolescent psychopathology*. Mahwah, NJ: Erlbaum.

Archer, R. P. (1997). *MMPI-A: Assessing adolescent psychopathology* (2nd ed.). Mahwah, NJ: Erlbaum.

Barkley, R. A. (1987). *Defiant children: A clinician's manual for parent training*. New York: Guilford Press.

Barkley, R. A. (1995). *Taking charge of ADHD*. New York: Guilford Press.

Barona, A., Reynolds, C., & Chastain, R. (1984). A demographically based index of premorbid intelligence for the WAIS-R. *Journal of Consulting and Clinical Psychology, 26,* 74–75.

Beck, A. T., Steer, R. A., & Brown, G. K. (1996). *Beck depression inventory* (2nd ed.). San Antonio, TX: The Psychological Corporation.

Beery, K. E., & Buktenica, N. A. (1997). *Developmental test of visual-motor integration* (4th ed.). Cleveland, OH: Modern Curriculum Press.

Bellak, L., & Abrams, D. M. (1997). *The Thematic Apperception Test; Children's Apperception Test; and Senior apperception technique in clinical use* (6th ed.). Needham Heights, MA: Allyn & Bacon.

Benton, A. L., & Hamsher, K. S. (1994). *Multilingual aphasia examination* (3rd ed.). Iowa City: AJA Associates.

Bond, M. H. (1996). *The handbook of Chinese psychology*. Hong Kong: Oxford University Press.

Bongar, B. M. (1991). *The suicidal patient: Clinical and legal standards of care.* Washington, DC: American Psychological Association.

Briere, J. (1997). *Psychological assessment of adult posttraumatic states.* Washington, DC: American Psychological Association.

Briere, J. N. (1995). *Traumatic symptom inventory professional manual.* Odessa, FL: Psychological Assessment Resources.

Briere, J. N. (1996). *Traumatic symptom checklist for children professional manual.* Odessa, FL: Psychological Assessment Resources.

Brown, T. E. (1996). *Brown attention-deficit disorders scales manual.* San Antonio, TX: The Psychological Corporation.

Brownell, R. (1983). *Expressive one-word picture vocabulary test–upper extension.* Novato, CA: Academic Therapy Publications.

Buck, J. N. (1966). *The house-tree-person technique: Revised manual.* Beverly Hills, CA: Western Psychological Services.

Busse, E. W., & Blazer, D. G. (1996). *Textbook of geriatric psychiatry* (2nd ed.). Washington, DC: American Psychiatric Press.

Butcher, J. N., Dahlstrom, W. G., Graham, J. R., Tellegen, A., & Kaemmer, B. (1989). *Manual for administration and scoring: MMPI-2.* Minneapolis: University of Minnesota Press.

Butcher, J. N., & Williams, C. L. (1992). *Essentials of MMPI-2 and MMPI-A interpretation.* Minneapolis: University of Minnesota Press.

Choca, J. P., & Van Denburg, E. (1997). *Interpretive guide to the Millon clinical multiaxial inventory* (2nd ed.). Washington, DC: American Psychological Association.

Cohen, M. J. (1997). *Manual for the children's memory scale.* San Antonio, TX: The Psychological Corporation.

Cohen, R. J. (1992). *Psychological testing and assessment* (2nd ed.). Mountain View, CA: Mayfield.

Conners, C. K. (1997). *CRS-R Manual.* North Tonawanda, NY: MHS.

Cushman, L. A., & Scherer, M. J. (1995). *Psychological assessment in medical rehabilitation.* Washington, DC: American Psychological Association.

D'Elia, L. F., Satz, P., Uchiyama, C. L., & White, T. (1996). *Color trails test professional manual.* Odessa, FL: Psychological Assessment Resources.

Dunn, L. M., Dunn, L. M., & Williams, K. T. (1997). *Peabody picture vocabulary test–III.* Circle Pines, MN: American Guidance Services.

Exner, J. E., Jr. (1991). *The Rorschach: A comprehensive system: Vol. 2. Interpretation* (2nd ed.). New York: Wiley.

Exner, J. E., Jr. (1993). *The Rorschach: A comprehensive system: Vol. 1. Basic foundations* (3rd ed.). New York: Wiley.

Exner, J. E., Jr. (1995a). *Issues and methods in Rorschach research.* Mahwah, NJ: Erlbaum.

Exner, J. E., Jr. (1995b). *The Rorschach: A comprehensive system: Vol. 3. Assessment of children and adolescents* (2nd ed.). New York: Wiley.

Finn, S. E., & Tonsager, M. E. (1995). Therapeutic effects of providing MMPI-2 test feedback to college students awaiting therapy. *Psychological Assessment, 4,* 278–287.

Folstein, M. F., Folstein, S. E., & McHugh, P. R. (1975). "Mini-mental state": A practical method for grading the cognitive state of patients for the clinician. *Journal of Psychiatric Research, 12,* 189–198.

Gardner, M. E. (1990). *Expressive one-word picture vocabulary test–revised.* Novato, CA: Academic Therapy Publications.

Geisinger, K. F. (1992). *Psychological testing of Hispanics.* Washington, DC: American Psychological Association.

Graham, J. R. (1993). *MMPI-2: Assessing personality and psychopathology* (2nd ed.). New York: Oxford University Press.

Greene, R. L. (1991). *The MMPI-2/MMPI: An interpretive manual.* Needham Heights, MA: Allyn and Bacon.

Groth-Marnat, G. (1997). *Handbook of psychological assessment* (3rd ed.). New York: Wiley.

Hare, R. D. (1995). *Hare psychopathy check list-revised manual.* San Antonio, TX: Psychological Corporation.

Heaton, R. K., Chelune, G. J., Talley, J. L., Kay, G. G., & Curtiss, G. (1993). *Wisconsin card sorting test manual—revised and expanded.* Odessa, FL: Psychological Assessment Resources.

Helmes, E. (1996). Use of the Barona method to predict premorbid intelligence in the elderly. *Clinical Neuropsychologist, 10,* 255–261.

Howes, R. D., & DeBlassie, R. R. (1989). Modal errors in the cross cultural use of the Rorschach. *Journal of Multicultural Counseling and Development, 17,* 79–84.

Impara, J. C., & Plake, B. S. (Eds.). (1998). *The thirteenth mental measurements yearbook* (13th ed.). Lincoln: University of Nebraska Press.

Jongsma, A. E., Jr., & Peterson, M. L. (1995). *The complete psychotherapy treatment planner.* New York: Wiley.

Jongsma, A. E., Jr., Peterson, M. L., & McInnis, W. P. (1996). *The child and adolescent psychotherapy treatment planner.* New York: Wiley.

Kaplan, E., Goodglass, H., & Weintraub, S. (1983). *The Boston naming test* (2nd ed.). Philadelphia: Lea & Febiger.

Kaszniak, W. A., & Ditraglia-Christenson, G. (1995). Differential diagnosis of dementia and depression. In M. Storandt & G. R. VandenBos (Eds.), *Neuropsychological assessment of dementia and depression* (pp. 81–117). Washington, DC: American Psychological Association.

Kaufman, A. S. (1994). *Intelligent testing with the WISC-III*. New York: Wiley.

Knoff, H. M. (1985). *Kinetic drawing system for family and school: A handbook*. Beverly Hills, CA: Western Psychological Services.

Koenig, H. G., Christison, C., Christison, G., & Blazer, D. G. (1996). Schizophrenia and paranoid disorders. In E. W. Busse & D. G. Blazer (Eds.), *The American psychiatric press textbook of geriatric psychiatry* (p. 265). Washington, DC: American Psychiatric Press.

Kohn, R., Westlake, R. J., Rasmussen, S. A., Marsland, R. T., & Norman, W. H. (1997). Clinical features of obsessive-compulsive disorder in elderly patients. *American Journal of Geriatric Psychiatry, 5*, 211–215.

Kovacs, M. (1992). *Children's depression inventory manual*. North Tonawanda, NY: MHS.

Levine, M. D. (1981a). *The Anser system parent questionnaire for developmental, behavioral, and health assessment of the preschool and kindergarten child (Form 1P)*. Cambridge, MA: Educators Publishing Service.

Levine, M. D. (1981b). *The Anser system school questionnaire for developmental, behavioral, and health assessment of the preschool and kindergarten child (Form 1S)*. Cambridge, MA: Educators Publishing Service.

Levine, M. D. (1985a). *The Anser system parent questionnaire for developmental, behavioral, and health assessment of the elementary school child (Form 2P)*. Cambridge, MA: Educators Publishing Service.

Levine, M. D. (1985b). *The Anser system school questionnaire for developmental, behavioral, and health assessment of the elementary school child (Form 2S)*. Cambridge, MA: Educators Publishing Service.

Levine, M. D. (1988a). *The Anser system parent questionnaire for developmental, behavioral, and health assessment of the secondary school child (Form 3P)*. Cambridge, MA: Educators Publishing Service.

Levine, M. D. (1988b). *The Anser system school questionnaire for developmental, behavioral, and health assessment of the secondary school child (Form 3S)*. Cambridge, MA: Educators Publishing Service.

Levine, M. D. (1994). *Educational care: A system for understanding and helping children with learning problems at home and in school*. Cambridge, MA: Educator's Publishing Service.

Lewis, M. (1996a). *Child and adolescent psychiatry: A comprehensive textbook* (2nd ed.). Baltimore: Williams & Wilkins.

Lewis, M. (1996b). Psychiatric assessment of infants, children, and adolescents. In M. Lewis (Ed.), *Child and adolescent psychiatry: A comprehensive textbook* (2nd ed., pp. 440–456). Baltimore: Williams & Wilkins.

Livesley, W. J. (1995). *The DSM-IV personality disorders.* New York: Guilford Press.

Maddox, T. (Ed.). (1992). *Tests: A comprehensive reference for assessments in psychology, education and business* (4th ed.). Austin, TX: Pro-Ed.

Mattis, S. (1988). *Dementia rating scale—professional manual.* Odessa, FL: Psychological Assessment Resources.

Maxmen, J. S., & Ward, N. G. (1995). *Essential psychopathology and its treatment* (2nd ed.). New York: Norton.

McArthur, D. S., & Roberts, G. E. (1982). *Roberts apperception test for children manual.* Beverly Hills, CA: Western Psychological Services.

Mecham, M. J. (1989). *The token test for children manual.* Austin, TX: Pro-Ed.

Mednick, S. A., Parnas, J., & Schulsinger, F. (1987). The Copenhagen high-risk project, 1962–1986. *Schizophrenia Bulletin, 13,* 485–495.

Melton, G. B., Petrila, J., Poythress, N. G., & Slobogin, C. (1987). *Psychological evaluations for the courts: A handbook for mental health professionals and lawyers.* New York: Guilford Press.

Meyer, R. G., & Deitsch, S. E. (1996). *The clinician's handbook* (4th ed.). Boston: Allyn & Bacon.

Meyers, J. E., & Meyers, K. R. (1995). *Rey complex figure test and recognition trial professional manual.* Odessa, FL: Psychological Assessment Resources.

Millon, T. (1993). *Manual for the MACI.* Minneapolis, MN: National Computer Systems.

Millon, T. (1994). *Manual for the MCMI-III.* Minneapolis, MN: National Computer Systems.

Milner, & Wimberely, (1979/1980). *Child abuse potential inventory (CAPI).*

Morgan, C., & Murray, H. A. (1935). A method for investigating fantasies. *AMA Archives of Neurology and Psychiatry, 65,* 237–254.

Murphy, L. L., Conoley, J. C., & Impara, J. C. (1994). *Tests in print IV: An index to tests, test reviews, and the literature on specific tests.* Lincoln: University of Nebraska Press.

Naglieri, J. A., McNeish, T. J., & Bardos, A. N. (1991). *Draw a person: Screening procedure for emotional disturbance.* Austin, TX: Pro-Ed.

Newmark, C. S. (1996). *Major psychological assessment instruments* (2nd ed.). Needham Height, MA: Allyn & Bacon.

Olin, S. S., Raine, A., Cannon, T. D., Parnes, J., Schulsinger, F., & Mednick, S. A. (1997). Childhood behavior precursors of schizotypal personality disorders. *Schizophrenia Bulletin, 23,* 93–103.

Pena, L. M., Megargee, E. I., & Brody, E. (1996). MMPI-A patterns of male juvenile delinquents. *Psychological Assessment, 8,* 388–397.

Pennington, B. F. (1991). *Diagnosing learning disorders: A neuropsychological framework.* New York: Guilford Press.

Phillips, K. A. (1986). *The broken mirror.* New York: Oxford University Press.

The Psychological Corporation. (1992). *Wechsler Individual Achievement Test (WIAT)*. San Antonio, TX: Author.

The Psychological Corporation. (1993). *Manual for the Beck Hopelessness Scale*. San Antonio, TX: Author.

The Psychological Corporation. (1997). *WAIS-III–WMS-III technical manual*. San Antonio, TX: Author.

Reynolds, C. R., Sanchez, S., & Willson, V. L. (1996). Normative tables for calculating the WISC-III performance and full scale IQs when symbol search is substituted for coding. *Psychological Assessment, 8*, 378–382.

Rodgers, R., Bagby, R. M., & Dickens, S. E. (1992). *Structured interview of reported symptoms*. Odessa, FL: Psychological Assessment Resources.

Ruff, R. M. (1996). *Ruff figural fluency test professional manual*. Odessa, FL: Psychological Assessment Resources.

Schneider, L. S., Reynolds, C. F., Lebowitz, B. D., & Friedhoff, A. J. (1994). *Diagnosis and treatment of depression in late life: Results of the NIH Consensus Development Conference*. Washington, DC: American Psychiatric Press.

Sparrow, S. S., Balla, D. A., & Cicchetti, D. V. (1984). *Vineland Adaptive Behavior Scales*. Circle Pines, MN: American Guidance Service.

Tarasoff v. Regents of the University of California, 529 P 2d 553, 118 California Reporter 129 (1974).

Tarasoff v. Regents of the University of California, 17 Cal 3d 425, 551 P 2d 334, 131 California Reporter (1976).

Tombaugh, T. N. (1995). *Test of memory malingering manual*. North Tonawanda, NY: MHS.

Trevisan, M. S. (1996). Review of the draw a person: Screening procedure for emotional disturbance. *Measurement and Evaluation in Counseling and Development, 28*, 225–228.

Uba, L. (1994). *Asian Americans: Personality patterns, identity, and mental health*. New York: Guilford Press.

Wechsler, D. (1989). *Manual for the Wechsler preschool and primary scale of intelligence—revised (WPPSI-R)*. San Antonio: The Psychological Corporation.

Wechsler, D. (1991). *Manual for the Wechsler intelligence scale for children* (3rd ed.). New York: Psychological Corporation.

Wechsler, D. (1997a). *WMS-III administration and scoring manual*. San Antonio: The Psychological Corporation.

Wechsler, D. (1997b). *WAIS-III administration and scoring manual*. San Antonio: The Psychological Corporation.

Wilkinson, G. S. (1993). *Wide range achievement test administration manual*. Wilmington, DE: Wide Range.

Woodcock, R. W., & Mather, N. (1989). *Woodcock-Johnson tests of achievement manual*. Allen, TX: DLM Teaching Resources.

Author Index

Subject Index